The Tropical Vegan Kitchen

COOKBOOKS BY DONNA KLEIN

The Mediterranean Vegan Kitchen
The PDQ (Pretty Darn Quick) Vegetarian Cookbook
Vegan Italiano
The Gluten-Free Vegetarian Kitchen
The Tropical Vegan Kitchen

The Tropical Vegan Kitchen

Meat-Free, Egg-Free, Dairy-Free Dishes from the Tropics

Donna Klein

HOME

A HOME BOOK
Published by the Penguin Group
Penguin Group (USA) Inc.
375 Hudson Street, New York, New York 10014, USA
Penguin Group (Canada), 90 Eglinton Avenue East, Suite 700, Toronto, Ontario M4P 2Y3, Canada
(a division of Pearson Penguin Canada Inc.)
Penguin Books Ltd., 80 Strand, London WC2R 0RL, England
Penguin Group Ireland, 25 St. Stephen's Green, Dublin 2, Ireland (a division of Penguin Books Ltd.)
Penguin Group (Australia), 250 Camberwell Road, Camberwell, Victoria 3124, Australia
(a division of Pearson Australia Group Pty. Ltd.)
Penguin Books India Pvt. Ltd., 11 Community Centre, Panchsheel Park, New Delhi—110 017, India
Penguin Group (NZ), 67 Apollo Drive, Rosedale, North Shore 0632, New Zealand
(a division of Pearson New Zealand Ltd.)
Penguin Books (South Africa) (Pty.) Ltd., 24 Sturdee Avenue, Rosebank, Johannesburg 2196,
South Africa

Penguin Books Ltd., Registered Offices: 80 Strand, London WC2R 0RL, England

While the author has made every effort to provide accurate telephone numbers and Internet addresses
at the time of publication, neither the publisher nor the author assumes any responsibility for errors,
or for changes that occur after publication. Further, the publisher does not have any control over and
does not assume any responsibility for author or third-party websites or their content.

First edition: January 2009

Library of Congress Cataloging-in-Publication Data

Klein, Donna (Donna M.)
    The tropical vegan kitchen : meat-free, egg-free, dairy-free dishes from the tropics / Donna Klein.—
1st ed.
        p. cm.
    Includes index.
    ISBN 978-1-55788-544-9
    1. Vegan cookery.   2. Cookery, Tropical.   I. Title.
    TX837.K5478 2009
    641.5'636—dc22   2008032671

PRINTED IN THE UNITED STATES OF AMERICA

10   9   8   7   6   5   4   3   2   1

PUBLISHER'S NOTE: The recipes contained in this book are to be followed exactly as written. The
publisher is not responsible for your specific health or allergy needs that may require medical super-
vision. The publisher is not responsible for any adverse reactions to the recipes contained in this
book.

Most Home books are available at special quantity discounts for bulk purchases for sales promotions,
premiums, fund-raising, or educational use. Special books, or book excerpts, can also be created to fit
specific needs. For details, write: Special Markets, Penguin Group (USA) Inc., 375 Hudson Street,
New York, New York 10014.

For Karen Carroll,
in lasting friendship

Contents

Acknowledgments

As always, I extend my sincere thanks to those who helped make this book possible: my amazing literary agent, Linda Konner; the truly talented staff and crew at Home Books, especially John Duff and Jeanette Egan; my very efficient recipe testers and beautiful daughters, Emma and Sarah; and my number one taste-tester and precious dog, Trevor.

Special thanks to the generous people of Hawaii, whose delicious polycultural cuisine largely inspired this book.

Introduction

The Tropics: A Vegan Garden of Eden

Sweet, spicy, hot, sour, light, juicy, refreshing, dazzling—tropical cuisine is a delightful fusion of diverse flavors, textures, and colors that excite the palate as well as the imagination. Scores of countries and islands lie within the tropics, the geographic region of the earth centered on the equator, bounded by the Tropic of Cancer on the north and the Tropic of Capricorn on the south. Because the sun is always high in the sky and rainfall is plentiful, the climate is warm and moist year-round—a magical endless summer, conducive to lush vegetation and an incredible array of exotic fruits and vegetables that transforms this torrid zone into a vegan paradise.

Some of the countries and islands found in the tropics include the Caribbean Isles, Mexico, Costa Rica, Brazil, Venezuela, Australia, Hawaii, Indonesia, Thailand, the Philippines, Singapore, Taiwan, Vietnam, India, Ghana, Kenya, and Mozambique, to name just a few. Common tropical foods such as coconut, mango, avocado, pineapple, banana, citrus, and fiery chilies unite these various cultures, but the use of spices and seasonings lend them their respective culinary accents. Take native rice dishes, for example. While coconut typically perfumes steamed or stir-fried dishes throughout the tropics, it's the jerk seasoning in the Caribbean, turmeric in Thailand, and curry powder in India that often reveals the country of origin.

These days, thanks to rapid air cargo and efficient distribution systems, tropical fruits and vegetables are widely available in most major supermarkets throughout North America. As luck would have it, several varieties are in season during the northern hemisphere's dreary winter months. So when it's cold and blustery outside and the sunny skies and balmy breezes of the tropics beckon, who needs the escape of travel when you can transport yourself to paradise by indulging in the recipes of *The Tropical Vegan Kitchen*?

Tropical Fruits and Vegetables

AVOCADO

Indigenous to Central America where it has been cultivated since pre-Columbian times, the avocado is now grown widely throughout the tropics and many subtropical climates. While there are about five hundred varieties of avocado, all are high in heart-healthy monounsaturated fat and abundant in the B vitamin group, vitamin E, and potassium. Most avocados are sold firm and unripe. Select an unblemished avocado that is heavy for its size. Leave to ripen for four to five days at room temperature; to quicken ripening, place in a brown paper bag in a cool, dry place. A ripe avocado will yield to gentle pressure from your thumb. Store ripe avocados in the refrigerator for up to five days. Peel shortly before using, as avocado flesh darkens quickly when in contact with air.

BANANA

Native to tropical Asia, bananas are today grown in every humid tropical region and constitute the fourth-largest fruit crop of the world, following the grape, citrus fruits, and the apple. Bananas can be as short as three inches and as long as eighteen inches. There are two general types: sweet (dessert) bananas, which are usually eaten raw, and a starchier type, called plantains (see Plantain, page 8), which are always cooked. The skin of the immature banana is generally green, becoming yellow as it ripens. When buying, look for plump, firm bananas free of breaks or blemishes. Ripe and ready-to-eat bananas begin to become flecked with tiny brown specks. Bananas still green along the ridges and at the tips require further ripening. To ripen bananas, leave uncovered at room temperature; for quicker ripening, place in a brown paper bag. Store ripe bananas in the refrigerator; the peel will darken but the flesh will remain fine to eat for several days.

CHAYOTE

Probably originating in Central America, chayote is a firm, pear-shaped, pale green squash with deep lengthwise ridges and a large edible center seed. Delicious raw in salads and slaws, chayote can also be boiled, baked, mashed, fried, and pickled. Select firm, smooth chayote without blemishes. Place in a plastic bag and refrigerate for up to three weeks. Always peel the skins from mature chayote, working under cold running water to prevent skin irritation from a sticky substance just beneath the surface. (This substance is destroyed by cooking.) If the chayote is small, peeling the skin is not necessary.

CHILIES

Hot chilies originated in the Americas, but are now grown extensively throughout the tropics. There are countless varieties of chilies, with wide ranges of size, color, and heat. Generally, smaller is hotter, and removing the seeds and membranes reduces the heat. Some chilies can be dangerously hot, so always avoid contact with the eyes when handling them and wear disposable plastic or surgical gloves, if practical. Select firm chilies that have unblemished and lustrous skins, avoiding those that look wrinkled or soft. Store them in a plastic bag in the refrigerator for up to one week.

COCONUT

While the exact origin of the coconut is often disputed, many historians believe it is native to Southeast Asia, probably originating in Malaysia. Today, the buoyant coconut palm, transported by sea currents, grows prolifically across much of the tropics and areas with subtropical climates. Perhaps the most versatile of the tropical fruits, the coconut has various uses, depending on ripeness. A young coconut is blond in color and shaped like the top of a sharpened pencil; it contains a slightly sweet, effervescent water, which makes a satisfying and highly nutritious drink. At this stage of growth, the flesh is soft and jellylike, and is eaten raw, usually as a light dessert. The hard flesh of mature coconuts is grated and used to produce coconut milk or is added to cooked dishes for its flavor and texture. Commercially, the mature flesh is also used to make cooking oils. There are a variety of other food products produced from the coconut palm. Hearts of palm, the growing tissue at the top of the tree where new fronds are generated, is considered a gourmet food, and can be eaten raw or cooked as a vegetable. The sap produced by the flower stem is fermented to produce an alcoholic drink or vinegar, or it is boiled and made into palm sugar. When buying young coconuts, select those that are heavy and nearly full of juice. There should be a slight sloshing sound to indicate the presence of liquid. Store unopened young coconuts in the refrigerator for two to three weeks. To ensure freshness, it is best to consume the young coconut water and/or young flesh shortly after opening. Mature coconuts should be at least one-third full of juice, and have dark brown, hard eyes. Soft or black eyes indicate decay. Store whole, unopened mature coconuts at room temperature in a dry location away from direct light for a couple months, depending on the degree of ripeness. Chunks of mature coconut meat can be submerged in the juice drained from the coconut (or water) in a tightly sealed container and refrigerated for up to five days. Seal grated fresh coconut in an airtight plastic bag and refrigerate for up to one week, or freeze for up to six months.

GINGER

Probably native to China, ginger is used widely throughout the tropics as a seasoning and a medicine. Mature gingerroot is fibrous and has a thin, brown skin that is removed before slicing or grating. It has a strong flavor and is added to many dishes as a flavoring. Young ginger has green stems, and a delicate thin skin, which allows the underlying yellow color to show through. The flavor is milder and the texture is less fibrous than mature ginger. It is often pickled or used in marinades. Select plump but firm pieces of gingerroot, light tan in color, with a tight skin. Wrinkled skin indicates dryness and age. Gingerroot keeps well for several weeks in the refrigerator.

GUAVA

Native to Mexico, the Caribbean, Central America, and northern South America, guavas are rich in vitamins A, B, and C, and also contain significant amounts of calcium. There are many varieties of guavas, which vary in size from that of a small egg to a medium apple. The skin of a ripe guava ranges in color from yellow to red and, sometimes, purple-black, and the flesh may be white, yellow, pink, or bright red. Some guavas are filled with inedible seeds, while others are seedless. Ripe guavas have a fragrant aroma and give to gentle pressure. To finish ripening a guava, enclose it in a paper bag with a banana and leave at room temperature until the guava starts to soften; use it before dark spots begin to appear. Refrigerate ripe guavas immediately, and use within two days.

JACKFRUIT

Probably native to southwestern India, Bangladesh, and Sri Lanka, jackfruit is the largest tree-borne fruit in the world and can weigh up to sixty pounds. Ripe jackfruit has a creamy yellow flesh and can be eaten raw. Unripe fruit can be used in cooking. Ripen fruit at room temperature until it is very soft to the touch. Ripe fruit can be stored in sealed containers in the refrigerator for three to five days or it can be frozen up to two months. To prevent gummy hands, coat hands lightly with vegetable oil when opening fruit. Open lengthwise like watermelon and slice into quarters. The pockets of flesh surrounding the seeds are the edible portions of jackfruit when eaten fresh. Seeds are edible when boiled and mashed like lima beans, or parboiled and roasted like chestnuts.

KIWIFRUIT

A native of southern China, kiwifruit is now widely cultivated in New Zealand, Israel, Italy, Chile, Spain, France, and California. Kiwifruit has a thin, fuzzy, brown skin and a fruity aroma. The flesh is green with shiny black seeds and succulent flesh. Select semi-firm, unblemished fruit with uniform skin. To ripen firm kiwifruit, place in a paper bag and leave at room temperature. Refrigerate ripe kiwifruit, away from other fruit, for up to one week.

LIME

Originally from Southeast Asia, limes are commonly found throughout the tropics in four varieties: the Tahitian lime, kaffir lime, kalamansi lime, and Key lime. The Tahitian lime, or Persian lime, is large, nearly round, with a thin green skin that turns yellow when ripe, although it is generally sold and used only while still green. Its abundant juice is made into drinks, and both the juice and peel (and, sometimes, flesh) are added to food to provide acidity and flavor. The kaffir lime has a rough green skin with dimples. It has little juice and its flesh is too bitter to eat. However, the grated skin and leaves are used to flavor cooked dishes, particularly in Thai cuisine. The kalamansi lime, native to the Philippines, is very small, round, thin-skinned, and green in color, changing to yellow as the lime ripens. The seeds are large, and the juice is very flavorful. The Key lime, or Mexican lime, is also very small, round to oval in shape, and has a thin skin that is greenish yellow at maturity. The juice is highly prized for its unique flavor. Select limes that are heavy for their size and full of juice. While skin blemishes are not important, avoid limes with soft spots or mold. Store limes in the refrigerator for up to three weeks.

MANGO

Native to India where it has been cultivated for more than four thousand years, the mango is now widely grown throughout the tropics, especially in Central America and the Caribbean. Known as the king of tropical fruit, it is an excellent source of vitamin A, and a good source of vitamin C, some B vitamins, potassium, and dietary fiber. Mangoes vary in color from green to gold or green-red. The ripe fruit has a remarkably refreshing taste and a nutty, soft texture. Select mangoes that have a fruity aroma and give slightly to the touch; avoid very soft or bruised fruit. Some mangoes ripen to a combination of red, orange, and green shades, while other varieties are golden yellow or green when ripe. Keep unripe mangoes at room temperature to ripen, which may take up to one week. Whole ripe mangoes can be kept in the refrigerator for about five days, or they can be sliced and frozen for up to two months with little loss of flavor.

MELON

There is a wide variety of melon available throughout the tropics. These include the honeydew and casaba melons, cantaloupe, and watermelon, among others. When selecting cantaloupes and similar melons, rub the stem spot and smell; there should be a slightly fruity aroma. Shake the melon; a sloshing sound indicates that the melon is overripe. When selecting watermelons, rap with a knuckle; a hollow sound indicates maturity. The white spot where the melon lay on the ground turns slightly yellow when it is ripe. For the fullest flavor, keep melons at room temperature away from direct sunlight and consume within one to two days. Refrigerate cut melons in plastic wrap for up to three days. Refrigerate whole ripe melons for up to five days.

PAPAYA

Now widely grown throughout tropical and subtropical countries, papaya is believed to be native to southern Mexico and neighboring Central America. Reputably called the "fruit of the angels" by Christopher Columbus, ripe papaya has a sweet and succulent orange-yellow flesh and is preferably eaten raw. Unripe green papaya does not have a strong taste and is cooked as a vegetable, pickled, or shredded raw in certain salads. If you are pregnant or trying to become pregnant, avoid eating unripe papaya, as the unripened fruit contains a latex substance that triggers uterine contractions and may cause a miscarriage. Anyone with latex allergies should also avoid eating unripe papaya. All papayas are picked green and allowed to ripen off the tree. Select fruit that is slightly soft with few black spots. Green papaya will ripen at room temperature within a few days. When ripe, the large Mexican variety will typically remain mostly green, while the smaller Hawaiian papaya will turn mostly golden. Ripe whole papaya can be placed in a plastic bag and refrigerated for up to three days to slow down the ripening process.

PASSION FRUIT

Native to South America, passion fruit is now frequently imported from New Zealand. A highly fragrant berry with a delicate flavor, the fruit consists of innumerable seeds and a jellylike pulp with a distinctly sour but pleasing taste. Choose fragrant, shriveled, wrinkled fruit that is rich in color. If the skin is smooth, ripen at room temperature and turn occasionally. The ripe fruit can be placed in a plastic bag and refrigerated for a few days, or frozen for up to a month with little loss of quality.

PINEAPPLE

Native to South America, the pineapple has become one of the leading commercial fruit crops of the tropics. Select fresh pineapple that feels heavy and has a plume of fresh green leaves. The rind can be dark green, yellow, or reddish yellow. A ripe pineapple will be about two-thirds yellow and smell sweet. It can be stored at room temperature for one or two days before consuming. A ripe whole pineapple can be placed in a perforated plastic bag and refrigerated for up to three days. It can also be peeled, sliced, or cubed, and refrigerated in an airtight container for a few days. While sliced or cubed pineapple can be frozen and stored in its own juices, it has a tendency to lose some of its flavor.

PLANTAIN

Thought to be native to Africa, plantains belong to the banana family and are now grown all around the Caribbean and Central and South America. Unlike bananas, plantains must be cooked prior to consumption to convert starches to sugar. Green plantains are very hard and starchy; they have little banana flavor, and no sweetness. They are generally used in the same ways as potatoes, and can be baked, boiled, or fried, or added to soups and stews. Yellow-ripe plantains are more tender, but can be used in these same ways, and will have a creamier texture. They are often mashed or grilled. Black-ripe plantains are also delicious prepared in any of these methods but have a sweeter flavor, and are frequently eaten as dessert. Select plantains that are firm and not mushy, moldy, or cracked. Ripen plantains in a loosely closed paper bag at room temperature. It takes six to eight days for a green plantain to fully ripen. Fully ripe black plantains should be firm like bananas, but not hard. Whole plantains can be refrigerated at any degree of ripeness, but the chill will stop them from ripening further.

STAR FRUIT (CARAMBOLA)

Probably native to Malaysia, Indonesia, or southern China, star fruit gets its name because its crosswise slices have a star shape. A ripe star fruit has a floral aroma, and is moderately firm with a thin, glossy, golden-yellow skin. Slightly brown tips are normal. Avoid star fruit that are soft, shriveled, blemished, or excessively brown at the edges. Allow greenish, unripe star fruit to ripen at room temperature. Once ripe, it will keep for two days at room temperature and about one week in the refrigerator, stored in a plastic bag. The fruit can be eaten out of hand without having to remove the skin.

TARO ROOT

Probably originating in Malaysia, taro root is now a major vegetable crop throughout much of the tropics, feeding more than 100 million people on a daily basis. The potatolike root can range in length from five inches to over a foot long. The flesh is often creamy white or pale pink and sometimes becomes purple-tinged once cooked. Used much like a potato, taro root can be boiled, baked, mashed, or fried. Select firm, brown-skinned taro roots with rings. Avoid those with soft spots or patches. To prepare the root, peel with a vegetable peeler under running water to avoid any skin sensitivity to its sticky juices. Toxic in its raw state, taro contains calcium oxalate crystals, so the root (as well as the leaves) must always be boiled to remove the crystals before other preparation.

TOMATILLO

Native to Mexico and Central America, the tomatillo is a small, green, tomato-like fruit with a tan husk. Used primarily in salsas and sauces, tomatillos can be eaten raw or cooked. Select small and firm tomatillos with supple and light brown (not shriveled and blackened) husks; check under the husk to make sure the fruit inside is not yellow, which indicates overripeness. Refrigerate tomatillos in their husks for up to three weeks in a paper bag. To prepare tomatillos for eating, remove the husks and rinse thoroughly under warm tap water to remove the natural stickiness. Use as directed in desired recipe.

YUCCA

Also known as yuca, cassava, tapioca, or manioc, yucca root has been cultivated in South America since around 1000 BC, and is now an important starch source throughout the tropics. The skin of the yucca root is brown and shiny, and the hard, white flesh turns yellowish and translucent after cooking and has a rich, buttery taste. The most popular use of yucca in the Western world is in the form of tapioca pearls, made from tapioca flour, which are used to make puddings. In the tropics, the yucca root is used in similar fashion to the potato, and is boiled, baked, mashed, or fried. Yucca roots are often waxed to prevent moisture loss. In the case of waxed yuccas, do not bake whole, as the wax will smoke and burn. Select yucca that smells fresh and has no mold or cracks. Store vegetables in a cool, dark place for up to seven days, but do not refrigerate.

Tropical Countries, Islands, and Regions

AFRICA

Central Africa
East Africa
North Africa (except Morocco and Tunisia)
Southern Africa (except Lesotho and Swaziland)
West Africa

ASIA

Bangladesh
Borneo
Brunei
Cambodia
India
Indonesia
Laos
Malaysia
Myanmar (Burma)
Philippines
Singapore
South China
   Sea Islands
Sri Lanka
Taiwan
Thailand
Vietnam

ATLANTIC OCEAN

Canary Islands (Spain)*
Florida Keys (USA)*

CARIBBEAN

Anguilla

Antigua

Aruba

Bahamas

Barbados

Bonaire and
  Curaçao (Neth-
  erlands Antilles)

British Virgin
  Islands

Cayman Islands

Cuba

Dominica

Haiti and Dominican
  Republic

French West Indies

Grenada

Jamaica

Puerto Rico

Saba

Saint Kitts and
  Nevis

Saint Lucia

St. Vincent and the
  Grenadines

Trinidad and
  Tobago

Turks and Caicos

U.S. Virgin Islands

CENTRAL AMERICA

Belize

Costa Rica

El Salvador

Guatemala

Honduras

Mexico

Nicaragua

Panama

INDIAN OCEAN

Australia

Maldives

Mauritius

MIDDLE EAST

Oman

Saudi Arabia

United Arab Emirates

Yemen

PACIFIC OCEAN

Melanesia (includes New Guinea, New Caledonia, Vanuatu, Fiji, and the Solo-
  mon Islands)

Micronesia (includes the Marianas, Guam, Wake Island, Palau, the Marshall
    Islands, Kiribati, Nauru, and the Federated States of Micronesia)
Polynesia (includes the Hawaiian Islands, Rotuma, the Midway Islands, Samoa,
    American Samoa, Tonga, Tuvalu, the Cook Islands, French Polynesia, and
    Easter Island)
New Zealand*

SOUTH AMERICA

Argentina	Ecuador	Peru
Bolivia	French Guiana	Suriname
Brazil	Galápagos Islands	Venezuela
Chile	Guyana	
Colombia	Paraguay	

*Geographically, does not lie within the tropics, but the cuisine is predominately tropical.

About the Nutritional Numbers

All of the nutritional analyses in this book were compiled using MasterCook Deluxe
4.06 Software, from SierraHome. However, as certain ingredients (fufu flour, galangal)
were unknown to the software at the time of compilation, substitutes of equivalent
caloric and nutritional value were used in their place. All of the recipes using broth have
been analyzed using low-sodium canned vegetable broth. All the recipes using rinsed
and drained canned beans have been analyzed using freshly cooked dried beans. Unless
salt is listed as a measured ingredient (versus to taste, with no preceding suggested mea-
surement) in the recipe, or unless otherwise indicated, no salt has been included in the
analysis; this applies to other seasonings (black pepper, cayenne, etc.) as well. None of
the recipes' optional ingredients, unless otherwise indicated, have been included in the
nutritional analyses. If there is a choice of two or more ingredients in a recipe (for example, low-sodium tamari or soy sauce), the first ingredient has been used in the analysis. Likewise, if there is a choice in the amounts of a particular ingredient in a recipe (for
example, 1 to 2 tablespoons low-sodium soy sauce), the first amount has been used in
the analysis. If there is a range in the number of servings a recipe yields (for example, 4
to 6 servings), the analysis has been based on the first amount.

Appetizers and Snacks

Serving appetizers with a tropical flair is a hit at any gathering. Ever-popular starters include Mexican tortilla chips with assorted salsas and guacamoles, Crispy Thai Spring Rolls with Assorted Dipping Sauces, and Singapore-Style Avocado and Cucumber Sushi with traditional wasabi and pickled ginger. Other enticing openers your guests are sure to welcome but may not have tried before are Caribbean Eggplant Spread, Canary Island–Style Wrinkled Potatoes with Red Pepper Mojo Sauce, or Taiwanese Black Sesame Foccacia, to name just a few. And not to worry—most of the recipes in this chapter can be made in advance, so you, too, can relax and enjoy these exotic offerings with your guests.

Singapore-Style Avocado-Cucumber Sushi Rolls

MAKES 20 TO 24 PIECES

Sushi bars and restaurants are popular throughout the tropical island of Singapore, which was occupied by the Japanese Empire from 1942 to 1945, and is now a prosperous and independent republic. Feel free to experiment with your own sushi fillings in this quick, easy, and delicious recipe. If you don't own a bamboo sushi mat, improvise with a flexible cutting board. Sushi-style, or glutinous rice (also known as sticky rice), and pre-toasted nori, or dry seaweed sheets, are available in Asian markets and many well-stocked supermarkets.

- 1 cup sushi-style (glutinous or sticky) white rice
- 1 cup water
- 3 tablespoons seasoned rice vinegar
- 1 tablespoon sugar
- ½ teaspoon salt
- 4 sheets pre-toasted nori (dry seaweed)
- ½ large cucumber (about 6 ounces), cut in half lengthwise, seeded, and sliced into thin lengthwise strips
- 1 ripe avocado, peeled, pitted, and thinly sliced lengthwise
- Wasabi, soy sauce, and pickled ginger, for condiments

Rinse the rice in a fine-meshed sieve under cold-running tap water until the water runs clear. Drain well.

Place the rice and water in a small saucepan and cover with a tight-fitting lid. Bring to a boil over high heat; immediately reduce the heat to medium and cook 5 minutes. Reduce the heat to low and cook 15 minutes. Remove from heat and let stand, covered, 10 minutes.

In a medium bowl, stir the rice vinegar, sugar, and salt until the sugar is dissolved. Add the hot rice, mixing continuously until the rice is barely warm, about 5 minutes. Set aside to cool to room temperature.

Place a sheet of nori on a bamboo mat, shiny side down. Using wet hands, spread one-fourth of the rice (about ¾ cup) evenly onto the sheet, leaving about a ¾-inch strip of nori uncovered on the long side farthest from you. Place one-fourth of the cucumber, then one-fourth of the avocado, horizontally along the center of the rice. To roll, hold the filling in place with your fingers as you curl the mat forward with your thumbs, pressing gently. When you reach the uncovered strip of nori, stop rolling and lift the bamboo mat up slightly; continue rolling over the uncovered strip of nori, sealing the roll (moisten with a little water to help seal, if desired). Remove the sushi roll and set aside. Repeat with remaining nori sheets, rice, and fillings.

With a sharp, wet knife, slice the rolls into 5 or 6 slices. Serve at room temperature, cut side up, accompanied by the sushi condiments. Sushi can be refrigerated, covered, up to 3 hours before serving chilled or returning to room temperature.

PER PIECE (1/20 of recipe): Calories 59 • Protein 1g • Total Fat 2g • Sat. Fat 0g • Cholesterol 0mg • Carbohydrate 11g • Dietary Fiber 1g • Sodium 57mg

Avocado-Mango Crostini

MAKES 6 SERVINGS

This refreshing crostini or bruschetta topping can also be served salsa-style with tortilla chips.

1 ripe yet firm avocado, peeled, pitted, and
chopped

1 cup chopped fresh mango

¼ cup finely chopped red, yellow, or green bell
pepper

2 tablespoons finely chopped fresh cilantro

1 tablespoon extra-virgin olive oil

1 tablespoon fresh lime juice

Salt and freshly ground black pepper, to taste

Toasted baguette rounds, to serve

In a medium bowl, toss all the ingredients, except the bread, gently to combine. Let stand a few minutes to allow the flavors to blend, and then toss again. Serve at room temperature, or cover and refrigerate 1 to 6 hours and serve chilled, accompanied by the baguette rounds.

PER SERVING (without bread): Calories 94 • Protein 1g • Total Fat 8g • Sat. Fat 1g • Cholesterol 0mg • Carbohydrate 8g • Dietary Fiber 2g • Sodium 4mg

Black Bean and Tropical Fruit Salsa

MAKES 8 SERVINGS

Wow your guests with this fabulous salsa at your next summertime fiesta.

¾ cup chopped fresh papaya

¾ cup chopped fresh mango

¾ cup chopped fresh pineapple

1 (15-ounce) can black beans, rinsed and drained

1 to 2 jalapeño chilies, seeded and finely chopped

½ cup finely chopped red onion

¼ cup finely chopped fresh cilantro

2 tablespoons canola oil

1 tablespoon fresh lime juice

1 tablespoon red wine vinegar

1 teaspoon sugar

½ teaspoon salt, or to taste

Freshly ground black pepper, to taste

Tortilla chips, to serve

In a medium bowl, toss all the ingredients, except the chips, until thoroughly combined. Let stand about 10 minutes at room temperature, then toss again and serve, accompanied by the tortilla chips. Alternatively, cover and refrigerate a minimum of 2 hours or up to 1 day and serve chilled or return to room temperature, accompanied by tortilla chips.

PER SERVING (without chips): Calories 104 • Protein 3g • Total Fat 4g • Sat. Fat 0g • Cholesterol 0mg • Carbohydrate 16g • Dietary Fiber 2g • Sodium 135mg

Thai-Style Glazed Cashews

MAKES 2 CUPS

These sweet yet spicy nuts are addictive. Serve with drinks, on their own as a snack, or tossed in salads and stir-fries.

3 tablespoons granulated white sugar

½ tablespoon palm sugar or light brown sugar

2 tablespoons canola oil

½ to 1 teaspoon crushed red pepper flakes

2 cups salted whole cashews

Line a baking sheet with waxed paper and set aside. In a small container, combine the sugars, and set aside.

In a large nonstick skillet, heat the oil over medium-high heat. Add the red pepper flakes and cook, stirring constantly with a wooden spoon, 30 seconds. Add the cashews and cook, stirring and tossing constantly with a spatula, until nuts are coated with the oil, about 30 seconds. Add the sugar mixture and cook, stirring and tossing constantly with a spatula until the sugar is dissolved, 45 to 60 seconds. Remove the skillet from heat and immediately transfer the nuts to the prepared baking sheet, quickly spreading in a single layer. Let cool to room temperature before serving. Completely cooled nuts can be stored in an airtight container at room temperature a few weeks.

PER ¼ CUP: Calories 239 • Protein 5g • Total Fat 19g • Sat. Fat 3g • Cholesterol 0mg • Carbohydrate 15g • Dietary Fiber 2g • Sodium 6mg

Butter Bean Guacamole

MAKES 4 SERVINGS

The butter bean is actually a type of lima bean that grows wild from Mexico to Argentina. Canned limas can replace the butter beans, if desired.

⅔ cup rinsed, drained canned butter beans

1 tablespoon fresh lemon juice

2 large cloves garlic, finely chopped

1 ripe avocado, peeled, pitted, and coarsely chopped

½ cup chopped red onion

2 tablespoons canned chopped green chilies

¼ teaspoon cayenne pepper, or to taste (optional)

¼ teaspoon salt

Freshly ground black pepper, to taste

1 medium tomato (about 6 ounces), seeded and finely chopped

3 scallions, white and green parts, thinly sliced

Tortilla chips, to serve

In a food processor fitted with the knife blade, process the beans, lemon juice, and garlic until smooth. Add the avocado, red onion, chilies, cayenne (if using), salt, and black pepper; pulse a few times or until chunky. Transfer to a medium bowl and stir in the tomato and scallions. Cover and refrigerate a minimum of 2 hours or up to 1 day and serve chilled, accompanied by tortilla chips.

PER SERVING (without chips): Calories 143 • Protein 5g • Total Fat 8g • Sat. Fat 1g • Cholesterol 0mg • Carbohydrate 16g • Dietary Fiber 5g • Sodium 146mg

Chipotle-Corn Salsa

MAKES ABOUT 3 CUPS

If you have any leftovers, use this spicy salsa to dress up plain rice.

2 medium tomatoes (about 6 ounces each), chopped

1 cup fresh or frozen yellow or white corn, cooked and cooled

¾ cup chopped red bell pepper

1 small red onion (about 4 ounces), chopped

¼ cup chopped fresh cilantro

Juice of 1 to 2 limes

1 tablespoon extra-virgin olive oil

1 to 2 jalapeño chilies, seeded and finely chopped

1 to 2 teaspoons chipotle puree (see Cook's Tip, page 112)

½ teaspoon coarse salt, or to taste

Freshly ground black pepper, to taste

Tortilla chips, to serve

In a medium bowl, toss all the ingredients, except the chips, until well combined. Cover and refrigerate a minimum of 1 hour or up to 2 days. Serve chilled or return to room temperature, accompanied by tortilla chips.

PER ¼ CUP (1/12 of recipe, without chips): Calories 35 • Protein 1g • Total Fat 1g • Sat. Fat 0g • Cholesterol 0mg • Carbohydrate 6g • Dietary Fiber 1g • Sodium 83mg

Citrus Salsa

MAKES 4 SERVINGS

Often used as a condiment for fish, this delightfully refreshing and vitamin-C rich salsa is wonderful with tortilla chips, over mixed greens, in lettuce cups, or all alone.

1 large pink grapefruit, peeled, and bitter white pith removed

1 navel orange, peeled, and bitter white pith removed

½ small red onion (about 2 ounces), finely chopped

2 tablespoons chopped fresh cilantro (optional)

Juice of 1 lime (about 2 tablespoons)

1 jalapeño chili, seeded and finely chopped

¼ teaspoon salt, or to taste

Freshly ground black pepper, to taste

Tortilla chips, to serve

With a small, sharp knife, over a medium bowl, cut grapefruit and orange segments from membranes, allowing juices to fall into the bowl. On a cutting board, carefully cut the segmented fruit into small pieces and add to the bowl, along with any accumulated juices on the cutting board. Add the remaining ingredients, except the chips, and toss gently to combine. Serve at room temperature, or cover and refrigerate a minimum of 2 hours or overnight and serve chilled, accompanied by tortilla chips.

PER SERVING (without chips): Calories 48 • Protein 1g • Total Fat 0g • Sat. Fat 0g • Cholesterol 0mg • Carbohydrate 12g • Dietary Fiber 2g • Sodium 135mg

Baked Wonton Crisps

MAKES 24 CRISPS

You can make these crispy wonton chips as hot or salty as you'd like. Egg-free wonton wrappers are available in Asian markets and health-food stores.

12 egg-free wonton wrappers

2 teaspoons Chinese hot oil, peanut oil, or plain sesame oil

Garlic salt or table salt, to taste (optional)

Preheat oven to 400F (205C).

Arrange the wonton wrappers on a large ungreased baking sheet and brush the tops evenly with half the oil. Turn over and brush with remaining oil. With a sharp knife, cut each wrapper diagonally in half. Sprinkle lightly with salt (if using). Bake on the center rack about 5 minutes, until golden, taking care not to burn. Let cool slightly before serving warm or at room temperature.

2 hours, or up to 2 days. Served chilled, accompanied by the bread.

Caribbean Eggplant Spread

MAKES 4 SERVINGS

This delicious spread or dip also makes a fine filling for flour tortilla wraps, which you can eat whole for lunch or cut into tiny appetizer servings.

- 1 large eggplant (about 1 pound), peeled and cut into bite-size chunks
- 1 small plum tomato (about 2 ounces), finely chopped
- 2 to 3 tablespoons very finely chopped red onion
- 2 to 3 tablespoons finely chopped fresh cilantro
- 1 to 2 tablespoons fresh lime juice
- 1 tablespoon canola oil
- 1 large clove garlic, finely chopped
- ½ teaspoon coarse salt
- ½ teaspoon sugar
- ¼ teaspoon jerk seasoning, or more to taste
- Freshly ground black pepper, to taste
- Toasted baguette rounds or other crusty bread, crackers, pita bread, or tortilla chips

Bring a large pot of liberally salted water (use about 2 tablespoons salt) to a boil over high heat; add the eggplant and return to a boil. Reduce the heat slightly and boil until very tender, 5 to 7 minutes. Drain well and transfer to a medium bowl.

Using a fork, mash the eggplant until slightly chunky. Add the remaining ingredients, except the bread, stirring well until mixture is a creamy dip consistency. Cover and refrigerate a minimum of

Taiwanese Black Sesame Focaccia

MAKES 4 GENEROUS, 8 MEDIUM, OR 16 SMALL APPETIZERS

Aside from making a splendid snack or appetizer, this exotic focaccia is also an excellent accompaniment to many of the book's soups, namely Cambodian Tomato Soup, page 39. Regular sesame seeds can be used in lieu of the black variety, which are available in Asian markets and specialty stores. Chinese hot oil can typically be located in the international aisle of well-stocked supermarkets.

- 1 (1-pound) package refrigerated pizza dough
- All-purpose flour, for dusting
- 2 teaspoons Chinese hot oil
- 1 teaspoon coarse salt
- 2 teaspoons toasted (dark) sesame oil
- 4 large cloves garlic, thinly sliced
- 2 teaspoons black sesame seeds

Preheat oven to 400F (205C). Lightly oil a baking sheet and set aside.

Divide the dough into 4 equal portions. On a lightly floured work surface, roll each portion to a ¼-inch thickness. Transfer to prepared baking sheet. Brush each portion with ½ teaspoon of the hot oil and sprinkle with ¼ teaspoon of the salt. Bake on the center rack 8 minutes. Remove the baking sheet from oven. Brush each portion with ½ teaspoon of the sesame oil, and then sprinkle with equal amounts of garlic and sesame seeds. Return to oven and bake 7 minutes, or until golden brown. Cut in halves or in quarters, if desired, and serve warm or at room temperature.

PER SERVING (¼ of recipe): Calories 302 • Protein 7g • Total Fat 8g • Sat. Fat 1g • Cholesterol 0mg • Carbohydrate 49g • Dietary Fiber 1g • Sodium 474mg

Kiwifruit Salsa

MAKES 4 SERVINGS

This slightly spicy yet very refreshing salsa is wonderful tossed with rice and beans, or steamed vegetables such as asparagus. It also makes a tasty topping for grilled eggplant and zucchini.

2 kiwifruit, peeled and finely chopped
½ tablespoon fresh orange juice
½ tablespoon chopped fresh mint
1 teaspoon cider vinegar
1 teaspoon finely chopped jalapeño chili
¼ teaspoon salt, or to taste
Freshly ground black pepper, to taste

In a small bowl, combine all the ingredients. Cover and refrigerate a minimum of 1 hour or up to 2 days. Serve chilled or return to room temperature.

PER SERVING: Calories 28 • Protein 1g • Total Fat 0g • Sat. Fat 0g • Cholesterol 0mg • Carbohydrate 7g • Dietary Fiber 2g • Sodium 136mg

Thai-Style Mango Salsa

MAKES 4 TO 6 SERVINGS

Traditionally used as a condiment for fish, this Asian-style mango salsa can wear many hats: dip for Baked Wonton Crisps (page 17), as well as for pita crisps and tortilla chips; dressing for countless steamed vegetables and plain rice; relish for veggie burgers, grilled or baked tofu, and grilled vegetables such as eggplant, portobello mushrooms, and zucchini. If you don't have time to make the Thai Sweet Chili Sauce, it can be purchased at Asian markets as well as the international aisle of many well-stocked supermarkets.

2 cups cubed mango (about 2 medium)
½ cup chopped fresh cilantro
1 to 1½ tablespoons Thai Sweet Chili Sauce (page 26) or store-bought sauce
1 tablespoon low-sodium tamari or soy sauce
1 tablespoon fresh lime juice
2 large cloves garlic, finely chopped
½ teaspoon sugar, or to taste (optional)
Salt and freshly ground black pepper, to taste
2 recipes Baked Wonton Crisps (page 17)

In a food processor fitted with the knife blade, pulse the mango until finely chopped but slightly chunky. Transfer to a small bowl and add the remaining ingredients, except the wonton crisps, stirring well to combine. Let stand about 10 minutes at room temperature to allow the flavors to blend; stir again and serve. Alternatively, cover and refrigerate a minimum of 2 hours or up to 2 days and serve chilled or return to room temperature.

PER SERVING (without Wonton Crisps): Calories 70 • Protein 2g • Total Fat 0g • Sat. Fat 0g • Cholesterol 0mg • Carbohydrate 17g • Dietary Fiber 2g • Sodium 160mg

Oven-Dried Mangoes

MAKES 12 SERVINGS

Here is a delicious and easy way of preserving mangoes to enjoy when they're not in season. The initial sugar-water bath is largely discarded, so the dried fruit is essentially unsweetened. For a sweeter fruit, sprinkle the slices as directed with additional sugar before placing in the oven.

3 cups water

1 cup sugar, plus additional, to taste

Juice of 1 lime (about 2 tablespoons)

2 pounds mangoes (about 2 extra-large or
    3 medium), peeled, pitted, and cut into
    5/16-inch-thick slices

Preheat oven to 125F (50C). Lightly oil a baking rack, set on a baking sheet, and set aside.

In a medium saucepan, combine the water, 1 cup sugar, and lime juice. Bring to a brisk simmer over medium-high heat, stirring until the sugar is dissolved. Add the mango slices, stir, and remove from heat. Let stand, uncovered, 20 minutes, stirring and turning the fruit a few times. Drain well in a colander.

Arrange the mango slices in a single layer on the prepared baking rack. Sprinkle with additional sugar, if desired. Place in the preheated oven 6 to 8 hours, until mangoes are leathery but still pliable. Let cool to room temperature before transferring to a self-sealing plastic bag. Store at room temperature a few weeks, or refrigerate or freeze a few months.

PER SERVING: Calories 43 • Protein 0g • Total Fat 0g • Sat. Fat 0g • Cholesterol 0mg • Carbohydrate 11g • Dietary Fiber 1g • Sodium 1mg

Nori Bundles with Peanut-Chutney Sauce

MAKES 8 APPETIZERS

The time-pressed host or hostess's quick answer to sushi, these colorful nori bundles are ideal finger food that can be served with a variety of Asian-style dips. They also make an easy yet elegant first course for four, with the sauce drizzled attractively over the top.

2 medium carrots (about 4 ounces each), cut in half
    widthwise, then cut lengthwise into 8 strips for a
    total of 32 strips

16 green beans, cut lengthwise in half

2 sheets nori, cut widthwise with scissors into 4
    equal strips for a total of 8 strips

Peanut-Chutney Sauce (page 27)

Bring a large stockpot of salted water to a boil over high heat. Add the carrots and boil 2 minutes. Add the green beans and boil until crisp-tender, another 2 minutes. Drain in a colander and rinse under cold-running water to cool. Drain well.

Arrange one-eighth of each vegetable (4 carrot strips and 4 bean halves) crosswise on each nori strip; roll up into bundles, pressing the ends of the nori to seal (if necessary, dampen a fingertip with water to help seal). Repeat with remaining vegetables and nori strips. (At this point, the nori bundles can be stored, covered, in the refrigerator up to 24 hours before serving.) Transfer to a serving platter and serve with Peanut-Chutney Sauce for dipping.

PER BUNDLE WITH ABOUT 1½ TABLESPOONS SAUCE: Calories 151 • Protein 7g • Total Fat 4g • Sat. Fat 1g • Cholesterol 0mg • Carbohydrate 26g • Dietary Fiber 9g • Sodium 206mg

Haitian Peanut Sauce with Raw and Steamed Vegetables

MAKES 6 SERVINGS (ABOUT 1½ CUPS SAUCE)

Also known as *mamba*, this spicy sauce's heat can be toned down if you use jalapeño chilies in lieu of the hotter Scotch bonnet variety.

- 1 tablespoon canola oil
- 1 small onion (about 4 ounces), finely chopped
- 4 large cloves garlic, finely chopped
- ½ Scotch bonnet chili or 2 jalapeño chilies, seeded and finely chopped
- 1 cup low-sodium vegetable broth
- ½ cup chunky peanut butter
- ½ teaspoon salt, or to taste
- Freshly ground black pepper, to taste
- 2 tablespoons chopped fresh flat-leaf parsley
- 1 teaspoon fresh lime juice, or more to taste
- 4 to 6 cups assorted raw and/or steamed vegetables, such as sliced raw cucumber and jicama or steamed broccoli and cauliflower florets, for dipping

In a small saucepan, heat the oil over medium heat. Add the onion and cook, stirring, until softened, about 3 minutes. Add the garlic and chili and cook, stirring constantly, until the onion begins to brown, 1 to 2 minutes. Add the broth, peanut butter, salt, and black pepper and bring to a simmer, stirring well to thoroughly incorporate. Remove from the heat and stir in the parsley and lime juice. Let cool to room temperature. Serve at room temperature, accompanied by the vegetables for dipping, or cover and refrigerate a minimum of 2 hours or up to 5 days and serve chilled or return to room temperature.

PER ¼ CUP (⅙ of recipe, without vegetables): Calories 169 • Protein 8g • Total Fat 13g • Sat. Fat 2g • Cholesterol 0mg • Carbohydrate 8g • Dietary Fiber 3g • Sodium 371mg

Caribbean-Spiced Popcorn

MAKES ABOUT 10 CUPS

This is fun party popcorn. For a little more kick, use the greater amount of jerk seasoning. For best results, season the popcorn while it's still quite hot.

- ½ to ¾ teaspoon garlic salt
- ¼ to ½ teaspoon jerk seasoning
- ¼ teaspoon mild curry powder
- ⅛ teaspoon lemon pepper seasoning
- 1 (2.9-ounce) package light natural-flavor microwave popcorn, freshly popped according to package directions, still hot

Combine the salt, jerk seasoning, curry powder, and lemon pepper seasoning in a small bowl. In a large bowl, place about one-third of the hot popcorn and sprinkle evenly with one-third of the seasoning mixture. Repeat with remaining popcorn and seasoning. (Do not toss.) Serve at once.

PER 1 CUP (⅒ of recipe): Calories 43 • Protein 1g • Total Fat 2g • Sat. Fat 0g • Cholesterol 0mg • Carbohydrate 6g • Dietary Fiber 1g • Sodium 326mg

Canary Island–Style Wrinkled Potatoes with Red Pepper Mojo Sauce

MAKES 8 SERVINGS

A specialty dish of the Canary Islands, wrinkled potatoes, or *papas arrugadas*, were originally cooked in seawater. Unless you must watch your sodium intake, don't be put off by the copious amount of salt, as all but about 2 tablespoons is drained away. If sodium is a concern, simply boil the potatoes in lightly salted water (see Thai-Style Curried Potato Puffs, page 23 for method). To serve, spear the potatoes with wooden picks, with the mojo sauce on the side for dipping.

> 1½ pounds small round red or white potatoes (1½ to 2 inches in diameter), unpeeled, left whole
>
> ½ cup coarse salt
>
> ½ recipe Canary Island–Style Red Pepper Mojo Sauce (opposite)

In a medium deep-sided skillet with a lid, add about 1 inch of water. Add the potatoes (they will not be completely immersed in the water) and salt and bring to a boil over high heat. Reduce the heat to medium-high and cook, partially covered, turning occasionally, until the potatoes are tender through the center, about 15 minutes. Drain the potatoes, leaving about ½ cup liquid in the skillet. Return the skillet to medium heat and cook, uncovered, stirring and shaking the skillet occasionally, until the potatoes are dried, covered with a whitish coat, and slightly wrinkled, about 5 minutes. Transfer the potatoes to a serving platter and serve at once, with the mojo sauce passed separately for dipping.

PER SERVING (based on 2 tablespoons total coarse salt coating finished potatoes): Calories 67 • Protein 2g • Total Fat 1g • Sat. Fat 0g • Cholesterol 0mg • Carbohydrate 13g • Dietary Fiber 1g • Sodium 1,414mg

Canary Island–Style Red Pepper Mojo Sauce

MAKES ABOUT 3/4 CUP

Toss this vitamin-C rich sauce with countless cooked vegetables. It also makes an excellent topping for grilled eggplant and portobello mushrooms, as well as a spread for toasted baguette rounds. Omit the coarse salt if serving with Canary Island–Style Wrinkled Potatoes (opposite).

> 1 large red bell pepper (about 8 ounces), cut into eighths
>
> 1½ tablespoons extra-virgin olive oil
>
> 1 large clove garlic, finely chopped
>
> 1 teaspoon ground cumin
>
> 1 teaspoon coarse salt
>
> ½ teaspoon sweet paprika
>
> ¼ teaspoon freshly ground black pepper
>
> Pinch cayenne pepper, or to taste (optional)

In a food processor fitted with the knife blade, combine all the ingredients; process until very smooth. Serve at room temperature. Sauce can be stored, covered, in the refrigerator up to 3 days. Return to room temperature before using.

PER 1 TABLESPOON (1/12 of recipe): Calories 21 • Protein 0g • Total Fat 2g • Sat. Fat 0g • Cholesterol 0mg • Carbohydrate 2g • Dietary Fiber 1g • Sodium 157mg

Thai-Style Curried Potato Puffs

MAKES 9 APPETIZERS

Perfect for parties, these tasty Thai potato parcels are easy to prepare with frozen puff pastry. Even better, the potato filling can be made a day ahead of assembling and baking.

½ pound medium boiling potatoes, peeled and quartered

3 teaspoons canola oil

1 large shallot, finely chopped

½ tablespoon turmeric

½ teaspoon sugar

1 large clove garlic, finely chopped

¼ teaspoon salt

⅛ teaspoon crushed red pepper flakes, or more to taste

Freshly ground black pepper, to taste

1 tablespoon finely chopped fresh basil and/or cilantro

1 sheet frozen puff pastry, thawed according to package directions

In a large saucepan, bring the potatoes and enough salted water to cover to a boil over high heat. Reduce the heat slightly and boil gently until tender, 15 to 20 minutes. Drain and return to pot; add 1 teaspoon of the oil and mash well.

Meanwhile, in a small nonstick skillet, heat the remaining oil over medium heat. Add the shallot and cook, stirring, until softened but not browned, about 3 minutes. Add the turmeric, sugar, garlic, salt, red pepper flakes, and black pepper; cook, stirring constantly, 1 minute. Remove the skillet from the heat and add the basil, mixing well to combine. Transfer the shallot mixture to the mashed potatoes, mixing well to thoroughly combine. Set aside to cool. (At this point, the filling can be refrigerated, covered, 24 hours before continuing with the recipe.)

Preheat oven to 400F (205C).

Cut the pastry sheet into 9 equal squares. Place about 1 heaping tablespoon of the potato filling in the middle of each square. Lift a corner to its opposite corner, forming a triangular parcel. Pinch the edges to seal. Repeat with remaining filling and pastry. Transfer to an ungreased baking sheet and prick each parcel once with a fork. Bake on the center rack until golden brown, about 20 minutes. Serve warm.

PER SERVING: Calories 167 • Protein 3g • Total Fat 9g • Sat. Fat 2g • Cholesterol 0mg • Carbohydrate 20g • Dietary Fiber 2g • Sodium 151mg

Sofrito-Grilled Bread

MAKES 4 SERVINGS

The Caribbean equivalent of Italian bruschetta, this quick-and-easy snack or appetizer takes advantage of jarred sofrito, available in most well-stocked supermarkets in the international aisle. If you would rather make your own, see the recipe on page 77.

½ baguette (about 5 ounces), cut in half lengthwise, then cut in half crosswise (4 pieces)

1 clove garlic, halved

8 teaspoons sofrito, heated

2 teaspoons extra-virgin olive oil

Dried oregano and/or whole cumin seed

Grill or toast the bread lightly on the cut sides. Rub the grilled sides with the flat sides of the cut garlic.

Spread each toasted side evenly with 2 teaspoons of the sofrito. Drizzle each with ½ teaspoon of the oil and sprinkle lightly with oregano and/or cumin seed, as desired. Serve at once.

PER SERVING: Calories 143 • Protein 4g • Total Fat 6g • Sat. Fat 1g • Cholesterol 0mg • Carbohydrate 19g • Dietary Fiber 1g • Sodium 305mg

Warm New Potatoes with Indonesian Peanut Sauce

MAKES 6 SERVINGS

If desired, any lightly cooked vegetable can be substituted for the potatoes; broccoli and cauliflower florets are especially delicious with the peanut sauce.

24 to 28 tiny new potatoes (1 to 1½ inches in diameter), scrubbed and left whole
Indonesian Peanut Sauce (opposite)

In a medium stockpot, bring the potatoes and enough salted water to cover to a boil over high heat. Reduce the heat and boil gently until potatoes are just tender, 10 to 15 minutes. Drain.

To serve, place the sauce in a small bowl in the center of a warmed serving platter and surround with the hot potatoes. Spear the potatoes with wooden picks and serve at once.

PER SERVING: Calories 148 • Protein 5g • Total Fat 6g • Sat. Fat 2g • Cholesterol 0mg • Carbohydrate 21g • Dietary Fiber 2g • Sodium 124mg

Indonesian Peanut Sauce

MAKES ABOUT ½ CUP

Serve this as a dipping sauce for countless raw and lightly cooked vegetables.

¼ cup creamy peanut butter
¼ cup water
2 tablespoons fresh lime juice
1 tablespoon light coconut milk
1 tablespoon sugar
1 teaspoon low-sodium soy sauce or tamari
1 teaspoon tomato ketchup
1 large clove garlic, finely chopped
½ teaspoon cayenne pepper, or to taste

In a small saucepan, bring all the ingredients to a boil over medium heat, stirring often. Reduce heat and simmer, uncovered, stirring occasionally, until reduced and thickened, about 10 minutes. Serve warm or at room temperature.

PER TABLESPOON: Calories 61 • Protein 2g • Total Fat 5g • Sat. Fat 1g • Cholesterol 0mg • Carbohydrate 4g • Dietary Fiber 1g • Sodium 71mg

Mexican-Spiced Mini Pretzels

MAKES 10 TO 12 SERVINGS

These easy-to-make mini pretzels can be made even spicier by doubling the spice ingredients. If you are watching your salt intake, low-sodium or no-salt pretzels can be used.

1 (16-ounce) bag salted mini pretzels

3 tablespoons canola oil

½ tablespoon chili powder

¼ teaspoon ground cumin

⅛ teaspoon onion powder

⅛ teaspoon garlic powder

⅛ teaspoon cayenne pepper

Preheat oven to 300F (150C). Lightly grease 2 rimmed baking sheets and set aside.

Place the pretzels in a large bowl. In a small bowl, whisk together the oil, chili powder, cumin, onion powder, garlic powder, and cayenne until thoroughly blended. Pour over the pretzels, tossing gently yet thoroughly to coat. Transfer to prepared baking sheets and spread in a single layer (some overlap is okay). Bake on center rack, without turning, 10 to 15 minutes, until the pretzels are glazed. Let cool on the baking sheet to room temperature. Store in a tightly covered container at room temperature up to 1 week.

PER SERVING: Calories 211 • Protein 4g • Total Fat 6g • Sat. Fat 1g • Cholesterol 0mg • Carbohydrate 36g • Dietary Fiber 2g • Sodium 782mg

Crispy Thai Spring Rolls with Dipping Sauces

MAKES 15 ROLLS

These scrumptious rolls can be assembled and refrigerated overnight before frying for easy entertaining. If you don't have time to make the Thai Sweet Chili Sauce or Thai Peanut Sauce, serve them with prepared plum sauce mixed with a little soy and Chinese chili paste, to taste.

1½ tablespoons peanut oil, plus additional for frying

2 shallots, thinly sliced

1 fresh red or green chili, seeded and finely chopped

1 tablespoon chopped peeled fresh ginger

3 large cloves garlic, finely chopped

1 cup shredded cabbage

4 scallions, white and green parts, thinly sliced

½ cup shredded carrot

½ cup thinly sliced fresh shiitake or cultivated white mushrooms

3 tablespoons low-sodium soy sauce or tamari

2 tablespoons fresh lime juice

½ tablespoon toasted (dark) sesame oil

1 teaspoon Chinese chili paste, or to taste

½ teaspoon sugar

1½ cups bean sprouts

½ cup chopped fresh basil

½ cup chopped fresh cilantro

15 (8-inch) round rice papers (see Cook's Tip, page 26)

Thai Sweet Chili Sauce (page 26) and/or Thai Peanut Sauce (page 29)

In a large nonstick skillet, heat the 1½ tablespoons peanut oil over medium-high heat. Add the shallots, chili, ginger, and garlic; cook, stirring constantly, until fragrant, 1 minute. Add the cabbage, scallions, carrot, and mushrooms; cook, stirring constantly, 2 minutes. Add the soy sauce, lime juice, sesame oil, chili paste, and sugar; cook, stirring constantly, 1 minute. Add the sprouts and toss to thoroughly combine. Remove from heat and add the basil and cilantro, tossing well to combine. Set aside.

Prepare a bowl of warm water large enough in which to dip the rice papers. Working with one at a time, dip the rice paper in the warm water 8 to 10 seconds, or until it begins to soften. Transfer to a flat work surface. Working quickly, put about ¼ cup filling on a wrapper. Fold the bottom of the wrapper up over the filling, and then fold each side toward the center. Roll from the bottom to the top of each roll, as tightly as you can without ripping the wrapper. Repeat with remaining papers and filling. (At this point, rolls can be covered with plastic wrap and refrigerated overnight. Bring to room temperature before proceeding with the recipe.)

Line a baking sheet or dinner plate with several layers of paper towels. In a wok, medium stockpot, or other high-sided pot or pan, heat between 1 and 1½ inches of peanut oil over medium-high heat. To test when oil is hot enough, using tongs, dip a corner of a spring roll in the oil; if oil begins to sizzle, the oil is ready. Working with a few at a time, carefully place the spring rolls in the oil. Fry the rolls until golden-brown, anywhere from a few seconds to 1 minute on each side, depending on the heat of the oil (oil will become hotter with each batch; if necessary, reduce the heat to medium). Transfer to the paper towel–lined baking sheet to absorb the excess oil. Repeat with remaining rolls. Serve hot, accompanied by sauces for dipping.

PER SPRING ROLL (without sauce, based on ¼ cup peanut oil absorbed during frying): Calories 88 • Protein 2g • Total Fat 6g • Sat. Fat 1g • Cholesterol 0mg • Carbohydrate 8g • Dietary Fiber 1g • Sodium 171mg

COOK'S TIP: *Rice papers, or spring roll skins, are available in Asian and gourmet markets, health food stores, and some well-stocked supermarkets. To avoid tearing as you roll them, make sure the filling ingredients are in small uniform pieces and that you only use about ¼ cup filling per 8-inch round rice paper.*

Thai Sweet Chili Sauce

MAKES ABOUT 1 CUP

This sweet-and-spicy chili sauce is also a fine condiment for grilled tofu and veggie burgers.

⅓ cup water
⅓ cup sugar
¼ cup plain rice vinegar
1 to 1½ tablespoons hot ground chili paste, such as Chinese chili paste or *sambal olek*
2 large cloves garlic, finely chopped
2 teaspoons cornstarch
½ teaspoon salt

In a small saucepan over medium heat, bring all ingredients to a boil, whisking often until the sugar dissolves. Reduce the heat to medium-low and simmer 5 minutes, stirring occasionally. Remove from heat and let cool to room temperature before using. The sauce can be stored, covered, in the refrigerator up to 1 week before using.

PER TABLESPOON: Calories 19 • Protein 0g • Total Fat 0g • Sat. Fat 0g • Cholesterol 0mg • Carbohydrate 5g • Dietary Fiber 0g • Sodium 67mg

Tofu Satay with Peanut-Chutney Sauce

MAKES 6 SERVINGS

Wonderful as appetizers, these yummy satays can also be served over brown rice, accompanied by steamed broccoli, for a memorable meal for four people; in this instance, use four skewers.

1 (15-ounce) package extra-firm tofu, well drained

1 tablespoon low-sodium tamari or soy sauce

1 tablespoon toasted (dark) sesame oil

1 tablespoon sherry

1 large red bell pepper (about 8 ounces), cut into
   1-inch squares

Peanut-Chutney Sauce (opposite)

Place the tofu on a deep-sided plate or shallow bowl. Top with a second plate and weight with a heavy can. Let stand for a minimum of 15 minutes (preferably 1 hour). Drain excess water. Cut the tofu into 1-inch cubes. In a medium bowl, combine the tamari, oil, and sherry. Add the tofu and toss gently to coat. Let marinate 30 minutes at room temperature, or cover and refrigerate 1 hour or overnight.

Soak 6 wooden skewers in water 15 minutes. Prepare a medium-hot charcoal grill or gas grill, or preheat a broiler. Position the grill or oven rack 4 to 6 inches from heat source. If broiling, lightly oil a large baking sheet and set aside. Or heat a large nonstick stovetop grilling pan with ridges over medium-high heat.

With a slotted spoon, remove the tofu from the marinade and reserve the marinade. Alternate tofu and bell pepper pieces on the skewers. Grill or broil until tofu is nicely browned and bell pepper is beginning to char, turning once, 10 to 12 minutes. Transfer to a warm platter and drizzle with the reserved marinade. Serve warm, with Peanut-Chutney Sauce for dipping.

PER SERVING: Calories 176 • Protein 9g • Total Fat 11g • Sat. Fat 2g • Cholesterol 0mg • Carbohydrate 12g • Dietary Fiber 3g • Sodium 348mg

Peanut Chutney-Sauce

MAKES ABOUT ¾ CUP

Use this versatile sauce as a dip for various steamed or raw vegetables, boiled new potatoes, and fried tofu cubes. It can be stored, covered, in the refrigerator up to 5 days; for best results, return to room temperature before using.

¼ cup creamy peanut butter

¼ cup water

3 tablespoons mango chutney

2 tablespoons fresh lime juice

1 tablespoon low-sodium tamari or soy sauce

1 large clove garlic, finely chopped

¼ teaspoon salt

¼ teaspoon crushed red pepper flakes

In a food processor fitted with the knife blade, or in a blender, combine all the ingredients; process or blend until smooth. Serve at room temperature.

PER TABLESPOON (1/12 of recipe): Calories 43 • Protein 1g • Total Fat 3g • Sat. Fat 1g • Cholesterol 0mg • Carbohydrate 4g • Dietary Fiber 1g • Sodium 121mg

Taiwan-Style Vegetable Wraps with Pineapple Five-Spice Dipping Sauce

MAKES 12 APPETIZER-SIZE WRAPS

These crunchy vegetable wraps can also be made with lightly blanched sugar snap peas instead of the snow peas, but increase the blanching time for the peas to about 1 minute.

1 cup snow peas

1 cup bean sprouts

1 cup shredded carrots

2 scallions, white and green parts, thinly sliced

¼ cup chopped peanuts

Pineapple Five-Spice Dipping
    Sauce (page 30)

Salt and freshly ground black pepper, to taste

12 (8-inch) round rice papers (see Cook's Tip,
    page 26)

Bring a medium stockpot filled with salted water to a boil over high heat. Add the snow peas and blanch until barely softened, 30 seconds. Drain and rinse under cold-running water until cooled. Drain well.

In a medium bowl, toss together the snow peas, sprouts, carrots, scallions, peanuts, 2 tablespoons of the dipping sauce, salt, and pepper until thoroughly combined. Let stand about 10 minutes, and then toss again.

Prepare a bowl of warm water large enough in which to dip the rice papers. Working with one at a time, dip the rice paper in the warm water 8 to 10 seconds, or until it begins to soften. Transfer to a flat work surface. Working quickly, put about ¼ cup vegetable filling on a wrapper. Fold the bottom of the wrapper up over the filling, and then fold each side toward the center. Roll from the bottom to the top of each roll, as tightly as you can without ripping the wrapper. Wrap in plastic wrap to keep from drying out. Repeat with remaining papers and filling. Serve at room temperature, with the remaining dipping sauce. Alternatively, refrigerate a minimum of 2 hours, or overnight, and serve chilled or return to room temperature.

Fried Tofu Nuggets with Thai Peanut Sauce

MAKES 8 SERVINGS

You can serve these tasty fried tofu nuggets with any of your favorite Asian-style dipping sauces—they are especially delicious with the Thai Sweet Chili Sauce (page 26). Provide wooden picks for easy dipping.

1 (15-ounce) package extra-firm tofu, well drained

⅓ cup sesame seeds

3 tablespoons all-purpose flour

2 tablespoons cornstarch

¼ teaspoon sugar

¼ cup peanut oil

Salt and freshly ground black pepper, to taste

Thai Peanut Sauce (page 29)

Place the tofu on a deep-sided plate or shallow bowl. Top with a second plate and weight with a heavy can. Let stand for a minimum of 15 minutes (preferably 1 hour). Drain excess water. Cut into 1-inch cubes.

Line a baking sheet with a few layers of paper towels and set aside.

In a small bowl, mix together the sesame seeds, flour, cornstarch, and sugar. Roll tofu in sesame mixture until well coated.

In a large nonstick skillet, heat the oil over medium-high heat. Add the tofu and cook, turning with a spatula every few minutes, until it is nicely browned on all sides, 6 to 8 minutes. Transfer to prepared baking sheet and season with salt and pepper. Let drain a few minutes before arranging on a warm serving platter, accompanied by Thai Peanut Sauce. Serve at once.

PER SERVING: Calories 241 • Protein 9g • Total Fat 19g • Sat. Fat 4g • Cholesterol 0mg • Carbohydrate 12g • Dietary Fiber 2g • Sodium 199mg

Thai Peanut Sauce

MAKES ABOUT 3/4 CUP

If you don't have tamarind paste, substitute with 1 to 2 teaspoons fresh lemon juice.

- ½ cup light coconut milk, plus additional, as necessary
- ⅓ cup chunky peanut butter
- 1½ to 3 teaspoons Chinese chili paste, *sambal olek*, or other chili paste
- 1 tablespoon light brown sugar
- ½ tablespoon low-sodium soy sauce or tamari
- ½ teaspoon tamarind paste
- ½ teaspoon ground ginger
- ½ teaspoon salt
- ¼ teaspoon coriander seed, crushed
- Freshly ground black pepper, to taste

In a small saucepan, bring all the ingredients to a gentle simmer over medium-high heat, stirring often. Reduce the heat to medium and cook, stirring, 1 minute. Remove from heat and let cool to room temperature before using. For a thinner sauce, add more coconut milk or water. The sauce can be stored, covered, in the refrigerator up to 3 days before using.

PER TABLESPOON: Calories 59 • Protein 2g • Total Fat 5g • Sat. Fat 2g • Cholesterol 0mg • Carbohydrate 4g • Dietary Fiber 1g • Sodium 153mg

Tomatillo Guacamole

MAKES ABOUT 2 CUPS

Canned tomatillos, available in Latin markets and the international aisle of many well-stocked supermarkets, make quick work of this tasty guacamole.

- 1 (11-ounce) can tomatillos, well drained, or ½ pound fresh tomatillos, husked, stemmed and rinsed under warm water to remove stickiness
- ⅓ cup packed fresh cilantro
- 1 to 2 tablespoons fresh lime juice
- 2 large cloves garlic, finely chopped
- ½ teaspoon sugar
- Salt and freshly ground black pepper, to taste
- 3 ripe avocados, pitted, peeled, and chopped
- Tortilla chips, to serve

If using fresh tomatillos, place in a small saucepan with cold water to cover. Bring to a boil over high heat. Immediately remove from heat and drain. Remove the cores, if desired.

In a food processor fitted with the knife blade, or in a blender, process the tomatillos, cilantro, lime juice, garlic, sugar, salt, and pepper until smooth and pureed. Transfer to a medium bowl and add the avocados, stirring well to combine. Cover and refrigerate 2 to 12 hours and serve chilled, accompanied by tortilla chips.

Pineapple Five-Spice Dipping Sauce

MAKES ABOUT 1 CUP

This pleasantly spiced sauce also makes a great dressing or marinade for raw or lightly steamed vegetables. Chinese five-spice powder, an aromatic blend typically made of anise, ginger, star anise, cinnamon, and cloves, can be located in the spice aisle of most well-stocked supermarkets.

½ cup pineapple preserves, at room temperature
¼ cup low-sodium soy sauce or tamari
¼ cup plain rice vinegar
2 teaspoons Chinese five-spice powder
½ teaspoon toasted (dark) sesame oil
Freshly ground black pepper, to taste

In a small bowl, whisk together all the ingredients until well combined. Serve at room temperature. The sauce can be stored, covered, in the refrigerator up to 1 week. Return to room temperature before using.

Soups

Imaginative soups and stews for all seasons abound in the tropics. Warm up in winter with a hearty bowl of Brazilian Black Bean Soup, redolent of citrus and sherry, or a rib-sticking bowl of African Groundnut Stew with Fufu, a porridge-like staple from equatorial Africa. On those blustery days of early spring, thaw out with a comforting bowl of Thai Coconut-Noodle Soup, fragrant with lemongrass and ginger. During the dog days of summer, chill out with a cool bowl of Chilled Australian Curried Mango Soup; no stovetop required. When all the leaves have fallen and the autumn skies grow bleak, cheer up with a lively bowl of Caribbean Pumpkin Soup. Served up in a pumpkin shell, it's sure to make you smile.

Quick Caribbean Black Bean Soup

MAKES 4 SERVINGS

This quick and easy version of the Caribbean classic is delicious garnished with broken tortilla chips or taco shells.

1 (14-ounce) can low-sodium vegetable broth

1 (14.5-ounce) can diced tomatoes with jalapeño chilies, juices included

¾ cup water

1 (14-ounce) can light coconut milk

1 (16-ounce) can refried vegetarian black beans

Salt and freshly ground black pepper, to taste

¼ cup chopped fresh cilantro

Hot pepper sauce (optional)

In a medium stockpot or large saucepan, bring the broth, tomatoes and their juices, and the water to a boil over high heat. Reduce the heat to medium and stir in the coconut milk, beans, salt, and pepper; cook, stirring often, until the beans are thoroughly blended. Reduce the heat to low and simmer, covered, 10 minutes, stirring occasionally. Stir in the cilantro and serve hot, with the hot pepper sauce passed separately (if using).

PER SERVING: Calories 269 • Protein 15g • Total Fat 12g • Sat. Fat 10g • Cholesterol 0mg • Carbohydrate 28g • Dietary Fiber 8g • Sodium 886mg

Caribbean Callaloo Soup

MAKES 6 SERVINGS

Callaloo is a creamy Caribbean soup consisting primarily of greens, such as spinach, and okra, a natural thickener. One serving yields about 20 percent of the Daily Recommended Value for both calcium and iron. Chopped kale, escarole, or arugula can replace the spinach, if desired.

2 tablespoons canola oil

1 medium onion (about 6 ounces), chopped

1 fresh green or red chili, seeded and chopped

3 large garlic cloves, finely chopped

2 cups low-sodium vegetable broth

1 (14-ounce) can light coconut milk

2 cups frozen chopped okra, thawed

½ teaspoon dried thyme leaves

½ teaspoon salt

Freshly ground black pepper, to taste

16 ounces fresh spinach, stemmed and coarsely chopped, or 1 (10-ounce) bag fresh spinach leaves, coarsely chopped

In a medium stockpot, heat the oil over medium heat. Add the onion and chili and cook, stirring, until softened, 3 to 5 minutes. Add the garlic and cook, stirring, until golden, about 2 minutes.

Add the remaining ingredients, except the spinach, and bring to a brisk simmer over medium-high heat. Gradually add the spinach, stirring and turning until wilted. Reduce the heat to low, cover, and simmer gently, stirring occasionally, until the okra is tender, about 10 minutes. Transfer about two-thirds of the soup to a food processor fitted with the knife blade, or to a blender; process or blend until smooth. Return to the stockpot and reheat over low heat, stirring occasionally. Serve warm.

PER SERVING: Calories 186 • Protein 9g • Total Fat 12g • Sat. Fat 7g • Cholesterol 0mg • Carbohydrate 13g • Dietary Fiber 5g • Sodium 438mg

PER SERVING: Calories 248 • Protein 12g • Total Fat 12g • Sat. Fat 10g • Cholesterol 0mg • Carbohydrate 29g • Dietary Fiber 5g • Sodium 607mg

Brazilian Corn Soup

MAKES 4 SERVINGS

Unlike most pureed soups, this simple yet flavorful Brazilian favorite is blended before cooking. For a milder version, substitute chopped pimiento for the chili, if desired. For a smokier flavor, use frozen roasted corn, available at Trader Joe's.

- 2 cups frozen regular or roasted yellow corn, thawed
- 2 cups low-sodium vegetable broth
- 1 (14-ounce) can light coconut milk
- 1 slice whole wheat bread, lightly toasted, crusts removed and crumbled
- 2 scallions, mostly green parts, thinly sliced
- ½ to 1 fresh red or green chili, seeded and chopped
- ½ teaspoon salt, or to taste
- Freshly ground black pepper, to taste
- 2 tablespoons chopped fresh parsley

In a food processor fitted with the knife blade, process the corn, broth, coconut milk, and bread until smooth but slightly chunky. Transfer to a medium stockpot or large saucepan and add the scallions, chili, salt, and pepper; bring to brisk simmer over medium-high heat, stirring occasionally. Reduce the heat and simmer gently, uncovered, stirring occasionally, about 15 minutes. Serve warm, garnished with the parsley.

Chilled Avocado Soup

MAKES 4 SERVINGS

From tropical Africa, this rich yet nutritious chilled soup makes a lovely luncheon or first course offering during the hot summer months.

- 2 ripe avocados, peeled and pitted
- 4 cups chilled low-sodium vegetable broth
- Juice of 1 lime (about 2 tablespoons)
- ¼ teaspoon crushed red pepper flakes, or to taste
- Salt and freshly ground black pepper, to taste
- Chopped fresh chives or the green parts of scallions, to garnish

In a food processor fitted with the knife blade, or in a blender, process the avocados until a smooth paste forms. Transfer to a large bowl and add the broth, lime juice, red pepper flakes, salt, and black pepper, whisking until thoroughly blended. Cover and refrigerate 1 to 6 hours and serve chilled, garnished with the chives.

PER SERVING: Calories 214 • Protein 13g • Total Fat 15g • Sat. Fat 3g • Cholesterol 0mg • Carbohydrate 10g • Dietary Fiber 6g • Sodium 528mg

Thai Hot-and-Sour Lemongrass Soup with Mushrooms and Tofu

MAKES 4 SERVINGS

This delicious vegetarian variation of the famous Thai hot-and-sour soup known as *tom yum* can be made without the coconut milk; simply replace it with 1¾ cups additional vegetable broth. For an even lighter soup, omit the tofu, as well. Both fresh lemongrass and kaffir lime leaves are available in Asian groceries and Whole Foods markets.

2 cups low-sodium vegetable broth

1 cup water

6 kaffir lime leaves or about 1 tablespoon chopped fresh lime peel

2 stalks fresh lemongrass, tough outer leaves removed, cut into 2- to 3-inch pieces, and lightly crushed, or 6 to 9 (3- to 4-inch-long) strips fresh lemon peel

1 (3-inch) piece fresh galangal (see Cook's Tip, opposite) or ginger, cut into 6 slices

1 sprig fresh cilantro

2 to 3 whole black peppercorns

1 (14-ounce) can light coconut milk

8 ounces extra-firm tofu, cubed

1 cup well-drained canned straw mushrooms

1 to 2 fresh red or green chilies, seeded and thinly sliced

1 to 2 tablespoons Chinese chili paste

1 to 2 tablespoons chopped fresh cilantro

1 tablespoon low-sodium soy sauce or tamari

Salt, to taste

1 to 2 tablespoons fresh lime juice

In a medium stockpot, combine the broth, water, lime leaves, lemongrass, galangal, cilantro sprig, and peppercorns. Bring to a boil over high heat; reduce heat to between low and medium-low, cover, and simmer 30 minutes. Strain through a sieve and return to the pot. Add the coconut milk, tofu, mushrooms, chilies, chili paste, chopped cilantro, soy sauce, and salt. Bring to a simmer over medium-high heat; reduce the heat and simmer gently, uncovered, 5 minutes, stirring occasionally. Stir in the lime juice and remove from heat. Serve warm.

PER SERVING: Calories 222 • Protein 15g • Total Fat 14g • Sat. Fat 10g • Cholesterol 0mg • Carbohydrate 14g • Dietary Fiber 4g • Sodium 507mg

COOK'S TIP: *A close relative of ginger, galangal is an important and popular ingredient in the foods of Southeast Asia, especially in Thailand and Indonesia. It is slightly more pungent than ginger, however, and should be used a bit more sparingly in recipes. Likewise, use a little more ginger if substituting for galangal. Unlike ginger, galangal does not require peeling before using. Galangal is available in Asian and international markets.*

Hawaiian Long Rice Soup

MAKES 4 SERVINGS

"Long rice" actually refers to the thin rice noodles that are the essential ingredient in Hawaii's best-loved chicken soup. Served with a tossed green salad this vegetarian variation makes a hearty main dish for two.

Hawaiian red sea salt contains purified Alae clay, which adds minerals and gives it a mild taste. Any coarse salt can be substituted.

> 4 ounces thin (vermicelli-style) rice noodles, soaked according to package directions until almost al dente (see Cook's Tip, page 44)
> 2 (14-ounce) cans low-sodium vegetable broth
> 1 tablespoon chopped peeled fresh ginger
> 4 to 6 scallions, white and green parts separated, thinly sliced
> ½ small carrot (about 1 ounce), thinly sliced
> ½ stalk celery, thinly sliced
> ½ cup drained canned straw mushroom pieces
> 1 tablespoon Hawaiian shoyu, tamari, or soy sauce
> 1 teaspoon toasted (dark) sesame oil
> Coarse salt, preferably Hawaiian red sea salt, to taste
> Freshly ground black pepper, to taste

Drain the soaked noodles well and rinse under cold-running water 30 seconds. Cut into 3-inch bunches and set aside.

In a medium stockpot, bring the broth, ginger, white parts of scallions, carrot, and celery to a boil over high heat. Reduce the heat to medium and simmer 5 minutes, stirring occasionally. Add the rice noodles, mushrooms, shoyu, oil, salt, and pepper. Continue to cook over medium heat, stirring occasionally, until the noodles are al dente, about 10 minutes, adding the scallion greens the last few minutes of cooking. Serve hot or warm.

PER SERVING: Calories 172 • Protein 11g • Total Fat 1g • Sat. Fat 0g • Cholesterol 0mg • Carbohydrate 30g • Dietary Fiber 4g • Sodium 750mg

Chilled Australian Curried Mango Soup

MAKES 4 SERVINGS

This is the quintessential no-cook tropical summer soup, ideal for easy yet elegant entertaining.

> 2 mangoes (about 12 ounces each), peeled, pitted, and chopped
> 2 cups low-sodium vegetable broth
> Juice of ½ lemon (about 1½ tablespoons), or more, to taste
> ½ cup light coconut milk
> ¼ teaspoon mild curry powder
> Salt and freshly ground black pepper, to taste
> Chopped fresh chives or green parts of scallions, for garnish

In a food processor fitted with the knife blade, or in a blender, process all the ingredients, except the chives, until very smooth. Transfer to a covered container and refrigerate a minimum of 2 hours, or overnight, and serve chilled, garnished with the chives.

PER SERVING: Calories 127 • Protein 7g • Total Fat 3g • Sat. Fat 3g • Cholesterol 0mg • Carbohydrate 21g • Dietary Fiber 4g • Sodium 273mg

Plantain Soup

MAKES 4 SERVINGS

Plantains are an excellent source of potassium, vitamins A and C, and also contain a significant amount of iron. Make sure you only use green plantains for this recipe; if you allow the peels to turn yellow or black the soup will be too sweet.

1 tablespoon extra-virgin olive oil

1 cup chopped onion

½ cup chopped carrot

¼ cup chopped celery

2 large cloves garlic, finely chopped

4 cups low-sodium vegetable broth

½ cup water, plus additional, as necessary

2 green plantains (about 1 pound), peeled, quartered lengthwise, and thinly sliced

1 cup chopped fresh cilantro

1 teaspoon ground cumin

½ teaspoon salt, or to taste

1 bay leaf

Freshly ground black pepper, to taste

In a medium stockpot or large saucepan, heat the oil over medium heat. Add the onion, carrot, and celery; cook, stirring, until softened, 3 to 5 minutes. Add the garlic and cook, stirring constantly, 1 minute. Add the broth and water and bring to a boil over high heat. Add the plantains, cilantro, cumin, salt, bay leaf, and pepper; return to a boil. Reduce heat to medium-low and simmer gently, uncovered, stirring occasionally, until the plantains are very tender, about 45 minutes. Remove and discard the bay leaf.

Transfer half of the soup to a food processor fitted with the knife blade, or a blender; process or blend until smooth. Return to the pot and reheat over medium-low heat as necessary, stirring occasionally and adding more water if a thinner consistency is desired. Serve hot.

PER SERVING: Calories 218 • Protein 13g • Total Fat 4g • Sat. Fat 1g • Cholesterol 0mg • Carbohydrate 37g • Dietary Fiber 7g • Sodium 802mg

Caribbean Pumpkin Soup

MAKES 4 SERVINGS

Available in Caribbean markets and some well-stocked supermarkets, the calabaza, or calabasa, is a dense and very flavorful pumpkinlike squash commonly used for soups. If you can't locate one, butternut squash is a good substitute. For a less spicy soup, use a jalapeño chili in lieu of the extremely hot Scotch bonnet or habanero varieties.

1½ tablespoons canola oil

1 pound (about 2½ cups) cubed calabaza or butternut squash

1 small onion (about 4 ounces), chopped

1 stalk celery, chopped

1 teaspoon finely chopped Scotch bonnet or habanero chili

2 large cloves garlic, finely chopped

3½ cups low-sodium vegetable broth

½ cup water

1 tablespoon light brown sugar

1 tablespoon finely chopped peeled fresh ginger or about ½ teaspoon ground ginger

½ teaspoon dried thyme

¼ teaspoon salt

Freshly ground black pepper, to taste

1 bay leaf

In a medium stockpot, heat the oil over medium heat. Add the squash, onion, celery, chili, and garlic; cook, stirring, until softened and fragrant, about 5 minutes. Add the remaining ingredients and bring to a boil over high heat. Reduce the heat, cover, and simmer, stirring occasionally, until the squash is tender, about 30 minutes. Remove and discard the bay leaf.

Working in batches, as necessary, transfer the

mixture to a food processor fitted with the knife blade, or to a blender; process until smooth and pureed. Return the pureed mixture to the pot and cook over medium heat until heated through, stirring occasionally, about 3 minutes. Serve warm.

PER SERVING: Calories 149 • Protein 11g • Total Fat 5g • Sat. Fat 0g • Cholesterol 0mg • Carbohydrate 16g • Dietary Fiber 6g • Sodium 599mg

over medium-high heat. Reduce the heat and simmer, covered, 10 minutes, stirring occasionally. Add the coconut milk, peanut butter, rice vinegar, and green parts of scallions, stirring well to thoroughly incorporate. Cook, stirring occasionally, about 3 minutes. Serve warm.

PER SERVING: Calories 237 • Protein 14g • Total Fat 10g • Sat. Fat 3g • Cholesterol 0mg • Carbohydrate 28g • Dietary Fiber 7g • Sodium 512mg

Thai Pumpkin Soup

MAKES 4 TO 6 SERVINGS

This scrumptious pumpkin soup can be made with papaya nectar, as well.

1 tablespoon peanut oil

4 scallions, thinly sliced, white and green parts separated

1 teaspoon grated peeled fresh ginger

2 large cloves garlic, finely chopped

¼ teaspoon crushed red pepper flakes

3½ cups low-sodium vegetable broth

1 (15-ounce) can pumpkin puree

1 (11.3-ounce) can mango nectar (about 1½ cups)

½ teaspoon grated fresh orange peel

Salt and freshly ground black pepper, to taste

¼ cup light coconut milk

2 tablespoons smooth or chunky peanut butter

1 tablespoon plain rice vinegar

In a medium stockpot, heat the oil over medium heat. Add the white parts of the scallions, ginger, garlic, and red pepper flakes; cook, stirring, 1 minute. Add the broth, pumpkin, mango nectar, orange peel, salt, and black pepper; bring to a boil

Thai Curried Red Pepper– Coconut Soup

MAKES 4 SERVINGS

This simple yet sophisticated soup is an ideal first course for a special meal.

1 tablespoon canola oil

1 medium onion (about 6 ounces), chopped

½ to 1 teaspoon Thai red or green curry paste

3 cups low-sodium vegetable broth

1 (12-ounce) jar roasted red peppers, well drained

½ teaspoon salt, or to taste

1 cup light coconut milk

2 tablespoons chopped fresh basil (optional)

In a large saucepan or medium stockpot, heat the oil over medium heat. Add the onion and cook, stirring, until softened, about 3 minutes. Add the curry paste and cook, stirring constantly, 1 minute. Add the broth, roasted peppers, and salt; bring to a boil over medium-high heat. Reduce the heat and simmer gently for 15 minutes, stirring occasionally.

Working in batches, as necessary, transfer the

mixture to a food processor fitted with the knife blade, or to a blender; process until smooth and pureed. Return to the pan and add the coconut milk; cook over medium-low heat, stirring occasionally, until heated through, about 5 minutes. Serve warm, garnished with the basil (if using).

PER SERVING: Calories 176 • Protein 11g • Total Fat 10g • Sat. Fat 6g • Cholesterol 0mg • Carbohydrate 14g • Dietary Fiber 5g • Sodium 700mg

Cold Tomatillo Soup

MAKES 4 SERVINGS

This refreshing first-course soup also makes a satisfying light lunch on a hot day when accompanied by a tossed salad.

2 tablespoons extra-virgin olive oil

1 medium onion (about 6 ounces), chopped

1 to 2 jalapeño chilies, seeded and chopped

2 pounds tomatillos, husked, stemmed, rinsed under warm water to remove stickiness, cored, and quartered

4 cups low-sodium vegetable broth

¼ cup chopped fresh cilantro, plus additional, for garnish (optional)

½ teaspoon salt, or to taste

Freshly ground black pepper, to taste

In a medium stockpot, heat the oil over medium-low heat. Add the onion and chilies and cook, stirring occasionally, until tender but not browned, 8 to 10 minutes. Add the tomatillos, broth, ¼ cup cilantro, salt, and pepper; bring to a boil over high heat.

Reduce the heat, cover, and simmer until tomatillos are tender, about 10 minutes, stirring occasionally.

Working in batches, as necessary, transfer the mixture to a food processor fitted with the knife blade, or to a blender; process or blend until smooth and pureed. Let cool to room temperature. Cover and refrigerate a minimum of 3 hours, or up to 2 days, and serve chilled, garnished with cilantro (if using).

PER SERVING: Calories 203 • Protein 14g • Total Fat 9g • Sat. Fat 1g • Cholesterol 0mg • Carbohydrate 20g • Dietary Fiber 8g • Sodium 786mg

Cambodian Tomato Soup

MAKES 4 SERVINGS

Serve this rich and creamy soup as an impressive opener for your next dinner party, or call it a delicious dinner with a piece of Taiwanese Black Sesame Focaccia (page 18) and a tossed green salad. On a hot summer's day, enjoy it chilled.

1 teaspoon canola oil

4 scallions, white and green parts, thinly sliced, 2 tablespoons green parts reserved

1 (15-ounce) can tomato sauce

¾ cup low-sodium vegetable broth

1 (14-ounce) can light coconut milk

1 tablespoon sugar

½ tablespoon Chinese chili paste, or to taste

½ tablespoon toasted (dark) sesame oil

1 teaspoon low-sodium soy sauce or tamari, or to taste

Salt and freshly ground black pepper, to taste

In a medium stockpot, heat the canola oil over medium heat. Add the scallions and cook, stirring, until softened, about 3 minutes. Add the tomato sauce and broth; bring to a brisk simmer over medium-high heat, stirring occasionally. Reduce the heat to low and add the coconut milk, sugar, chili paste, sesame oil, soy sauce, salt, and pepper; cook, stirring occasionally, until heated through, about 5 minutes. Serve warm or at room temperature, garnished with the reserved scallion greens. Alternatively, cover and refrigerate a minimum of 3 hours or up to 2 days and serve chilled.

PER SERVING: Calories 211 • Protein 7g • Total Fat 14g • Sat. Fat 10g • Cholesterol 0mg • Carbohydrate 18g • Dietary Fiber 3g • Sodium 832mg

HEARTIER SOUPS AND STEWS

Brazilian Black Bean and Vegetable Stew

MAKES 6 SERVINGS

Originally based on a simple Portuguese stew of beans and vegetables, *feijoada* (pronounced "fay-zhwa-duh"), considered the national dish of Brazil, is now heavily meat-laden. This delicious vegetarian version is a tribute to its healthier roots. If using spinach instead of kale, double the amount, as it will shrivel considerably more.

3 tablespoons extra-virgin olive oil

1 medium sweet potato (about 6 ounces), peeled and coarsely chopped

1 medium red bell pepper (about 6 ounces), chopped

1 medium green bell pepper (about 6 ounces), chopped

1 medium onion (about 6 ounces), chopped

4 large cloves garlic, finely chopped

2 teaspoons dried thyme leaves

1 teaspoon ground cumin

1 teaspoon chipotle puree (see Cook's Tip, page 112), or to taste

2 (15-ounce) cans black beans, rinsed and drained

1 cup chopped fresh kale or 2 cups fresh spinach

1 cup low-sodium vegetable broth

1 large ripe tomato (about 8 ounces), seeded and chopped

1 teaspoon salt

½ teaspoon chopped fresh orange peel

Freshly ground black pepper, to taste

Juice of 1 lime (about 2 tablespoons)

1 medium navel orange, thinly sliced, for garnish (optional)

¼ cup chopped fresh cilantro, for garnish (optional)

4½ to 6 cups hot cooked rice (see Cook's Tip, page 79)

In a large deep-sided nonstick skillet with a lid, heat the oil over medium heat. Add the sweet potato, bell peppers, and onion; cook, stirring, until softened, about 5 minutes. Add the garlic, thyme, cumin, and chipotle puree; cook, stirring, 2 minutes. Add the beans, kale, broth, tomato, salt, orange peel, and black pepper; bring to a brisk simmer over medium-high heat. Reduce the heat and simmer, covered, stirring occasionally, until all the vegetables are tender, 15 to 20 minutes. Stir in the lime juice.

For a traditional presentation, transfer to a shallow serving dish and garnish with the orange slices and cilantro (if using). Serve at once, accompanied by the rice. Alternatively, ladle the stew over individual portions of rice, top with the garnishes (if using), and serve at once.

PER SERVING: Calories 436 • Protein 15g • Total Fat 8g • Sat. Fat 1g • Cholesterol 0mg • Carbohydrate 77g • Dietary Fiber 8g • Sodium 460mg

African Black Barley Stew with Okra and Tomatoes

MAKES 4 TO 6 SERVINGS

Black barley, also known as Ethiopian barley, is available in health food and specialty stores. Pearl barley can be substituted, if desired.

2 tablespoons canola oil

1 medium onion (about 6 ounces), finely chopped

2 large cloves garlic, finely chopped

5 cups water

1 (14.5-ounce) can diced tomatoes with jalapeño chilies, juices included

1 (14-ounce) can low-sodium vegetable broth

1¼ cups black or pearl barley

½ teaspoon ground cumin

½ teaspoon coriander seed, crushed

¼ teaspoon ground cinnamon

2 whole cloves, crushed

Salt and freshly ground black pepper, to taste

1½ cups frozen cut okra, cooked according to package directions, drained

In a medium stockpot, heat the oil over medium heat. Add the onion and cook, stirring, until softened, about 3 minutes. Add the garlic and cook, stirring, 1 minute. Add the water, tomatoes and

their juices, broth, barley, cumin, coriander, cinnamon, cloves, salt, and pepper; bring to a boil over high heat. Reduce the heat to medium-low and cook, covered, stirring occasionally, until the barley is tender but still slightly chewy, about 45 minutes. Add the okra and cook, uncovered, stirring occasionally, until heated through, about 5 minutes. Serve warm.

PER SERVING: Calories 386 • Protein 15g • Total Fat 9g • Sat. Fat 1g • Cholesterol 0mg • Carbohydrate 67g • Dietary Fiber 16g • Sodium 468mg

Mexican Black Bean and Brown Rice Soup

MAKES 4 SERVINGS

Serve this protein-packed, fiber-rich whole-grain soup with a tossed green salad for a satisfying meal.

1 tablespoon extra-virgin olive oil

1 medium onion (about 6 ounces), finely chopped

½ cup chopped carrot

¼ cup chopped celery

2 large cloves garlic, finely chopped

3½ cups low-sodium vegetable broth

1 (15-ounce) can black beans, rinsed and drained

1 (16-ounce) can vegetarian refried black beans

1 cup water

1 cup frozen yellow corn

½ cup mild or medium picante sauce

½ cup instant brown rice

Salt and freshly ground black pepper, to taste

2 bay leaves

Juice of 1 lime

In a medium stockpot, heat the oil over medium heat. Add the onion, carrot, and celery; cook, stirring, until softened, about 5 minutes. Add the garlic and cook, stirring, 1 minute. Add the remaining ingredients, except the lime juice, and bring to a boil over high heat, stirring to thoroughly incorporate the refried beans. Reduce the heat to medium-low and simmer, uncovered, stirring occasionally, until the rice is tender, about 10 minutes. Discard the bay leaves, stir in the lime juice, and serve warm.

PER SERVING: Calories 422 • Protein 26g • Total Fat 6g • Sat. Fat 1g • Cholesterol 0mg • Carbohydrate 70g • Dietary Fiber 14g • Sodium 1,108mg

Brazilian Black Bean Soup

MAKES 4 TO 6 SERVINGS

This winter-warming soup, redolent of citrus, cinnamon, and cloves, is a meal in itself, accompanied by crusty bread and a tossed green salad.

1 cup dry black beans, soaked overnight in cold water to cover

½ teaspoon salt, plus additional, to taste

1 tablespoon extra-virgin olive oil

1 medium onion (about 6 ounces), chopped

½ medium green bell pepper (about 3 ounces), chopped

½ small carrot (about 1 ounce), chopped

3 to 4 large cloves garlic, finely chopped

2 cups cooked brown or white rice

1 cup low-sodium vegetable broth

¾ cup fresh orange juice

1 medium tomato (about 6 ounces), seeded and chopped

½ tablespoon sugar

1 teaspoon ground cumin

½ teaspoon dried thyme

¼ teaspoon ground cloves

⅛ to ¼ teaspoon cayenne pepper, or to taste

Freshly ground black pepper, to taste

½ cup chopped fresh flat-leaf parsley and/or cilantro

2 scallions, white and green parts, thinly sliced

½ cinnamon stick

½ bay leaf

½ tablespoon cider vinegar

½ tablespoon dry sherry (optional)

Drain the beans and place in a medium stockpot with water to cover by 1 inch. Add the ½ teaspoon salt and bring to a boil over high heat. Reduce the heat to between low and medium-low, cover, and simmer, stirring occasionally, until the beans are tender, about 1½ hours. Set aside and do not drain.

Meanwhile, in a medium deep-sided skillet with a lid, heat the oil over medium heat. Add the onion, bell pepper, and carrot; cook, stirring, until softened, about 5 minutes. Reduce the heat to low and add the garlic; cook, stirring occasionally, until all the vegetables are tender, about 10 minutes. Add the vegetables to the stockpot containing the cooked beans and their liquid, along with the rice, broth, orange juice, tomato, sugar, cumin, thyme, cloves, cayenne, and black pepper; bring to a simmer over medium-high heat, stirring occasionally.

Remove from heat and transfer one-third of the soup to a food processor fitted with the knife blade, or to a blender; process until smooth and pureed. Return to the pot and stir in the parsley, scallions, cinnamon stick, and bay leaf; return to a simmer over medium-high heat. Reduce the heat and simmer, uncovered, stirring occasionally, about 15 minutes. Season with additional salt, if needed. Stir in the vinegar and sherry (if using). Discard the cinnamon stick and bay leaf and serve warm.

PER SERVING: Calories 396 • Protein 18g • Total Fat 6g • Sat. Fat 1g • Cholesterol 0mg • Carbohydrate 72g • Dietary Fiber 13g • Sodium 415mg

African Curried Coconut Soup with Chickpeas

MAKES 4 SERVINGS

Black-eyed peas can replace the chickpeas, if desired. For a lighter soup, the rice can be omitted.

2 tablespoons canola oil

1 medium onion (about 6 ounces), chopped

1 medium red bell pepper (about 6 ounces), chopped

1 jalapeño chili, seeded and finely chopped

2 large cloves garlic, finely chopped

2 cups low-sodium vegetable broth

1 (15-ounce) can chickpeas, rinsed and drained

1 cup chopped tomatoes, seeded and peeled, fresh or canned (see Cook's Tip, opposite)

1 teaspoon mild curry powder

½ teaspoon salt, or to taste

Freshly ground black pepper, to taste

1 (14-ounce) can light coconut milk

¾ cup cooked white or brown rice

2 tablespoons chopped fresh cilantro or parsley

In a medium stockpot, heat the oil over medium heat. Add the onion, bell pepper, and chili; cook, stir-

ring, until softened, about 5 minutes. Add the garlic and cook, stirring constantly, 1 minute. Add the broth, chickpeas, tomatoes, curry powder, salt, and black pepper; bring to a boil over high heat. Reduce the heat and simmer gently, uncovered, stirring occasionally, about 10 minutes. Add the remaining ingredients and cook, stirring occasionally, until heated through, about 5 minutes. Serve warm.

PER SERVING: Calories 401 • Protein 17g • Total Fat 20g • Sat. Fat 10g • Cholesterol 0mg • Carbohydrate 43g • Dietary Fiber 7g • Sodium 576mg

COOK'S TIP: To peel fresh tomatoes, bring a medium stockpot filled with water to a boil over high heat; drop in the tomatoes and boil 20 seconds. Drain and rinse under cold-running water. Peel off the skins.

Indian Black-Eyed Pea Soup

MAKES 4 SERVINGS

The black-eyed pea is actually a small, almost-white bean with a black spot. It is an important protein in vegetarian Indian, African, and Caribbean cuisines.

1½ cups dried black-eyed peas, soaked overnight in cold water to cover, drained

1½ tablespoons canola oil

1 small onion (about 4 ounces), chopped

½ fresh green or red chili, seeded and finely chopped

1 large clove garlic, finely chopped

¾ teaspoon ground cumin

½ teaspoon ground cinnamon

½ teaspoon whole coriander seeds, crushed

¼ teaspoon dried oregano

3 cups low-sodium vegetable broth

1 cup water

1 large ripe tomato (about 8 ounces), peeled,
    seeded, and chopped

½ tablespoon light brown sugar

½ teaspoon salt

⅛ teaspoon cayenne pepper, or to
    taste

Freshly ground black pepper, to taste

¼ cup chopped fresh cilantro and/or basil

In a medium stockpot, bring the peas and enough water to cover by 1 inch to a boil over high heat. Reduce the heat to between medium and medium-high and simmer briskly until just tender, about 30 minutes. Drain and set aside.

Meanwhile, in another medium stockpot, heat the oil over medium heat. Add the onion and cook, stirring, until beginning to brown, about 5 minutes. Add the chili and garlic and cook, stirring constantly, 1 minute. Add the cumin, cinnamon, coriander, and oregano; cook, stirring constantly, 30 seconds. Add the broth, water, peas, tomato, sugar, salt, cayenne, and black pepper; bring to a simmer over medium-high heat. Reduce the heat to medium-low and simmer gently, stirring occasionally, until the peas are tender and the soup is slightly thickened, 25 to 30 minutes. Stir in the cilantro about 5 minutes or so before cooking is complete. Serve warm.

PER SERVING: Calories 328 • Protein 24g • Total Fat 6g • Sat. Fat 1g • Cholesterol 0mg • Carbohydrate 47g • Dietary Fiber 10g • Sodium 672mg

Thai Coconut-Noodle Soup with Lemongrass

MAKES 4 MAIN-COURSE OR 6 FIRST-COURSE SERVINGS

Light, lovely, and fragrant describe this nourishing noodle soup from Thailand.

8 ounces thin (vermicelli-style) rice noodles, soaked
    according to package directions until tender yet
    firm to the bite (see Cook's Tip, page 44)

4 cups low-sodium vegetable broth

1 cup water

1 cup chopped carrots

2 stalks fresh lemongrass, tough outer leaves
    removed, cut into 2- to 3-inch pieces, lightly
    crushed, or 6 to 9 (3- to 4-inch-long) strips fresh
    lemon peel

1 teaspoon finely chopped peeled fresh ginger

3 cups chopped broccoli florets

2 cups chopped bok choy

1 cup light coconut milk

¼ cup low-sodium soy sauce or tamari

Salt and freshly ground black pepper, to taste

Drain the soaked noodles well and rinse under cold-running water 30 seconds. Divide equally among 4 soup bowls.

Meanwhile, in a medium stockpot, bring the broth, water, carrots, lemongrass, and ginger to a boil over high heat. Add the broccoli and bok choy and return to a boil. Reduce heat to medium and cook, stirring occasionally, until the vegetables are tender, 3 to 5 minutes. Add the coconut milk, soy sauce, salt, and pepper and reduce heat to low; cook, stirring, until just heated through, about 5 minutes. Remove and discard the lemongrass.

Ladle equal amounts of broth and vegetables over each serving of noodles. Serve at once.

PER SERVING: Calories 351 • Protein 16g • Total Fat 5g • Sat. Fat 4g • Cholesterol 0mg • Carbohydrate 62g • Dietary Fiber 7g • Sodium 1,189mg

COOK'S TIP: *There are at least two ways to soak rice noodles, for either further cooking or immediate use in a recipe. For the quicker hot-soak method, using 8 ounces of flat (stir-fry or linguine-style) rice noodles or thin (vermicelli-style) rice noodles, bring 4 to 6 cups of water to a boil in a large stockpot. Remove from heat and stir in the rice noodles. If noodles are to be cooked further in stir-fries, soups, or other dishes, let stand, stirring occasionally, until noodles are soft yet still quite chewy (almost al dente), 4 to 6 minutes for the thin noodles, 6 to 8 minutes for the flat noodles. If noodles require no additional cooking in the recipe, add 4 to 5 minutes to the total soaking time of either variety, or until the noodles are tender yet firm to the bite. After the noodles have soaked the appropriate amount of time, drain well and rinse under cold-running water 30 seconds. Noodles are now ready for either further cooking or immediate use in the recipe.*

For a longer cold-soak method recommended mainly for noodles that are to be cooked further in recipes, soak either variety of rice noodle about 30 minutes in like amount of cold water. Drain well and proceed to cook as directed in the recipe.

Thai Corn Chowder with Lime and Basil

MAKES 4 SERVINGS

This light and exotic chowder is ideal to make in the summer months when fresh corn is available, although the frozen variety yields an excellent soup in winter, as well. If using fresh corn, you will need about four medium ears.

2 tablespoons canola oil

¼ cup chopped red bell pepper

3 medium shallots, thinly sliced

1 fresh green or red chili, seeded and finely chopped

1 tablespoon chopped peeled fresh ginger

2 cups low-sodium vegetable broth

3 kaffir lime leaves or about ½ tablespoon chopped fresh lime peel

1 (14-ounce) can light coconut milk

2 cups fresh or frozen yellow corn kernels, thawed if frozen

Salt and freshly ground black pepper, to taste

8 fresh basil leaves, cut into thin strips

2 limes, quartered (optional)

In a medium stockpot, heat the oil over medium heat. Add the bell pepper, shallots, chili, and ginger; cook, stirring, until softened, 3 to 5 minutes. Add the broth and lime leaves and bring to a boil over high heat. Reduce the heat to medium-high and stir in the coconut milk, corn, salt, and pepper. When the mixture comes to a brisk simmer, reduce heat to low and simmer gently, stirring occasionally, until the corn is tender, about 5 minutes. Remove pot from heat.

Remove and discard the lime leaves and transfer about 2 cups of the soup to a food processor fitted with the knife blade, or to a blender; process until smooth and pureed. Add the pureed soup back to the pot and stir in the basil. Reheat, if necessary, over low heat. Serve hot or warm, with the lime quarters (if using).

PER SERVING: Calories 304 • Protein 12g • Total Fat 18g • Sat. Fat 10g • Cholesterol 0mg • Carbohydrate 28g • Dietary Fiber 4g • Sodium 303mg

African Groundnut Stew with Fufu

MAKES 6 SERVINGS

A staple food of tropical Africa, fufu (also spelled foofoo, foufou, or fu fu) is a thick starchy paste or porridge usually made from yams, cassava, plantains, maize, or potato flakes. It is a traditional accompaniment to groundnut, or peanut, stew, where the fufu is shaped into a large mound from which diners break off pieces to use as scoops for the stew. For a less authentic yet equally tasty method, simply place this fragrant stew over individual balls of fufu. It is also wonderful over polenta, couscous, or rice.

2 tablespoons peanut oil

1 large onion (about 8 ounces), chopped

1 large green bell pepper (about 8 ounces), chopped

3 large cloves garlic, finely chopped

3 tablespoons finely chopped peeled fresh ginger

1 tablespoon coriander seed, crushed

½ teaspoon crushed red pepper flakes, or to taste

1 (28-ounce) can crushed tomatoes

1 extra-large sweet potato (about 12 ounces), peeled and cut into small cubes

1 medium eggplant (about 12 ounces), cubed (salting is not necessary)

1 large zucchini (about 8 ounces), cubed

1 cup water, plus additional, as necessary

Salt and freshly ground black pepper, to taste

¼ cup creamy or crunchy peanut butter

Fufu (below)

In a medium stockpot, heat the oil over medium heat. Add the onion and bell pepper and cook, stirring, until fragrant and very soft but not quite browned, 5 to 7 minutes. Add the garlic, ginger, coriander, and red pepper flakes and increase the heat to medium-high; cook, stirring constantly, 2 minutes, or until the vegetables are just beginning to brown. Add the tomatoes, sweet potato, eggplant, zucchini, 1 cup water, salt, and black pepper; bring to a brisk simmer, stirring occasionally. Reduce the heat to medium-low and simmer, covered, stirring occasionally, until the potato is tender, about 45 minutes. Add the peanut butter, stirring well to thoroughly incorporate. Simmer, uncovered, stirring occasionally, until thickened, about 5 minutes. For a thinner consistency, add water as desired. Serve warm, with the fufu, below.

PER SERVING (with Fufu): Calories 446 • Protein 12g • Total Fat 11g • Sat. Fat 2g • Cholesterol 0mg • Carbohydrate 80g • Dietary Fiber 10g • Sodium 366mg

Fufu

MAKES 6 SERVINGS

Fufu is traditionally made by boiling starchy root vegetables such as cassava, plaintains, and yams in water and pounding with a large mortar and pestle until the desired consistency is achieved. This virtually instant recipe uses fufu flour, a blend of plantain, cassava, and potatoes, which is available in African and Caribbean markets, as well as some health food stores. Feel free to serve fufu with any vegetable stews of your liking.

3 cups water

2 cups fufu flour

In a large saucepan, stir together the water and flour until a thick paste forms. Place over medium heat and cook, kneading constantly with a wooden spoon, until a smooth but thick consistency forms, about 5 minutes. Remove from heat and let cool slightly.

When fufu is cool enough to handle but still warm, using your hands, form into 6 individual balls and place in individual soup bowls or deep-sided plates. Cover with equal amounts of stew and serve at once.

PER SERVING: Calories 209 • Protein 5g • Total Fat 1g • Sat. Fat 0g • Cholesterol 0mg • Carbohydrate 48g • Dietary Fiber 4g • Sodium 20mg

Vietnamese Noodle Soup

MAKES 6 SERVINGS

You can also use Japanese soba or somen noodles, or Italian vermicelli, cooked according to the package directions until al dente, with success in the following recipe.

12 ounces thin (vermicelli-style) rice noodles, soaked according to package directions until al dente (see Cook's Tip, page 44)

½ (15-ounce) package firm or extra-firm tofu, drained, cut into ½-inch cubes

2 tablespoons toasted (dark) sesame oil

Vietnamese-Style Vegetable Broth (opposite page), heated to simmering

Salt and freshly ground black pepper, to taste

½ cup bean sprouts

½ cup shredded cabbage

½ cup baby spinach, torn into bite-size pieces

½ cup basil leaves, coarsely chopped

½ cup fresh cilantro, coarsely chopped

3 scallions (white and green parts), thinly sliced

3 tablespoons chopped unsalted peanuts

1 to 2 fresh green or red chilies, seeded and thinly sliced (optional)

1 lime, cut into 6 wedges

Low-sodium soy sauce or tamari, to taste

Drain the soaked noodles well and rinse under cold-running water 30 seconds. Divide equally among 6 bowls and set aside.

Add the tofu and sesame oil to the simmering broth and season with salt and pepper. Simmer, stirring occasionally, until the tofu is heated through, about 5 minutes. Remove the tofu with a slotted spoon and arrange equal portions over the noodles.

To assemble the soup, place equal portions of the bean sprouts, cabbage, spinach, basil, cilantro, scallions, and peanuts on top of the noodles and tofu. Ladle equal portions of the hot broth onto the noodle mixture. Garnish with the sliced chilies (if using), and a lime wedge. Serve at once, with salt, freshly ground black pepper, and soy sauce passed separately.

PER SERVING: Calories 418 • Protein 22g • Total Fat 9g • Sat. Fat 1g • Cholesterol 0mg • Carbohydrate 67g • Dietary Fiber 10g • Sodium 912mg

Vietnamese-Style Vegetable Broth

MAKES 8 CUPS

I prefer to use tamari for this light and fragrant broth instead of regular soy sauce, which is a bit stronger in flavor. Eight-pointed pods of star anise are available in Asian markets and specialty stores; if necessary, substitute with ½ teaspoon of whole anise seed or fennel seed, crushed, for each pod.

    8 cups low-sodium clear vegetable broth (do not
        use a tomato-based variety)
    2 to 3 tablespoons low-sodium tamari or soy sauce
    6 large cloves garlic, crushed
    1 small onion (about 4 ounces), coarsely chopped
    1 (2-inch) piece ginger, cut into 5 or 6 pieces
    2 cinnamon sticks
    2 pods star anise
    2 large bay leaves

In a large stockpot, bring all the ingredients to a boil over medium heat. Reduce the heat to medium-low and simmer, partially covered, 30 minutes, stirring a few times.

Strain the broth through a fine-mesh sieve. Add water as necessary to equal 8 cups. Use as directed in the recipe. Completely cooled broth can be stored, covered, in the refrigerator up to 3 days before using, or freeze up to 3 months.

PER CUP: Calories 68 • Protein 12g • Total Fat 0g • Sat. Fat 0g • Cholesterol 0mg • Carbohydrate 6g • Dietary Fiber 0g • Sodium 669mg

Lentil-Pomegranate Stew with Spinach and Raisins

MAKES 6 SERVINGS

This comforting stew is in order on a dreary winter day. Dark raisins can replace the golden variety, if desired.

    2 tablespoons extra-virgin olive oil
    1 medium onion (about 6 ounces), chopped
    4 cups low-sodium vegetable broth
    4 cups water
    1 cup lentils, rinsed and drained
    1 cup long-grain white rice
    1 teaspoon ground turmeric
    1 teaspoon salt
    Freshly ground black pepper, to taste
    1 cup pomegranate juice
    ½ cup chopped fresh parsley
    4 scallions, white and green parts, thinly sliced
    ½ cup golden raisins
    8 ounces fresh baby spinach leaves, coarsely
        chopped

In a medium stockpot, heat the oil over medium heat. Add the onion and cook, stirring, until softened, about 3 minutes. Add the broth, water, lentils, rice, turmeric, salt, and pepper; bring to a boil over high heat. Reduce the heat to between low and medium-low and simmer, covered, 30 minutes. Add the juice, parsley, scallions, and raisins; simmer, covered, until lentils are tender, another 15 minutes, stirring in the spinach during the last few minutes of cooking. Serve warm.

PER SERVING: Calories 385 • Protein 21g • Total Fat 5g • Sat. Fat 1g • Cholesterol 0mg • Carbohydrate 66g • Dietary Fiber 15g • Sodium 747mg

African Pineapple and Peanut Stew with Kale

MAKES 4 TO 6 SERVINGS

Serve this yummy vitamin-C rich stew over fufu or hot cooked rice. You can use spinach in lieu of the kale, if desired, but increase the amount to 6 cups and cook it a few minutes less.

    2 tablespoons peanut oil
    1 medium red onion (about 6 ounces), chopped
    2 large cloves garlic, finely chopped
    2 (8-ounce) cans crushed pineapple in juice
        (undrained)
    ½ teaspoon crushed red pepper flakes, or to taste
    ½ teaspoon salt
    Freshly ground black pepper, to taste
    4 cups chopped fresh kale
    ½ cup chunky peanut butter
    ½ cup low-sodium vegetable broth or water, plus
        additional, as necessary
    ½ cup chopped fresh cilantro
    Fufu (page 45) or hot cooked rice (see Cook's Tip,
        page 79)
    Hot red pepper sauce, to taste (optional)

In a large deep-sided nonstick skillet with a lid, heat the oil over medium heat. Add the onion and cook, stirring often, until lightly browned, 7 to 10 minutes, adding the garlic the last few minutes of cooking. Add the pineapple and its juice, red pepper flakes, salt, and black pepper; bring to a simmer over medium-high heat. Stir in the kale, cover, and simmer over medium-low heat, stirring occasionally, until the kale is just tender, about 5 minutes. Stir in the peanut butter, broth, and cilantro; simmer, uncovered, stirring occasionally, until the kale is tender, about 5 minutes. If a thinner consis-

tency is desired, add additional broth or water, as necessary. Serve warm, over the fufu or rice, with the hot pepper sauce passed separately (if using).

PER SERVING (without the fufu or rice):
Calories 384 • Protein 13g • Total Fat 24g • Sat.
Fat 4g • Cholesterol 0mg • Carbohydrate 38g •
Dietary Fiber 6g • Sodium 521mg

Vietnamese-Style Pot Sticker Soup

MAKES 6 SERVINGS

Cooking time for the pot stickers, or *gyoza*, may vary slightly according to the brand used. Vegetable pot stickers are available in the frozen-food section of Asian markets and specialty stores; most are egg-free, as well, but check the label carefully. For a lighter soup, omit the peas, if desired.

    1 tablespoon peanut oil
    1 cup chopped carrots
    4 scallions, white and green parts separated, thinly
        sliced
    1 large clove garlic, finely chopped
    Vietnamese-Style Vegetable Broth (page 47)
    Salt and freshly ground black pepper, to taste
    1 pound frozen egg-free vegetable pot stickers
        (*gyoza*)
    1 cup frozen green peas
    2 tablespoons chopped fresh cilantro or parsley
    1 tablespoon toasted (dark) sesame oil
    Low-sodium soy sauce or tamari, to taste (optional)

In a medium stockpot, heat the peanut oil over medium heat. Add the carrots and white parts of the scallions and cook, stirring, until softened, about 5 minutes. Add the garlic and cook, stirring constantly, 1 minute. Add the broth, salt, and pepper and bring to a boil over high heat. Add the pot stickers and return to a boil. Reduce the heat slightly and cook until the pot stickers are almost tender, 2 to 3 minutes, stirring occasionally. Add the peas and cook, stirring, until pot stickers are cooked al dente, 1 to 2 minutes. Remove from heat and stir in the scallion greens, cilantro, and sesame oil. Serve warm, with soy sauce passed separately (if using).

PER SERVING: Calories 313 • Protein 23g • Total Fat 6g • Sat. Fat 1g • Cholesterol 0mg • Carbohydrate 45g • Dietary Fiber 10g • Sodium 1,204mg

Salads

One of the best things about tropical cuisine is the salads. Natural showoffs, tropical salads are simply dressed to make the most of their distinctive looks and flavor. The Luau Salad offers a delightful taste of Hawaii by tossing pineapple, mango, macadamia nuts, crystallized ginger, crunchy chow mein noodles, and mixed greens with a light and lovely Sesame-Guava Vinaigrette with Ginger. From tropics of a different longitude comes the spicy Thai Green Papaya and Peanut Salad with a slightly sweet tamarind-lime dressing, or the St. Martin–Style Orange and Red Onion Salad with a subtle accent of tarragon, a nod to the French influence upon Caribbean island cuisine. Several tropical salads move vegetables or legumes to center plate. Consider the Peruvian Purple Potato Salad with scallions, bell peppers, carrots, and olives; Mexico's Fiesta Black Bean and Corn Salad; or Singapore-Style Green Bean and Sprout Salad. Many tropical salads are substantial enough for dinner, such as the Vietnamese "Bun-Style" Herbed Rice Noodle Salad or the New Zealand–Style Brown Rice Salad with Kiwifruit and Apple. Whatever your preference, these healthy and refreshing recipes are sure to satisfy everyone at the table.

Arugula and Star Fruit Salad with Pineapple Vinaigrette

MAKES 6 SERVINGS

The sweetness of pineapple and tangy tartness of star fruit is a delightful contrast to peppery arugula in this delicious tropical salad. Spinach can replace the arugula, if desired.

1 (10-ounce) package ready-washed arugula or spinach

1 ripe star fruit (carambola), thinly sliced (see Cook's Tip, page 55)

3 scallions, white and green parts, thinly sliced

6 tablespoons chopped macadamia nuts or slivered almonds, toasted if desired (see Cook's Tip, page 55)

Pineapple Vinaigrette (opposite)

Divide the arugula equally among 6 salad bowls. Top with equal portions of the star fruit, and then sprinkle evenly with the scallions and nuts. Drizzle each serving with about 2 tablespoons of the vinaigrette. Serve at once.

PER SERVING: Calories 170 • Protein 2g • Total Fat 16g • Sat. Fat 2g • Cholesterol 0mg • Carbohydrate 8g • Dietary Fiber 2g • Sodium 199mg

Pineapple Vinaigrette

MAKES ABOUT 3/4 CUP

Use this versatile vinaigrette on any salad greens as well as lightly steamed or blanched vegetables such as snow peas, sugar snaps, green beans, and asparagus.

¼ cup pineapple juice

¼ cup extra-virgin olive oil

2½ tablespoons red wine vinegar

½ tablespoon cider vinegar

1 teaspoon light brown sugar

½ teaspoon Dijon mustard

½ teaspoon salt

Freshly ground black pepper, to taste

In a small bowl, whisk together all the ingredients until thoroughly blended. Serve at room temperature. The vinaigrette can be refrigerated, covered, up to 5 days before returning to room temperature and using.

PER TABLESPOON: Calories 45 • Protein 0g • Total Fat 5g • Sat. Fat 1g • Cholesterol 0mg • Carbohydrate 1g • Dietary Fiber 0g • Sodium 92mg

Avocado and Mango Salad with Arugula and Red Onion

MAKES 4 SERVINGS

Serve this tasty salad on its own or as an accompaniment to enchiladas, tacos, burritos, and other Mexican-style fare.

½ teaspoon ground cumin

½ teaspoon chili powder

¼ teaspoon garlic salt

1 large mango (about 14 ounces), peeled, pitted, and chopped

1 ripe avocado, halved, seeded, peeled, and chopped

½ cup thinly sliced red onion, soaked in cold water to cover for 10 minutes, well drained

2 tablespoons extra-virgin olive oil

2 tablespoons fresh lime juice

4 cups arugula or baby spinach

Freshly ground black pepper, to taste

In a small bowl, combine the cumin, chili powder, and garlic salt. Mix with a fork until blended. Set aside. In a medium bowl, toss together the mango, avocado, onion, oil, and lime juice until combined. Set aside.

Divide the arugula among 4 salad bowls or plates. Top with equal amounts of the avocado mixture. Using your fingers, drop pinches (to taste) of the spice mixture over the salads. Grind some pepper over the tops and serve at once.

PER SERVING: Calories 202 • Protein 2g • Total Fat 15g • Sat. Fat 2g • Cholesterol 0mg • Carbohydrate 19g • Dietary Fiber 3g • Sodium 144mg

Hawaiian Sesame-Cabbage Salad

MAKES 8 SERVINGS

This Hawaiian-style coleslaw is always a hit at a party or a potluck, or why not at your next luau? Though op-

tional, the fried chow mein noodles and almonds lend it added crunch and interest.

1 (16-ounce) bag shredded coleslaw mix

6 scallions, white and green parts, thinly sliced

1 cup frozen green peas, thawed

½ cup chopped red bell pepper

¼ cup canola oil

3 tablespoons plain rice vinegar or cider vinegar

2 tablespoons sugar

1 tablespoon sesame seeds, toasted if desired (see Cook's Tip, page 153)

½ tablespoon toasted (dark) sesame oil

Salt and freshly ground black pepper, to taste

1 cup egg-free fried chow mein noodles (optional)

¼ cup slivered almonds, toasted if desired (optional)

Mix all ingredients (except the chow mein noodles and almonds) until well combined. Cover and refrigerate a minimum of 3 hours or up to 1 day. Just before serving, toss with the chow mein noodles and almonds (if using). Serve chilled or let return to room temperature.

PER SERVING: Calories 122 • Protein 2g • Total Fat 9g • Sat. Fat 1g • Cholesterol 0mg • Carbohydrate 11g • Dietary Fiber 3g • Sodium 33mg

Avocado and Maui Onion Salad over Mixed Greens with Papaya Vinaigrette

MAKES 6 SERVINGS

This colorful salad can be prepared with any salad green. Maui onion is a sweet variety grown only in the deep red, volcanic soil on the upper slopes of Haleakala, Maui's world-famous dormant volcano. Thinly sliced Vidalia onion, or red onion, soaked in cold water to cover for ten minutes, drained well, can be substituted, if necessary.

1 (10-ounce) package ready-washed mixed greens

1 ripe avocado, peeled, pitted, and thinly sliced

½ cup thinly sliced Maui onion or other sweet onion, such as Vidalia

½ recipe (about 1 cup) Papaya Vinaigrette (below), plus additional, to taste

Divide the greens equally among 6 salad bowls. Top with equal portions of the avocado, and then garnish with the onion. Drizzle each serving with about 2½ tablespoons of the vinaigrette. Serve at once, with remaining vinaigrette passed separately, if desired.

PER SERVING (with ½ recipe Papaya Vinaigrette): Calories 144 • Protein 2g • Total Fat 11g • Sat. Fat 1g • Cholesterol 0mg • Carbohydrate 11g • Dietary Fiber 3g • Sodium 106mg

Papaya Vinaigrette

MAKES ABOUT 2 CUPS

The natural sweetness of papaya nicely balances the tanginess of cider vinegar in this tasty tropical dressing; it is also wonderful drizzled over grilled vegetables. Mango can replace one, or both, of the papayas, if desired.

2 small ripe papayas (about 1 pound each), peeled, seeded, and chopped (see Cook's Tip, below)

⅓ cup canola oil

¼ cup cider vinegar

1 tablespoon sugar

½ teaspoon salt

Freshly ground black pepper, to taste

1 to 2 tablespoons water or orange juice, as necessary

In a food processor fitted with the knife blade, or in a blender, process all the ingredients until smooth. For a thinner consistency, add water, as necessary. If not serving immediately, cover and refrigerate up to 3 days. For best results, return the dressing to room temperature before using.

PER TABLESPOON: Calories 29 • Protein 0g • Total Fat 2g • Sat. Fat 0g • Cholesterol 0mg • Carbohydrate 2g • Dietary Fiber 0g • Sodium 34mg

COOK'S TIP: *A ripe papaya will have skin that is turning from green to yellow and will yield to gentle pressure from the thumb; avoid papayas that feel mushy and have a very sweet scent. To prepare a papaya, cut it in half lengthwise and scrape out the seeds with a spoon. Place both halves cut sides down on a flat work surface and remove the skin with a long sharp knife. Slice crosswise into wedges. Chop, cube, shred, or julienne the flesh as directed in desired recipe.*

Thai Fruit Salad with Hot Peanut Dressing

MAKES 6 SERVINGS

This scrumptious fruit salad is not for the fainthearted, although you can always leave the hot chilies out, as well as the jicama and cucumber, and serve it as a splendid dessert. Fresh mango can replace the papaya, if desired.

> 3 tablespoons dry roasted peanuts
> ½ cup packed light brown sugar
> 1 tablespoon tamarind paste, dissolved in ⅓ cup water
> 1 to 2 fresh red or green chilies, seeded and sliced
> ½ tablespoon fresh lime juice, or more to taste
> 2 cups cubed fresh pineapple
> 1 small cucumber (about 6 ounces), peeled, seeded, and julienned
> 1 cup julienned jicama
> 1 cup cubed ripe yet firm papaya
> 1 ripe star fruit, thinly sliced (see Cook's Tip, opposite)
> 1 firm tart apple, cubed

In a food processor fitted with the knife blade, process the peanuts until finely chopped. Add the sugar, tamarind mixture, chilies, and lime juice; process until a smooth paste forms.

In a large bowl, toss together the remaining ingredients. Add the peanut-sugar mixture and toss well to thoroughly coat. Serve at once.

PER SERVING: Calories 168 • Protein 2g • Total Fat 3g • Sat. Fat 0g • Cholesterol 0mg • Carbohydrate 37g • Dietary Fiber 4g • Sodium 49mg

COOK'S TIP: *Ripe star fruit, also called carambola, is mostly bright yellow with light tinges of green. The skin of a star fruit is edible. To prepare for eating, simply cut off the dark tip along each ridge, and then cut off the stem end. Slice the star fruit crosswise into "stars," removing any seeds with the tip of a sharp knife.*

Singapore-Style Green Bean and Sprout Salad

MAKES 4 SERVINGS

You can prepare fresh asparagus in the same manner, if desired.

> 1 pound fresh green beans, trimmed
> 2 tablespoons plain rice vinegar
> 1 tablespoon toasted (dark) sesame oil
> 1 tablespoon low-sodium tamari or soy sauce, plus additional, as necessary
> ½ tablespoon finely chopped peeled fresh ginger
> 1 teaspoon toasted sesame seeds (see Cook's Tip, page 153) (optional)
> 1 teaspoon light brown sugar
> 1 large clove garlic, finely chopped
> Salt and freshly ground black pepper, to taste
> 1 cup bean sprouts
> ¼ cup thinly sliced red onion, soaked in cold water to cover for 10 minutes, well drained (see Cook's Tip, page 56)

In a large stockpot filled with boiling salted water, cook the green beans until just tender, 3 to 5 minutes. Meanwhile, prepare an ice water bath large enough to comfortably hold the green beans. Drain the green beans and immediately place in the ice water bath until cool, about 5 minutes. Drain well.

In a large bowl, whisk together the vinegar, sesame oil, tamari, ginger, sesame seeds (if using), sugar, garlic, salt, and pepper. Let stand about 5 minutes at room temperature, and then whisk again. Add the green beans, bean sprouts, and onion; toss gently yet thoroughly to combine. Let stand about 15 minutes at room temperature to allow the flavors to blend, and then toss again. Serve at room temperature, or cover and refrigerate a minimum of 1 hour or up to 1 day and serve chilled.

PER SERVING: Calories 90 • Protein 3g • Total Fat 4g • Sat. Fat 1g • Cholesterol 0mg • Carbohydrate 13g • Dietary Fiber 5g • Sodium 159mg

COOK'S TIP: *Soaking raw onion rings in cold water for 10 minutes helps minimize their pungency.*

Peruvian Lima Bean and Red Radish Salad

MAKES 4 SERVINGS

Serve this unusual and delicious salad over mixed greens or in lettuce cups, if desired. To save time, pick up some finely shredded or grated red radishes at your local supermarket salad bar. White hominy, a staple of American Southern cooking, is also highly popular in Latin and South American cuisines; if you can't locate it among the canned vegetables, look in the international food aisle.

2 tablespoons fresh lemon juice
2 tablespoons extra-virgin olive oil
2 large cloves garlic, finely chopped

½ teaspoon salt, preferably the coarse variety
Freshly ground black pepper, to taste
1 cup thinly sliced red onion, soaked in cold water to cover 10 minutes, drained well
1 cup rinsed, drained canned lima beans
1 cup finely shredded red radishes
1 cup rinsed, drained canned white hominy
2 tablespoons chopped fresh mint
2 tablespoons chopped fresh cilantro
1 to 2 tablespoons drained chopped pimiento
1 to 2 tablespoons chopped black olives (optional)

In a large bowl, whisk together the lemon juice, oil, garlic, salt, and pepper. Add the remaining ingredients and toss well to combine. Let stand about 15 minutes at room temperature before tossing again and serving. Alternatively, cover and refrigerate a minimum of 2 hours or up to 1 day and serve chilled or return to room temperature.

PER SERVING: Calories 170 • Protein 5g • Total Fat 8g • Sat. Fat 1g • Cholesterol 0mg • Carbohydrate 22g • Dietary Fiber 6g • Sodium 364mg

Costa Rican–Style Mango-Avocado Salad with Cabbage and Lime

MAKES 4 TO 6 SERVINGS

This refreshing and colorful salad makes a lovely first course or light lunch.

1½ cups shredded cabbage
1 large mango (about 14 ounces), peeled, pitted, and chopped (see Cook's Tip, opposite page)

1 medium red bell pepper (about 6 ounces),
   chopped

1 ripe avocado, peeled, pitted, and chopped

6 scallions, white and green parts, thinly sliced

½ cup chopped cucumber

¼ cup chopped fresh cilantro

Juice of 2 limes (about 4 tablespoons)

2 tablespoons extra-virgin olive oil

1 teaspoon sugar

1 large clove garlic, finely chopped

Salt and freshly ground black pepper, to taste

In a medium bowl, toss all the ingredients until well combined. Cover and refrigerate a minimum of 1 hour, or overnight. Serve chilled.

PER SERVING: Calories 213 • Protein 3g • Total Fat 15g • Sat. Fat 2g • Cholesterol 0mg • Carbohydrate 22g • Dietary Fiber 5g • Sodium 17mg

COOK'S TIP: *Ripe mangoes vary in color according to variety, yet all are pleasantly fragrant when held close to the nose and yield easily to pressure from the thumb. Avoid mangoes with a strong scent and that feel mushy. To prepare a mango, make a slice down one side of the mango stone or pit, and then make a slice on the other side of the stone. You will now have three parts: two "cheeks" plus the stone. Using a serrated knife, score each cheek lengthwise, and then crosswise, creating cubes; holding each cheek in your palm, spoon out the cubed flesh. Cut away the peel from around the stone, and then cut the remaining fruit from around the stone. Chop, shred, or julienne the flesh as directed in desired recipe.*

St. Martin–Style Orange and Red Onion Salad with Tarragon-Citrus Vinaigrette

MAKES 4 SERVINGS

The subtle use of tarragon in this refreshing salad can be traced to the French influence upon Caribbean cuisine.

Juice of 1 lime (about 2 tablespoons)

1 tablespoon extra-virgin olive oil

1 tablespoon fresh tarragon leaves or 1 teaspoon
   dried

1 teaspoon chopped fresh orange peel

½ teaspoon chopped fresh lime peel

½ teaspoon coarse salt

Freshly ground black pepper, to taste

4 medium seedless oranges, peeled and segmented

1 cup thinly sliced red onion, soaked in cold water
   to cover 10 minutes, drained well

In a medium bowl, stir together the lime juice, oil, tarragon, orange peel, lime peel, salt, and pepper until thoroughly blended. Let stand at room temperature about 10 minutes to allow the flavors to blend. Add the remaining ingredients and toss gently to thoroughly combine. Serve at room temperature. Alternatively, cover and refrigerate a minimum of 2 hours or overnight and serve chilled, or return to room temperature.

PER SERVING: Calories 113 • Protein 2g • Total Fat 4g • Sat. Fat 1g • Cholesterol 0mg • Carbohydrate 21g • Dietary Fiber 3g • Sodium 238mg

Brazilian Palm and Tomato Salad

MAKES 4 SERVINGS

Serve this attractive salad as an elegant first course or light lunch, accompanied by a bowl of Brazilian Corn Soup (page 33).

2 tablespoons extra-virgin olive oil

2 tablespoons fresh lemon juice

1 large clove garlic, finely chopped

Salt and freshly ground black pepper, to taste

2 ounces red onion (about ½ small), very thinly
   sliced into half-rings, soaked in cold water to
   cover 10 minutes, drained well

1 (4-ounce) heart of romaine, washed and torn into
   bite-size pieces (about 4 cups loosely packed)

1 (16-ounce) can hearts of palm, drained and cut
   into 2-inch pieces

2 medium ripe tomatoes (about 6 ounces each), cut
   into wedges

In a small bowl, whisk together the oil, lemon juice, garlic, salt, and pepper until thoroughly blended. Stir in the onion and let stand at room temperature about 20 minutes to allow the flavors to blend, turning the onion a few times.

To serve, divide the romaine evenly among 4 salad plates or bowls. Arrange hearts of palm and tomatoes on lettuce. Arrange onions on top of vegetables, drizzling evenly with remaining dressing. Serve at once.

PER SERVING: Calories 124 • Protein 4g • Total Fat 8g • Sat. Fat 1g • Cholesterol 0mg • Carbohydrate 13g • Dietary Fiber 5g • Sodium 493mg

Papaya, Jicama, and Avocado Salad with Sour Orange Dressing

MAKES 4 SERVINGS

This lovely and refreshing composed salad can be made with mango in lieu of the papaya, if desired.

¼ cup fresh orange juice

1 tablespoon fresh lime juice

1 tablespoon canola oil

1 teaspoon sugar

½ teaspoon cider vinegar

¼ teaspoon salt

Freshly ground black pepper, to taste

1 ripe yet firm small papaya (about 1 pound),
   peeled, seeded, cut crosswise into ½-inch-thick
   slices

1 ripe yet firm avocado, peeled, pitted, cut lengthwise into thin slices

½ medium jicama (about 8 ounces), peeled, cut into
   matchstick-size strips

In a small container, stir together the orange juice, lime juice, oil, sugar, vinegar, salt, and pepper until thoroughly blended.

To serve, arrange papaya and avocado slices on each of 4 rimmed salad plates. Top with jicama and drizzle evenly with the orange dressing. Serve at once.

PER SERVING: Calories 161 • Protein 2g • Total Fat 11g • Sat. Fat 2g • Cholesterol 0mg • Carbohydrate 16g • Dietary Fiber 4g • Sodium 141mg

Thai Green Papaya and Peanut Salad

MAKES 5 TO 6 SERVINGS

This is one of Thailand's most popular and delicious salads. However, if you are pregnant or trying to become pregnant, avoid eating unripe or green papaya. A papaya that is at all unripe contains a latex substance that triggers uterine contractions and may cause a miscarriage. Anyone with latex allergies should also avoid eating unripe papaya. Green unripe mango can replace the papaya, if desired. Tamarind paste, also known as Thai fruit paste, can be found in Asian markets, as well as many specialty stores. If you can't locate it, either omit from the recipe or add a tablespoon or so of fresh lemon juice—the salad will still be quite tasty.

- 1 tablespoon tamarind paste blended with
    3 tablespoons warm water
- 2 tablespoons fresh lime juice
- 2 tablespoons low-sodium soy sauce or tamari
- 2 tablespoons peanut oil
- 1 tablespoon light brown sugar
- 2 large cloves garlic, finely chopped
- Salt and freshly ground black pepper, to taste
- 3 scallions, white and green parts, thinly sliced
- 1 to 2 fresh red or green chilies, seeded and finely chopped
- 4 cups julienned green papaya, from about 1 extra-large (2½- to 3-pound) green papaya or 3 small (about 1-pound each) green papaya
- 3 large plum tomatoes (about 3 ounces each), cut into bite-size pieces
- 1½ cups bean sprouts
- ¼ cup chopped salted peanuts

In a large bowl, whisk together the tamarind paste mixture, lime juice, soy sauce, oil, sugar, garlic, salt, and pepper until thoroughly blended. Stir in the scallions and chilies and let stand a few minutes to allow the flavors to blend. Stir again. Add the remaining ingredients except the peanuts and toss well to combine. Let stand at room temperature about 15 minutes before tossing again and serving at room temperature, garnished with the peanuts. Or cover and refrigerate a minimum of 2 hours or overnight and serve chilled or return to room temperature.

PER SERVING: Calories 180 • Protein 5g • Total Fat 9g • Sat. Fat 2g • Cholesterol 0mg • Carbohydrate 23g • Dietary Fiber 4g • Sodium 258mg

Thai-Style Romaine Salad with Creamy Coconut-Tamari Dressing

MAKES 4 SERVINGS

You can make this tasty salad with any green; spinach is especially delicious.

- 1 (10-ounce) bag ready-washed romaine lettuce
- 1 cup cherry tomatoes, halved
- ½ cup thinly sliced red onion, soaked in cold water to cover 10 minutes, well drained
- ½ small cucumber (about 3 ounces), peeled, seeded, and thinly sliced
- 2 tablespoons chopped fresh basil
- Creamy Coconut-Tamari Dressing (page 60)

In a large bowl, toss together the lettuce, tomatoes, onion, cucumber, and basil with half of the dressing. Transfer to 4 salad bowls or plates and drizzle evenly with the remaining dressing. Serve at once.

Creamy Coconut-Tamari Dressing

MAKES ABOUT 2/3 CUP

You can easily reduce the heat of this creamy dressing by omitting the chili and replacing with a pinch or two of cayenne, if desired. For best results, use full-fat coconut milk.

- 6 tablespoons unsweetened coconut milk
- 2 tablespoons fresh lime juice
- 2 tablespoons low-sodium tamari or soy sauce
- 2 large cloves garlic, finely chopped
- 2 teaspoons light brown sugar
- 1 to 1½ teaspoons finely chopped fresh red chili, or cayenne pepper, to taste

In a small bowl, whisk together all the ingredients until the sugar dissolves. Serve at room temperature. Dressing can be stored, covered, in the refrigerator up to 5 days. For best results, return to room temperature before using.

Baby Spinach Salad with Pomegranates and Almonds

MAKES 4 SERVINGS

This pretty spinach salad, flecked with ruby-red pomegranate seeds, is an ideal opener for a special dinner, particularly around the holidays.

- 2 tablespoons extra-virgin olive oil
- 2 tablespoons fresh orange juice
- 2 tablespoons fresh lemon juice
- 1 tablespoon sugar
- ½ teaspoon Dijon mustard
- ¼ teaspoon salt
- Freshly ground black pepper, to taste
- 1 (6-ounce) bag ready-washed baby spinach
- ¼ cup very thinly sliced red onion, cut into half-rings, soaked in cold water to cover 10 minutes, well drained
- ½ cup pomegranate seeds
- ¼ cup slivered almonds

In a large bowl, whisk together the oil, orange juice, lemon juice, sugar, mustard, salt, and pepper until thoroughly blended. Add the spinach and onion; toss well to combine. Divide evenly among each of 4 salad bowls or salad plates and garnish with equal amounts of the pomegranate seeds and almonds. Serve at once.

Aussie-Style Curried Sweet Potato Salad with Orange

MAKES 4 SERVINGS

This is a wonderful potato salad. To serve as a light lunch or first course, serve over spinach leaves and garnish with pumpkin or sunflower seeds, or nuts.

1 extra-large sweet potato (12 to 14 ounces), peeled and cut into 2-inch chunks

2 tablespoons canola oil

1 tablespoon fresh orange juice

½ tablespoon cider vinegar

¼ teaspoon mild curry powder

Salt and freshly ground black pepper, to taste

2 tablespoons finely chopped red onion

2 scallions, white and green parts, thinly sliced

1 tablespoon chopped fresh orange peel

1 large navel orange (about 8 ounces), peeled and segmented

In a large saucepan, bring the sweet potato and enough salted water to cover to a boil over high heat. Reduce the heat slightly and cook until tender through the center, about 15 minutes. Drain and let cool about 15 minutes.

In a medium bowl, whisk together the oil, orange juice, vinegar, curry powder, salt, and pepper. Stir in the red onion, scallions, and orange peel and set aside to let the flavors blend.

Cut the cooled potatoes into bite-size cubes and add to the dressing mixture; toss gently yet thoroughly to combine. Let stand a few minutes, then add the orange segments; toss gently yet thoroughly to combine. Serve at room temperature. Alternatively, cover and refrigerate a minimum of 2 hours or up to 1 day and serve chilled or return to room temperature.

PER SERVING: Calories 175 • Protein 2g • Total Fat 7g • Sat. Fat 1g • Cholesterol 0mg • Carbohydrate 27g • Dietary Fiber 4g • Sodium 13mg

Caribbean Potato Salad

MAKES 5 TO 6 SERVINGS

Awesome aptly describes this refreshing and colorful potato salad.

1¼ pounds medium round red or white potatoes, peeled if desired, cut into halves or quarters, depending on size

2½ tablespoons mango chutney

2 tablespoons canola oil

1 tablespoon fresh lime juice

1 tablespoon cider vinegar

1 tablespoon finely chopped jalapeño chili

½ teaspoon salt

Freshly ground black pepper, to taste

4 scallions, white and green parts, thinly sliced

2 large plum tomatoes (about 3 ounces each), cut into bite-size pieces

1 cup cubed fresh papaya, mango, or cantaloupe

¼ cup thinly sliced green bell pepper

¼ cup thinly sliced celery

Place the potatoes in a large saucepan with enough salted water to cover; bring to a boil over high heat. Reduce the heat slightly and boil until tender through the center but not mushy, about 15 minutes. Drain and let cool 10 minutes.

In a large bowl, stir together the chutney, oil, lime juice, vinegar, chili, salt, and black pepper until thoroughly blended. Add the warm potatoes and scallions; toss gently to combine. Add the remaining ingredients and toss again. Serve slightly warm or at room temperature. Alternatively, cover and refrigerate a minimum of 3 hours or up to 1 day and serve chilled.

PER SERVING: Calories 162 • Protein 3g • Total Fat 6g • Sat. Fat 0g • Cholesterol 0mg • Carbohydrate 27g • Dietary Fiber 3g • Sodium 232mg

Hawaiian-Style Seasoned Soybean Sprout Salad

MAKES 4 TO 6 SERVINGS

The Asian influence upon the cuisine of Hawaii is apparent in this simple yet delicious side salad, popular at luaus. Soybean sprouts, loaded with essential protein, are available in Asian markets, health food stores, and some well-stocked supermarkets. Mung bean sprouts can easily be substituted; however, while the dish will contain about half the calories and fat, it will lose almost three-fourths of its protein.

1 pound soybean sprouts, stringy tails and any bean husks removed

½ cup water

1 tablespoon peanut oil

1 tablespoon toasted (dark) sesame oil

1 tablespoon low-sodium soy sauce or tamari

1 large clove garlic, finely chopped

¼ teaspoon crushed red pepper flakes, or more to taste

Salt and freshly ground black pepper, to taste

2 scallions, white and green parts, thinly sliced

1 teaspoon toasted sesame seeds

In a tightly covered medium stockpot, bring the sprouts and water to a boil over high heat; boil 2 minutes. Drain well.

In a medium bowl, whisk together the peanut oil, sesame oil, soy sauce, garlic, red pepper flakes, salt, and black pepper. Stir in the scallions and sesame seeds and let stand a few minutes to allow the flavors to blend. Stir again and add the warm sprouts, mixing well to combine. Bring to room temperature before tossing again and serving. Or cover and refrigerate up to 1 day and return to room temperature before serving.

PER SERVING: Calories 209 • Protein 15g • Total Fat 15g • Sat. Fat 2g • Cholesterol 0mg • Carbohydrate 13g • Dietary Fiber 2g • Sodium 168mg

Tomato Salad with Chilies and Lime

MAKES 4 SERVINGS

Reminiscent of salsa, this side salad makes a fine addition to a Mexican-style buffet.

1½ tablespoons extra-virgin olive oil

1 tablespoon fresh lime juice

¼ teaspoon Dijon mustard

¼ teaspoon coarse salt, plus additional, to taste

Freshly ground black pepper, to taste

1 pound vine-ripened tomatoes, seeded and cut
    into bite-size pieces
1 jalapeño chili, seeded and thinly sliced

In a medium bowl, stir together the oil, lime juice, mustard, salt, and black pepper until thoroughly blended. Add the remaining ingredients and toss gently to combine. Let stand at room temperature a few minutes to allow the flavors to blend; toss again. Serve at room temperature. Alternatively, cover and refrigerate a minimum of 2 hours or up to 1 day and serve chilled, or return to room temperature.

PER SERVING: Calories 77 • Protein 1g • Total Fat 5g • Sat. Fat 1g • Cholesterol 0mg • Carbohydrate 8g • Dietary Fiber 1g • Sodium 132mg

Peruvian Purple Potato Salad

MAKES 8 SERVINGS

This is an excellent potato salad, ideal for a picnic or potluck.

2 pounds small purple, red, or Yukon gold potatoes,
    scrubbed, left whole
¼ cup extra-virgin olive oil
3 tablespoons white wine vinegar
2 tablespoons coarsely ground mustard
1 tablespoon chopped fresh thyme leaves, or 1
    teaspoon crumbled dried thyme leaves
2 large cloves garlic, finely chopped
1 teaspoon chipotle puree, or more to taste (see
    Cook's Tip, page 112)

1 teaspoon coarse salt
Freshly ground black pepper, to taste
1 medium carrot (about 4 ounces), thinly sliced
1 large red or yellow bell pepper (about 8 ounces),
    chopped
½ cup chopped red onion
6 scallions, white and green parts, thinly
    sliced
¼ cup chopped black olives, preferably oil cured
    (optional)

Place the potatoes in a large saucepan or medium stockpot with enough salted water to cover; bring to a boil over high heat. Reduce the heat to a gentle boil and cook until the potatoes are just tender, about 15 minutes, depending on size. Drain and set aside to cool slightly.

Meanwhile, in a large bowl, whisk together the oil, vinegar, mustard, thyme, garlic, chipotle puree, salt, and black pepper. Let stand a few minutes to allow the flavors to blend.

As soon as the potatoes are cool enough to handle, yet still quite warm, cut them in half or in quarters, depending on size. Stir the reserved dressing a few times, and then add the warm potatoes along with the remaining ingredients. Toss gently yet thoroughly to combine. Serve slightly warm or at room temperature. Alternatively, let cool to room temperature and refrigerate, covered, a minimum of 3 hours, or up to 2 days, and serve chilled or return to room temperature.

PER SERVING: Calories 177 • Protein 4g • Total Fat 7g • Sat. Fat 1g • Cholesterol 0mg • Carbohydrate 26g • Dietary Fiber 3g • Sodium 301mg

Mexican Barley, Corn, and Bean Salad in Cabbage Cups

MAKES 6 SERVINGS

You can omit the cabbage cups and enjoy this wonderful fiber-rich barley salad all by itself.

5 cups water

1 cup pearl barley, rinsed under cold-running water, drained

2 cups frozen yellow corn kernels, thawed

1 cup rinsed, drained canned pinto, kidney, or black beans

¼ cup cider vinegar

3 tablespoons extra-virgin olive oil

½ tablespoon Dijon mustard

2 large cloves garlic, finely chopped

1 teaspoon ground cumin

1 teaspoon salt

½ teaspoon dried oregano

¼ teaspoon freshly ground black pepper

1 cup chopped red bell pepper

3 scallions, white and green parts, thinly sliced

½ cup chopped fresh cilantro

¼ cup pitted black olives, sliced (optional)

6 large whole red or green cabbage leaves, rinsed and drained

In a large saucepan or medium stockpot, bring the water to a boil over high heat. Add the barley, reduce heat to between low and medium-low, and simmer, covered, until the barley is tender, about 50 minutes. Stir in the corn and beans the last 10 minutes of simmering, increasing the heat momentarily to maintain a simmer. Drain in a colander and let cool about 10 minutes.

In a large bowl, whisk together the vinegar, oil, mustard, garlic, cumin, salt, oregano, and black pepper. Add the barley mixture, bell pepper, scallions, cilantro, and olives (if using), tossing well to combine. Let stand about 15 minutes at room temperature to allow the flavors to blend, and then toss again. (At this point, the barley salad can be refrigerated, covered, up to 2 days before serving chilled or returning to room temperature.)

To serve, fill each cabbage leaf with equal amounts of the barley salad.

PER SERVING: Calories 281 • Protein 8g • Total Fat 8g • Sat. Fat 1g • Cholesterol 0mg • Carbohydrate 48g • Dietary Fiber 9g • Sodium 383mg

Fiesta Black Bean and Corn Salad

MAKES 4 SERVINGS

This delightful dinner salad can be thrown together in minutes with the use of ready-shredded iceberg lettuce, available in many major supermarkets.

½ cup fresh orange juice

¼ cup chopped fresh cilantro

3 tablespoons red wine vinegar

2 tablespoons extra-virgin olive oil

2 large cloves garlic, finely chopped

½ teaspoon salt

¼ teaspoon cayenne pepper, or to taste

¼ teaspoon sugar

Freshly ground black pepper, to taste

1 (15-ounce) can black beans, rinsed and drained

1 (11-ounce) can Mexican-style corn, drained well

4 large plum tomatoes (about 3 ounces each),
    coarsely chopped

4 scallions, white and green parts, thinly sliced

8 cups shredded iceberg lettuce

4 ounces crushed tortilla chips

In a large bowl, stir together the orange juice, cilantro, vinegar, oil, garlic, salt, cayenne, sugar, and black pepper. Add the beans, corn, tomatoes, and scallions and toss well to combine. Let stand at room temperature a few minutes to allow the flavors to blend. Add the remaining ingredients, tossing well to thoroughly combine. Serve at once.

PER SERVING: Calories 384 • Protein 12g • Total Fat 15g • Sat. Fat 3g • Cholesterol 0mg • Carbohydrate 55g • Dietary Fiber 9g • Sodium 574mg

Tropical Couscous Salad

MAKES 4 TO 6 SERVINGS

This salad is also delicious made with orzo pasta in lieu of the couscous.

1 cup water

½ teaspoon salt, plus additional, to taste

1 cup instant couscous, preferably whole wheat

¼ cup fresh lime juice

2 tablespoons canola oil

½ teaspoon ground cumin

Freshly ground black pepper, to taste

1½ cups cubed fresh mango

1 cup cubed fresh pineapple

½ cup chopped fresh cilantro

¼ cup chopped red onion

¼ cup golden raisins

In a medium saucepan, bring the water and salt to a boil over high heat. Stir in the couscous, cover, and remove from heat. Let stand until all the liquid has been absorbed, about 7 minutes. Fluff with a fork and let cool to room temperature.

Meanwhile, in a medium bowl, whisk together the lime juice, oil, cumin, salt, and pepper. Add the mango, pineapple, cilantro, onion, and raisins and toss well to combine. Add the couscous and toss well to combine. Serve at room temperature. Alternatively, cover and refrigerate a minimum of 3 hours or up to 1 day and serve chilled, or return to room temperature.

PER SERVING: Calories 323 • Protein 7g • Total Fat 8g • Sat. Fat 1g • Cholesterol 0mg • Carbohydrate 59g • Dietary Fiber 4g • Sodium 275mg

Luau Salad

MAKES 4 SERVINGS

While freshly prepared fried chow mein noodles usually contain egg, most commercial brands are egg-free, but check the label carefully. If you are using unsalted nuts, increase the amount of salt in the vinaigrette.

1 (10-ounce) bag mixed salad greens or romaine lettuce

1 medium mango (about 10 ounces), peeled, pitted, and cut into small chunks

1 cup cubed fresh pineapple

1 cup egg-free fried chow mein noodles

1 medium red bell pepper (about 6 ounces), sliced into thin strips

1 small cucumber (about 6 ounces), thinly sliced

½ medium red onion (about 3 ounces), sliced into thin half-rings, soaked in cold water to cover 10 minutes, well drained

¼ cup chopped crystallized ginger

½ recipe (about ½ cup) Sesame-Guava Vinaigrette with Ginger (opposite), plus additional, as desired

½ cup shredded carrot

2 scallions, white and green parts, thinly sliced

¼ cup chopped salted macadamia nuts or peanuts

In a large bowl, toss the salad greens, mango, pineapple, ½ cup of the chow mein noodles, bell pepper, cucumber, onion, and half of the ginger until well combined. Add the vinaigrette, and toss again. Divide the mixture equally among 4 salad bowls. Garnish with the carrot, scallions, nuts, remaining ginger, and remaining chow mein noodles. Serve at once, with additional dressing passed separately, if desired.

PER SERVING (with ½ recipe Sesame-Guava Vinaigrette): Calories 356 • Protein 5g • Total Fat 21g • Sat. Fat 3g • Cholesterol 0mg • Carbohydrate 34g • Dietary Fiber 7g • Sodium 294mg

Sesame-Guava Vinaigrette with Ginger

MAKES ABOUT 1 CUP

Any fruit nectar can replace the guava variety, if desired. The vinaigrette can be refrigerated up to five days before returning to room temperature and serving.

¼ cup canola oil

¼ cup guava nectar

¼ cup plain rice vinegar

2 tablespoons toasted (dark) sesame oil

1 tablespoon mirin

1 tablespoon low-sodium soy sauce or tamari

1 tablespoon finely chopped fresh ginger

1 shallot, finely chopped

½ teaspoon light brown sugar, or to taste

½ teaspoon salt

Freshly ground black pepper, to taste

In a small bowl, whisk together all the ingredients until thoroughly blended. Let stand at room temperature about 15 minutes to allow the flavors to blend; whisk again. Serve at room temperature.

PER TABLESPOON: Calories 52 • Protein 0g • Total Fat 5g • Sat. Fat 1g • Cholesterol 0mg • Carbohydrate 1g • Dietary Fiber 0g • Sodium 105mg

Thai Glass Noodle Salad

MAKES 4 SERVINGS

For added protein, garnish each serving with chopped peanuts.

1 (7.75-ounce) package cellophane (mung bean) noodles

2 cups lightly packed fresh cilantro, finely chopped

½ large red bell pepper (about 4 ounces), thinly sliced

2 medium plum tomatoes (about 2 ounces each), cut into small pieces

4 to 6 scallions, white and green parts, thinly sliced

2 jalapeño chilies, seeded and finely chopped

1 stalk lemongrass, finely chopped (see Cook's Tip, opposite), or 1 teaspoon grated fresh lemon peel

¼ cup low-sodium soy sauce or tamari

Juice of 1 lime (about 2 tablespoons)

1 tablespoon peanut oil

1 tablespoon toasted (dark) sesame oil

Salt and freshly ground black pepper, to taste

Soak the noodles in hot water according to package directions until translucent, about 15 minutes. Drain in a colander and rinse under cold-running water to cool; drain well. Cut into 6-inch bunches and transfer to a large bowl. Add the remaining ingredients and toss well to combine. Serve at room temperature, or cover and refrigerate a minimum of 2 hours or up to 2 days and serve chilled.

PER SERVING: Calories 297 • Protein 3g • Total Fat 8g • Sat. Fat 1g • Cholesterol 0mg • Carbohydrate 56g • Dietary Fiber 5g • Sodium 616mg

COOK'S TIP: *Fresh lemongrass is available in Asian markets, specialty stores, and some well-stocked supermarkets. When buying lemongrass, select stalks that are fragrant, tightly formed, and of a lemony-green color toward the lower stalk. Avoid purchasing stalks that are brown and coming apart.*

To prepare lemongrass, pull off and discard the tough outer leaves until you reach the softer inner yellow section of the stalk, which is primarily used in cooking. Cut off and discard the lower bulb. Depending upon the recipe, cut the yellow stalk into 2- or 3-inch lengths with a sharp knife, and then crush or bruise by bending the pieces several times or pounding in a mortar and pestle. Alternatively, cut the yellow stalk into smaller pieces and chop in a food processor fitted with the knife blade. Use as directed in desired recipe.

Sesame Noodle Salad with Dried Pineapple

MAKES 4 TO 6 SERVINGS

Any dried tropical fruit or fruit blend—pineapple, mango, papaya—works well in this tasty noodle salad.

12 ounces dried soba or somen noodles

¼ cup low-sodium tamari or soy sauce

¼ cup plain rice vinegar

3 tablespoons toasted sesame seeds (see Cook's Tip, page 153)

1 tablespoon sugar

1 tablespoon toasted (dark) sesame oil

¼ teaspoon cayenne pepper, or more to taste

1 large red bell pepper (about 8 ounces), cut into thin strips

¾ cup shredded carrots

6 scallions, white and green parts, thinly sliced

½ cup chopped dried pineapple

In a large stockpot filled with boiling salted water, cook the soba noodles according to package directions until just tender to the bite, about 5 minutes. Drain and rinse well under cold-running water. Drain again.

In a large bowl, stir together the tamari, vinegar, sesame seeds, sugar, oil, and cayenne until well blended. Add the noodles and toss well to combine. Add the remaining ingredients and toss well to combine. Serve at room temperature, or cover and refrigerate a minimum of 2 hours or up to 2 days and serve chilled, or return to room temperature.

PER SERVING: Calories 482 • Protein 16g • Total Fat 8g • Sat. Fat 1g • Cholesterol 0mg • Carbohydrate 97g • Dietary Fiber 7g • Sodium 1,289mg

Vietnamese "Bun-Style" Herbed Rice Noodle Salad

MAKES 4 SERVINGS

Pronounced "boon," bun-style rice noodle salads are popular throughout Vietnam, and every cook seems to have their own favorite toppings. Feel free to experiment with your own.

8 ounces thin (vermicelli-style) rice noodles, soaked according to package directions until soft yet firm to the bite (see Cook's Tip, page 44)
Vietnamese Dipping Sauce (page 68)
2 cups coarsely torn red leaf lettuce
2 cups mung bean sprouts
1 cup peeled, seeded, and julienned cucumber
¼ cup chopped fresh mint

¼ cup chopped fresh cilantro
¼ cup chopped fresh basil
2 tablespoons peanut oil
½ (2.9-ounce) package deep-fried tofu or bean curd (about 5 squares), cut into thin strips
½ large red bell pepper (about 4 ounces), cut into strips
1 cup shredded cabbage
4 scallions, white and green parts, thinly sliced
1 fresh red or green chili, seeded and chopped
2 large cloves garlic, finely chopped
Salt and freshly ground black pepper, to taste
¼ cup chopped roasted peanuts (optional)
Fresh cilantro sprigs, for garnish (optional)

Drain the soaked noodles well and rinse under cold-running water, 30 seconds. Set aside to drain, about 15 minutes. Transfer to a large bowl and add about ⅓ cup of the dipping sauce; let stand at room temperature about 30 minutes, tossing and folding the noodles in the sauce a few times (at this point, the noodles can be covered and refrigerated up to 1 day before returning to room temperature and continuing with the recipe).

In a medium bowl, mix together the lettuce, sprouts, cucumber, mint, cilantro, and basil. Divide among 4 bowls. Set aside.

In a medium nonstick skillet, heat the oil over medium-high heat. Add the tofu, bell pepper, cabbage, scallions, chili, and garlic; cook, stirring constantly, until the bell pepper is crisp-tender, 3 to 4 minutes. Remove from heat and season with salt and black pepper. Set aside.

Top the lettuce mixture with equal amounts of the rice noodles. Top with equal amounts of the warm tofu mixture and garnish with the peanuts and cilantro sprigs (if using). Serve at once, with remaining dipping sauce on the side.

PER SERVING: Calories 456 • Protein 8g • Total Fat 13g • Sat. Fat 2g • Cholesterol 0mg • Carbohydrate 82g • Dietary Fiber 7g • Sodium 838mg

Vietnamese Dipping Sauce

MAKES ABOUT 1¼ CUPS

You can store this sauce, covered, in the refrigerator a few days before bringing to room temperature and serving.

- ½ cup fresh lime juice
- ⅓ cup low-sodium soy sauce or tamari
- ¼ cup sugar
- 3 tablespoons warm water
- 1 tablespoon toasted (dark) sesame oil
- 1 to 2 fresh red or green chilies, seeded and finely chopped
- 1 to 2 large cloves garlic, finely chopped

In a small bowl, combine the lime juice, soy sauce, sugar, water, and sesame oil; stir until the sugar is dissolved. Add the chilies and garlic and let stand 1 hour at room temperature before serving, stirring a few times.

PER ¼ OF RECIPE: Calories 105 • Protein 2g • Total Fat 4g • Sat. Fat 1g • Cholesterol 0mg • Carbohydrate 19g • Dietary Fiber 1g • Sodium 801mg

Tropical Pasta Salad

MAKES 3 TO 4 MAIN-COURSE OR 6 SIDE-DISH SERVINGS

Though optional, peanuts lend protein and crunch to this tasty tropical pasta salad, perfect for a picnic or potluck. Fresh papaya can replace the mango, if desired.

- 8 ounces rotelle or other twist pasta
- 1 medium green bell pepper (about 6 ounces), chopped
- 2 tablespoons peanut oil
- 1 tablespoon plain rice vinegar
- ½ teaspoon ground cardamom
- ½ teaspoon salt
- ¼ teaspoon freshly ground black pepper
- 4 scallions, white and green parts, thinly sliced
- 1 large mango (about 14 ounces), peeled, pitted, and chopped
- 8 ounces plum tomatoes, chopped
- 2 tablespoons finely chopped fresh cilantro
- ¼ cup chopped peanuts (optional)

In a large stockpot filled with boiling salted water, cook the pasta according to package directions until al dente. While the pasta is cooking, place the chopped bell pepper in a colander set in a sink. Slowly drain the cooked pasta over the bell pepper. Rinse under cold-running water until cooled and drain well.

Meanwhile, in a large bowl, whisk together the oil, vinegar, cardamom, salt, and black pepper. Stir in the scallions and let stand about 5 minutes to allow the flavors to blend. Add the pasta and bell pepper mixture, mango, tomatoes, and cilantro; toss well to thoroughly combine. Serve at room temperature, sprinkled with the peanuts (if using). Or cover and refrigerate a minimum of 2 hours or up to 2 days, and serve chilled or return to room temperature.

PER SERVING: Calories 443 • Protein 12g • Total Fat 11g • Sat. Fat 2g • Cholesterol 0mg • Carbohydrate 77g • Dietary Fiber 6g • Sodium 374mg

New Zealand–Style Brown Rice Salad with Kiwifruit and Apple

MAKES 4 MAIN-COURSE OR 6 SIDE-DISH SERVINGS

This versatile salad is ideal for a special luncheon, or a party buffet, as it holds up well at room temperature. Any sweet red apple can replace the Fuji variety, if desired.

- 1 cup brown rice, cooked according to package directions and cooled
- 2 kiwifruit, peeled and sliced into thin half-rounds
- 1 Fuji apple, cut into ½-inch cubes
- ½ cup thinly sliced celery
- ½ cup chopped red bell pepper
- ¼ cup chopped walnuts, toasted if desired (see Cook's Tip, page 130)
- 2 scallions, white and green parts, thinly sliced
- 2 tablespoons cider vinegar
- 2 tablespoons extra-virgin olive oil
- Salt and freshly ground black pepper, to taste

In a large bowl, toss all the ingredients until well combined. Let stand at room temperature about 15 minutes to allow the flavors to blend, and then

toss again. Serve at room temperature. Alternatively, cover and refrigerate up to 24 hours before serving chilled or returning to room temperature.

PER SERVING: Calories 336 • Protein 6g • Total Fat 13g • Sat. Fat 2g • Cholesterol 0mg • Carbohydrate 52g • Dietary Fiber 4g • Sodium 19mg

Brazilian Rice Salad

MAKES 6 TO 8 SERVINGS

You can use any bean in this tasty tropical salad from Brazil, ideal for summer picnics or a winter holiday buffet.

- 2 cups long-grain white rice
- 2¼ cups water
- 1¾ cups light coconut milk
- 1 teaspoon ground turmeric
- 1 teaspoon ground cumin
- 1 teaspoon sugar
- 1 teaspoon salt, plus additional, to taste
- 1 (15-ounce) cans black beans, rinsed and drained
- ½ cup chopped red onion
- ½ cup chopped red, yellow, and/or green bell pepper
- 2 large plum tomatoes (about 3 ounces each), chopped
- ¼ cup finely chopped fresh cilantro
- 3 tablespoons extra-virgin olive oil
- 3 tablespoons fresh lime juice, or to taste
- Freshly ground black pepper, to taste

In a medium deep-sided skillet with a lid, bring the rice, water, coconut milk, turmeric, cumin, sugar, and salt to a boil over high heat. Reduce the heat, cover, and simmer gently until all the liquid is absorbed, 17 to 20 minutes. Fluff with a fork and set aside to cool about 20 minutes.

In a large bowl, combine the rice with the remaining ingredients, tossing well to combine. Season with additional salt, as needed. Serve slightly warm or at room temperature. Alternatively, cover and refrigerate up to 24 hours, and return to room temperature before serving.

PER SERVING: Calories 445 • Protein 11g • Total Fat 15g • Sat. Fat 8g • Cholesterol 0mg • Carbohydrate 68g • Dietary Fiber 4g • Sodium 388mg

Curried Quinoa Salad with Mango

MAKES 4 SERVINGS

Quinoa (pronounced "keen-wa") is an ancient South American grain that has more protein than any other grain. It is available in health food stores and some well-stocked supermarkets.

    1 cup quinoa, rinsed well under cold-running water
       and drained
    2 tablespoons canola oil
    1 tablespoon cider vinegar
    1 tablespoon mango chutney (mostly liquid part)
    1 teaspoon mild curry powder
    ½ teaspoon salt
    ⅛ teaspoon dry mustard
    Freshly ground black pepper, to taste
    1 cup chopped fresh mango
    1 cup chopped unpeeled seedless cucumber
    4 scallions, white and green parts, thinly sliced

Bring a large saucepan filled with salted water to a boil over high heat. Add the quinoa, reduce the heat to medium, and cook until tender yet firm to the bite, about 12 minutes, stirring occasionally. Drain well and set aside to cool.

In a medium bowl, whisk together the oil, vinegar, chutney, curry powder, salt, mustard, and pepper until thoroughly blended. Add the cooled quinoa, mango, cucumber, and scallions, tossing gently yet thoroughly to combine. Serve at room temperature, or cover and refrigerate a minimum of 2 hours or up to 1 day and served chilled, or return to room temperature.

PER SERVING: Calories 268 • Protein 6g • Total Fat 10g • Sat. Fat 1g • Cholesterol 0mg • Carbohydrate 42g • Dietary Fiber 5g • Sodium 281mg

Caribbean Pigeon Pea and Brown Rice Salad

MAKES 6 SERVINGS

If you don't have fresh thyme sprigs, add a couple pinches of additional dried thyme to the rice before simmering.

3 cups water

1½ cups brown rice

½ teaspoon garlic salt

3 sprigs fresh thyme

¼ cup fresh lemon juice

¼ cup extra-virgin olive oil

2 cloves garlic, finely chopped

1 tablespoon jerk seasoning, or more to taste

½ tablespoon sugar

1 teaspoon dried thyme leaves

½ teaspoon coarse salt, plus additional, to taste

Freshly ground black pepper, to taste

1 (15-ounce) can pigeon peas or black-eyed peas, rinsed and drained

2 large plum tomatoes (about 3 ounces each), chopped

1 large red bell pepper (about 8 ounces), chopped

4 scallions, white and green parts, thinly sliced

1 stalk celery, thinly sliced

In a medium saucepan, bring the water to a boil over high heat. Stir in the rice, garlic salt, and thyme sprigs; cover, reduce the heat to between low and medium-low, and simmer until all the liquid has been absorbed, about 45 minutes. Transfer to a large bowl, fluff with a fork, and set aside to cool about 20 minutes.

In another large bowl, whisk together the lemon juice, oil, garlic, jerk seasoning, sugar, dried thyme, coarse salt, and black pepper. Add the peas, tomatoes, bell pepper, scallions, and celery; toss well to combine. Let stand about 10 minutes, and toss again.

Add the pea mixture to the rice and toss well to combine; season with additional salt and pepper as needed. Serve slightly warm or at room temperature. Alternatively, cover and refrigerate a minimum of 2 hours or up to 2 days, and serve chilled or return to room temperature.

PER SERVING: Calories 338 • Protein 8g • Total Fat 11g • Sat. Fat 2g • Cholesterol 0mg • Carbohydrate 55g • Dietary Fiber 3g • Sodium 451mg

Main Dishes

Tropical dinners are bold, colorful, and fun, not to mention full of flavor. Depending on the geographic region, everyday meals can be seasoned with fresh chilies, chipotle chilies, curry pastes, red pepper flakes, ginger, cinnamon, turmeric, cumin, coriander seeds, allspice, cardamom, lemongrass, kaffir lime leaves, scallions, garlic, citrus, rice vinegar, mirin, miso, tamarind paste, basil, cilantro, mint, almonds, cashews, macadamias, peanuts, peanut butter, pistachios, sesame seeds, and toasted sesame oil. Condiments appear on every table: chili sauces, salsas, soy sauces, peanut sauces, wasabi dipping sauces, chutneys, sambals, adobo sauces, mojo sauces, hot mustards, pickled chilies, peppercorns, and sea salts. Palm sugar is frequently used for sweetening and coconut milk is commonly added for creaminess, as well as to mitigate some of the heat from the chilies. Entrées can include vegetable, potato, and legume combinations, which can also contain a fruit. There are entrées such as main-course salads, soups, and stews found in other chapters. Almost always there is rice, whether in grain or noodle form. Often there are wheat noodles, and, sometimes, corn, barley, and quinoa. Always there is fearless flavor, so as you prepare the following recipes, don't be shy. Why not use the suggested amount of chilies and give the real tropical experience a try?

Indian Black-Barley Pilaf with Bananas and Oranges

MAKES 4 SERVINGS

Black barley is actually purple in color; regular barley can be substituted.

2 tablespoons extra-virgin olive oil

1 cup chopped onion

¼ cup chopped carrot

1 fresh green or red chili, seeded and finely chopped

1 cup black or regular barley, rinsed under cold water until the water runs clear

3 scallions, white and green parts, thinly sliced

2 large cloves garlic, finely chopped

3½ cups low-sodium vegetable broth

2 bay leaves

1 teaspoon whole coriander seed, crushed

½ teaspoon ground cinnamon

½ teaspoon salt, or to taste

Freshly ground black pepper, to taste

1 large or 2 small ripe yet firm bananas, peeled and cut into bite-size pieces

1 large navel orange, peeled and chopped

¼ cup chopped fresh cilantro or flat-leaf parsley

In a medium deep-sided skillet with a lid, heat the oil over medium heat. Add the onion, carrot, and chili; cook, stirring, until softened, about 5 minutes. Add the barley, scallions, and garlic; cook, stirring, 2 minutes. Add the broth, bay leaves, cori-

ander, cinnamon, salt, and pepper; bring to a boil over medium-high heat. Reduce the heat, cover, and simmer gently, stirring occasionally, until the barley is just tender, 45 to 50 minutes. Remove from heat and let stand, covered, 10 minutes. Add the banana, orange, and cilantro, stirring gently to combine. Serve at once.

PER SERVING: Calories 356 • Protein 17g • Total Fat 8g • Sat. Fat 1g • Cholesterol 0mg • Carbohydrate 59g • Dietary Fiber 14g • Sodium 732mg

African Beans and Potatoes

MAKES 4 SERVINGS

Serve this delicious dish with lots of crusty bread and a tossed green salad for a warm and comforting meal. Sweet potatoes can replace half or all of the white variety, if desired.

2 tablespoons peanut oil

1 large red onion (about 8 ounces), thinly sliced

2 stalks celery, chopped

2 large cloves garlic, finely chopped

2 cups low-sodium vegetable broth

1 pound round red or white potatoes, peeled and coarsely chopped

½ teaspoon salt

1 (15-ounce) can chickpeas, rinsed and drained

1 cup rinsed, drained canned pinto beans

2 tablespoons tomato paste

½ teaspoon crushed red pepper flakes, or to taste

¼ cup chopped peanuts or pumpkin seeds (optional)

Hot pepper sauce (optional)

In a medium deep-sided skillet with a lid, heat the oil over medium heat. Add the onion and cook, stirring often, until lightly browned, 7 to 10 minutes, adding the celery and garlic the last few minutes of cooking. Add the broth, potatoes, and salt; bring to a boil over high heat. Reduce the heat to medium and simmer briskly, partially covered, until the potatoes are tender, about 10 minutes. Stir in the chickpeas, pinto beans, tomato paste, and red pepper flakes; simmer, uncovered, stirring often from the bottom to prevent sticking, until the mixture is thickened, about 8 minutes. Serve warm, garnished with the peanuts (if using), and passing the hot pepper sauce (if using).

PER SERVING: Calories 346 • Protein 18g • Total Fat 9g • Sat. Fat 1g • Cholesterol 0mg • Carbohydrate 52g • Dietary Fiber 11g • Sodium 620mg

Costa Rican Beans and Rice

MAKES 4 SERVINGS

Gallo pinto is a beloved dish in Costa Rica and for good reason; it's simply delicious.

- ½ pound dried black beans, soaked overnight in water to cover
- ½ teaspoon salt, plus additional, to taste
- 2 tablespoons extra-virgin olive oil
- 1 cup long-grain white rice
- 1 small onion (about 4 ounces), finely chopped
- ½ cup finely chopped red or green bell pepper
- ¼ cup finely chopped fresh cilantro, plus additional, for garnish
- 2 large cloves garlic, finely chopped
- 1½ cups low-sodium vegetable broth or water
- ¼ teaspoon crushed red pepper flakes, or to taste (optional)
- Freshly ground black pepper, to taste

Drain the beans and place in a medium stockpot with enough water to cover by 1 inch. Add the ½ teaspoon salt and bring to a boil over high heat. Reduce the heat to between low and medium-low, cover, and simmer, stirring occasionally, until the beans are very soft, about 2 hours. Set aside, undrained.

In a medium deep-sided skillet with a lid, heat 1 tablespoon of the oil over medium heat. Add the rice and cook, stirring constantly, 2 minutes. Add half of the onion, and half of the bell pepper; cook, stirring constantly, 1 minute. Add half of the cilantro and all the garlic; cook, stirring constantly, 1 minute. Add the broth, red pepper flakes (if using), salt, and black pepper; bring to a boil over high heat. Reduce the heat to low, cover, and simmer until the rice has absorbed the liquid, 18 to 20 minutes.

Add the cooked black beans and their liquid, remaining oil, onion, bell pepper, and cilantro to the skillet; bring to a brisk simmer over medium-high heat. Reduce the heat to low and simmer, stirring occasionally, until slightly thickened, 3 to 5 minutes. Serve warm, garnished with additional chopped cilantro.

PER SERVING: Calories 456 • Protein 20g • Total Fat 8g • Sat. Fat 1g • Cholesterol 0mg • Carbohydrate 76g • Dietary Fiber 11g • Sodium 467mg

Black Bean and Avocado Enchiladas with Chipotle Sauce

MAKES 6 SERVINGS

These tasty enchiladas can also be made with pinto or kidney beans. For a spicier enchilada, use the greater amount of chipotle sauce, available in Latin markets and the international aisle of many well-stocked supermarkets.

1¾ cups crushed canned tomatoes

4 to 6 tablespoons chipotle sauce

2 tablespoons fresh lime juice

1 tablespoon sugar

1 tablespoon canola oil

1 medium onion (about 6 ounces), chopped

2 large cloves garlic, finely chopped

2 (15-ounce) cans black beans, rinsed and drained

2 teaspoons ground cumin

½ teaspoon salt

Freshly ground black pepper, to taste

1 to 2 tablespoons water

6 (8-inch) flour tortillas, preferably whole wheat

1 ripe yet firm avocado, peeled, pitted, and cut into 12 slices

Preheat oven to 375F (190C). Lightly oil a 13 × 9-inch baking dish and set aside.

In a small bowl, mix together the tomatoes, chipotle sauce, ½ tablespoon of the lime juice, and sugar until thoroughly combined. Spread 1 cup along the bottom of the prepared dish. Set aside.

In a medium deep-sided skillet, heat the oil over medium heat. Add the onion and cook, stirring, until softened but not browned, about 3 minutes.

Add the garlic and cook, stirring, 1 minute. Add the beans, remaining lime juice, cumin, salt, and pepper; cook, stirring, 1 minute. Remove from heat and transfer half of the bean mixture and 1 tablespoon water to a food processor fitted with a knife blade, or to a blender; process until smooth and pureed, adding the extra 1 tablespoon water, if necessary, to achieve a smooth consistency. Return to skillet and toss well with remaining bean mixture to thoroughly combine.

To assemble enchiladas, spread one-sixth of the bean mixture (about ½ cup) down the center of each tortilla and top with 2 of the avocado slices. Roll up each tortilla, tucking in both ends; place, seam sides down, in the prepared baking dish. Spread evenly with ½ cup of the remaining chipotle sauce mixture. Cover with foil (lightly oil underside if foil will touch sauce) and bake 45 minutes. Remove from oven and spread evenly with remaining chipotle sauce mixture. Return to oven and bake, uncovered, 5 minutes. Serve warm.

PER SERVING: Calories 342 • Protein 13g • Total Fat 11g • Sat. Fat 2g • Cholesterol 0mg • Carbohydrate 51g • Dietary Fiber 7g • Sodium 503mg

Black Beans with Sofrito over Rice

MAKES 4 SERVINGS

While this classic bean dish is traditionally served over white rice, the brown variety contains more fiber and is equally tasty to boot.

1 tablespoon extra-virgin olive oil

½ cup chopped onion

2 large cloves garlic, finely chopped

½ teaspoon cumin seed

¼ teaspoon coriander seed, lightly crushed

1 (15.5-ounce) can black beans, rinsed and drained

½ cup diced canned tomatoes, juices included

¼ cup Basic Sofrito Sauce (below)

2 tablespoons canned diced mild green chilies, drained

½ teaspoon ground cumin

½ teaspoon salt, or to taste

Freshly ground black pepper, to taste

3 cups hot cooked brown or white rice (see Cook's Tip, page 79)

In a small saucepan, heat the oil over medium heat. Add the onion and cook, stirring, until softened, about 3 minutes. Add the garlic, cumin seed, and coriander; cook, stirring, 1 minute. Add the remaining ingredients, except the rice. Bring to a simmer over medium heat, stirring occasionally. Reduce the heat to low, cover, and cook 10 minutes, stirring occasionally.

To serve, divide the rice evenly among 4 dinner plates. Top with equal portions of the bean mixture and serve at once.

PER SERVING: Calories 334 • Protein 11g • Total Fat 6g • Sat. Fat 1g • Cholesterol 0mg • Carbohydrate 60g • Dietary Fiber 4g • Sodium 370mg

Basic Sofrito Sauce

MAKES ABOUT 1¼ CUPS

Originating in Spain, *sofrito* is a fundamental cooking sauce consisting primarily of onion, bell peppers, and tomatoes. It is essential in the preparation of authentic Caribbean and Latin American rice and bean dishes, soups, and stews. For a less spicy sauce, omit the crushed red pepper flakes.

2 tablespoons extra-virgin olive oil

1 cup chopped onion

½ cup chopped green bell pepper

½ cup chopped red bell pepper

3 large cloves garlic, finely chopped

½ cup chopped fresh tomatoes

¼ cup finely chopped fresh cilantro

¼ cup water

1 tablespoon tomato paste

½ teaspoon dried oregano

¼ teaspoon crushed red pepper flakes, or to taste

¼ teaspoon freshly ground black pepper

¼ teaspoon salt

1 bay leaf

In a small heavy saucepan, heat the oil over medium heat. Add the onion and bell peppers and cook, stirring, until softened, about 3 minutes. Add the garlic and cook, stirring, 1 minute. Add the remaining ingredients and bring to a simmer over medium-high heat. Reduce the heat and simmer gently, uncovered, until the sauce is reduced and thickened, about 10 minutes, stirring occasionally. Remove and discard the bay leaf.

Transfer to a food processor fitted with the knife blade, or to a blender; process until smooth. Use as directed in desired recipe. Completely cooled sauce can be stored, covered, in the refrigerator up to 3 days, or frozen up to 1 month.

PER TABLESPOON: Calories 19 • Protein 0g • Total Fat 1g • Sat. Fat 0g • Cholesterol 0mg • Carbohydrate 2g • Dietary Fiber 0g • Sodium 34mg

Traditional Cuban Black Beans over Rice

MAKES 8 SERVINGS

Not too spicy, not too sweet, these Cuban black beans live up to their time-honored tradition of all-around appeal. Use them as a topping for baked white or sweet potatoes; as a filling for tacos, burritos, and quesadillas; or as a dip for tortilla chips in lieu of refried beans.

¼ cup extra-virgin olive oil

1 large onion (about 8 ounces), chopped

1 medium green bell pepper (about 6 ounces), chopped

4 large cloves garlic, finely chopped

5 cups water

1 pound dried black beans, soaked overnight in cold water to cover, and drained

1 (6-ounce) can tomato paste

2 tablespoons chopped pimientos (optional), drained

1 tablespoon cider vinegar

1 tablespoon sugar

½ tablespoon salt

1 teaspoon ground cumin

½ teaspoon dried oregano

¼ teaspoon freshly ground black pepper

¼ teaspoon crushed red pepper flakes, or to taste

2 bay leaves

6 cups hot cooked white rice (see Cook's Tip, opposite page)

In a medium stockpot, heat the oil over medium heat. Add the onion and bell pepper and cook, stirring, until softened, about 5 minutes. Add the garlic and cook, stirring, 2 minutes. Add the water, beans, tomato paste, pimientos (if using), vinegar, sugar, salt, cumin, oregano, black pepper, red pepper flakes, and bay leaves. Bring to a boil over high heat. Reduce heat to between low and medium-low, cover, and simmer about 1½ to 2 hours, stirring occasionally, or until beans are tender. Discard the bay leaves. Serve warm, over the rice.

PER SERVING: Calories 478 • Protein 18g • Total Fat 8g • Sat. Fat 1g • Cholesterol 0mg • Carbohydrate 85g • Dietary Fiber 11g • Sodium 575mg

Philippine-Style Eggplant in Coconut Cream over Rice

MAKES 4 TO 6 SERVINGS

This saucy eggplant dish is also delicious served over couscous. For a milder dish, use half the amount of *sambal olek.*

1 medium eggplant (about ¾ pound), unpeeled, cut into 1-inch cubes, sprinkled with salt, and set in a colander to drain 30 minutes (salting is optional)

½ tablespoon canola oil

4 scallions, white and green parts separated, thinly sliced

2 large cloves garlic, finely chopped

1 (14-ounce) can light coconut milk

2 tablespoons low-sodium soy sauce or tamari

1 teaspoon *sambal olek* or Chinese chili paste, or to taste

1 teaspoon light brown sugar

½ teaspoon salt

Juice of ½ lime (about 1 tablespoon)

4 to 6 cups hot cooked rice (see Cook's Tip, below)

Preheat oven to 425F (220C). Lightly oil an 8-inch-square baking dish and set aside.

Rinse the drained eggplant under cold-running water. Dry between paper towels. Set aside.

In a small saucepan, heat the oil over medium heat. Add the white parts of the scallions and the garlic and cook, stirring constantly, until fragrant but not browned, about 2 minutes. Stir in the coconut milk, soy sauce, *sambal olek*, sugar, and salt. Bring to a simmer over medium-high heat, stirring occasionally. Remove from the heat and stir in the green parts of the scallions and the lime juice.

Place the eggplant in the prepared baking dish and cover with the warm coconut milk mixture. Cover with foil and bake 40 minutes. Remove the baking dish from the oven and turn the eggplant over in the sauce. Bake, covered, another 15 minutes, until the eggplant is very tender. Uncover and bake another 5 to 10 minutes, until the sauce is slightly reduced and bubbly. Serve warm, over equal portions of the rice.

PER SERVING: Calories 418 • Protein 10g • Total Fat 13g • Sat. Fat 10g • Cholesterol 0mg • Carbohydrate 66g • Dietary Fiber 3g • Sodium 615mg

COOK'S TIP: *One-third cup uncooked regular long-grain white rice, basmati rice, or jasmine rice will yield about 1 cup cooked. One-quarter cup uncooked brown rice will yield about 1 cup cooked. To make 4 cups cooked long-grain white rice, combine 1⅓ cups white rice and 2⅔ cups salted water in a medium saucepan; bring to a boil over high heat. Reduce heat to low, cover, and simmer until all the water has been absorbed, 17 to 20 minutes. Fluff with a fork and serve. To make 4 cups cooked brown rice, combine 1 cup brown rice and 2¼ cups salted water in a medium saucepan. Cook as directed for white rice, increasing cooking time to 35 to 40 minutes.*

Island Bean Burgers with Caribbean-Style Creole Sauce

MAKES 4 SERVINGS

For a spicier burger, add a dash of hot pepper sauce or a pinch of cayenne pepper to the bean mixture before cooking.

1 cup rinsed and drained canned black beans

1 cup cooked brown rice, preferably warm

2 tablespoons finely chopped onion

1½ tablespoons tomato ketchup

1 teaspoon chili powder, or more to taste

½ teaspoon dried oregano

¼ teaspoon ground cumin

1 large garlic clove, finely chopped

Salt and freshly ground black pepper, to taste

1 tablespoon peanut oil

4 hamburger buns, preferably whole wheat

Caribbean-Style Creole Sauce, to taste (page 80)

In a large bowl, mix together the beans, rice, onion, ketchup, chili powder, oregano, cumin, garlic, salt, and pepper until well combined. Mash well with a potato masher. Divide mixture into 4 balls. With wet hands, form each ball into an even patty.

In a medium nonstick skillet, heat the oil over medium heat. Add the patties and cook until browned, 4 to 5 minutes per side. Place each patty inside a hamburger bun and serve at once, with the Creole sauce passed separately.

Caribbean-Style Creole Sauce

MAKES ABOUT 1 CUP

This spirited sauce is also fabulous on the Sweet Potato Patties (page 105), and most veggie burgers.

1 tablespoon canola oil

2 tablespoons finely chopped red onion

1 large clove garlic, finely chopped

1 tablespoon finely chopped fresh flat-leaf parsley or cilantro

¼ teaspoon dried thyme

½ cup tomato ketchup

¼ cup water

½ tablespoon cider vinegar

½ tablespoon fresh lime juice, or more to taste

1 teaspoon molasses

⅛ to ¼ teaspoon hot pepper sauce, or more to taste

Salt and freshly ground black pepper, to taste

In a small saucepan, heat the oil over medium heat. Add the onion and garlic and cook, stirring constantly, 2 minutes. Add the parsley and thyme and cook, stirring constantly, 1 minute. Stir in the ketchup, water, vinegar, lime juice, molasses, hot pepper sauce, salt, and pepper. Bring to a boil, stirring occasionally; reduce the heat to low and simmer, uncovered, 3 minutes, stirring occasionally. Remove from heat and let cool to room temperature. Mixture can be stored, covered, in the refrigerator up to 5 days.

Bengali-Style Black-Eyed Peas with Mushrooms over Basmati Rice

MAKES 4 SERVINGS

You can use about 2 cups rinsed and drained canned black-eyed peas in lieu of the frozen variety, if desired.

3 tablespoons canola oil

1 tablespoon whole cumin seed

1 cinnamon stick

1 medium yellow onion (about 6 ounces), finely chopped

8 ounces thinly sliced fresh white mushrooms

4 large cloves garlic, finely chopped

1 (14-ounce) can diced tomatoes with jalapeño chilies, juices included

2 teaspoons ground turmeric

1 teaspoon ground cumin

1 teaspoon whole coriander seed, crushed

1 teaspoon salt

¼ teaspoon cayenne pepper, or to taste (optional)

Freshly ground black pepper, to taste

1 (16-ounce) package frozen black-eyed peas, cooked according to package directions, drained

¼ cup chopped fresh cilantro

3 to 4 cups hot cooked basmati rice (see Cook's Tip, page 79)

In a large deep-sided nonstick skillet with a lid, heat the oil over medium-high heat. Add the cumin seed and cinnamon stick and cook, stirring constantly, about 10 seconds. Add the onion and cook, stirring, until the onion is beginning to brown, 4 to 5 minutes. Add the mushrooms and garlic and cook, stirring, until mushrooms are just softened, 2 to 3 minutes. Add the tomatoes and their juices, turmeric, ground cumin, coriander, salt, cayenne (if using), and black pepper; bring to a brisk simmer, stirring often. Cover, reduce heat to low, and cook about 10 minutes. Add the peas and cilantro and cook, uncovered, over medium heat, stirring occasionally, until the peas are heated through and the mixture is slightly thickened, about 5 minutes. Serve warm, over the rice.

PER SERVING: Calories 445 • Protein 14g • Total Fat 12g • Sat. Fat 1g • Cholesterol 0mg • Carbohydrate 73g • Dietary Fiber 11g • Sodium 760mg

Puerto Rican Pink Beans and White Rice

MAKES 4 TO 6 SERVINGS

Recaito is a Caribbean cooking sauce consisting of cilantro, green bell pepper, onion, and garlic; it can be found in Caribbean and Latin markets as well as the international aisle of many well-stocked supermarkets.

2 tablespoons extra-virgin olive oil

1 medium onion (about 6 ounces), chopped

1 medium green bell pepper (about 6 ounces), chopped

1 large clove garlic, finely chopped

2 (15-ounce) cans pink beans, rinsed and drained

1 (15-ounce) can tomato sauce

1 medium round red or white potato (about 4 ounces), peeled and cut into small cubes

½ cup low-sodium vegetable broth

2 tablespoons recaito sauce

½ teaspoon adobo seasoning (or a combination of dried oregano, paprika, and ground cumin)

Salt and freshly ground black pepper, to taste

3 to 4½ cups hot cooked rice (see Cook's Tip, page 79)

In a medium deep-sided skillet with a lid, heat the oil over medium heat. Add the onion and bell pepper and cook, stirring, until softened and beginning to brown, 5 to 7 minutes. Add the garlic and cook, stirring, until golden, about 2 minutes. Add the remaining ingredients, except the rice, and bring to a brisk simmer over medium-high heat, stirring often. Reduce the heat to medium-low and simmer, covered, stirring occasionally, until the potato is tender, about 20 minutes. Serve warm, over the rice.

PER SERVING: Calories 503 • Protein 19g • Total Fat 8g • Sat. Fat 1g • Cholesterol 0mg • Carbohydrate 90g • Dietary Fiber 11g • Sodium 745mg

Costa Rican Cabbage-Stuffed Tortillas

MAKES 4 SERVINGS; 8 TORTILLAS

Cabbage, an important crucifer, stars in these tasty Costa Rican–style tortillas. You can make the filling up to a day in advance, although the cabbage will not be quite as crunchy. The filling can also be used for tacos or as a topping for tostadas. For a milder yet less authentic dish, omit the hot pickled peppers.

8 corn tortillas or 8 snack-size (6-inch) flour tortillas

2 cups shredded cabbage

1 cup rinsed and drained canned black beans

1 medium tomato (about 6 ounces), seeded and finely chopped

2 scallions, white and green parts, thinly sliced

3 to 4 tablespoons chopped fresh cilantro

1 tablespoon extra-virgin olive oil

½ tablespoon fresh lemon or lime juice

½ tablespoon cider vinegar

1 teaspoon cumin seed

1 teaspoon sugar

Salt and freshly ground black pepper, to taste

Cayenne pepper, to taste (optional)

1 ripe avocado, peeled, pitted, and thinly sliced

Sliced hot pickled banana peppers or pickled jalapeño chilies, to taste

Preheat oven to 200F (95C).

Arrange the tortillas on a large ungreased baking sheet (some overlap is okay). Heat in the oven until softened and warmed, about 10 minutes.

Meanwhile, in a medium bowl, toss together the cabbage, beans, tomato, scallions, cilantro, oil, lemon juice, vinegar, cumin, sugar, salt, black pepper, and cayenne (if using) until well combined.

Let stand at room temperature about 10 minutes to allow the flavors to blend; toss again.

To serve, top the warm tortillas with equal amounts (about ½ cup) of the cabbage mixture. Top with equal amounts of the avocado and pickled hot peppers. Roll up and serve at once.

PER TORTILLA: Calories 153 • Protein 4g • Total Fat 7g • Sat. Fat 1g • Cholesterol 0mg • Carbohydrate 22g • Dietary Fiber 4g • Sodium 49mg

Aussie-Style Fettuccine with Basil-Macadamia Pesto

MAKES 3 TO 4 MAIN-COURSE OR 6 PASTA-COURSE SERVINGS

From Australia, this delicious pasta dish showcases the versatility of its famous native nut, the macadamia, which contains a high percentage of heart-healthy monounsaturated fats. For a smoother sauce, use the optional coconut milk.

2 cups loosely packed fresh basil leaves

¼ cup oil-packed sun-dried tomatoes, drained

3 tablespoons low-sodium vegetable broth

¼ cup chopped macadamia nuts

2 tablespoons macadamia nut oil or extra-virgin olive oil

2 to 3 large cloves garlic, finely chopped

¼ teaspoon coarse salt

Freshly ground black pepper, to taste

8 ounces egg-free fettuccine or linguine, cooked according to package directions until al dente, and drained

¼ cup light coconut milk (optional)

Place the basil, tomatoes, broth, half of the nuts, the oil, garlic, salt, and pepper in a food processor fitted with the knife blade; process until smooth and well combined. Transfer to a large bowl and combine with the pasta and coconut milk (if using), tossing to thoroughly coat. Serve at once, sprinkled with the remaining nuts.

PER SERVING: Calories 491 • Protein 14g • Total Fat 20g • Sat. Fat 3g • Cholesterol 0mg • Carbohydrate 65g • Dietary Fiber 3g • Sodium 224mg

Spicy Bolivian-Style Lentils over Rice

MAKES 4 TO 6 SERVINGS

These lentils are also delicious spooned over polenta, used as a filling for tacos or burritos, or served on their own as a side dish.

1 cup dried lentils, rinsed and picked over

4 large cloves garlic, 3 finely chopped, 1 crushed

1 bay leaf

1 teaspoon salt, plus additional, to taste

2 tablespoons extra-virgin olive oil

1 large onion (about 8 ounces), finely chopped

2 medium tomatoes (about 6 ounces each), chopped

½ cup finely chopped fresh flat-leaf parsley

½ cup low-sodium vegetable broth

1 teaspoon chipotle puree (see Cook's Tip, page 112), or more to taste

Freshly ground black pepper, to taste

3 to 4½ cups hot cooked rice (see Cook's Tip, page 79)

In a medium saucepan, bring the lentils, the crushed garlic, bay leaf, 1 teaspoon salt, and enough water to cover by 1 inch to a boil over high heat. Reduce the heat to medium and simmer, uncovered, until the lentils are just tender, 20 to 25 minutes, stirring occasionally. Place a lid over the saucepan and briefly drain the lentils. Remove and discard the garlic and bay leaf. Set aside.

Meanwhile, in a medium deep-sided nonstick skillet, heat the oil over medium heat. Add the onion and cook, stirring, until softened and translucent, 5 to 7 minutes. Add the chopped garlic and cook, stirring constantly, until lightly golden, about 2 minutes. Add the tomatoes, parsley, broth, chipotle puree, salt, and pepper; bring to a simmer over medium-high heat. Reduce the heat to medium-low and simmer, uncovered, until reduced and thickened, about 15 minutes, stirring occasionally. Stir in the lentils and cook, covered, until the lentils are heated through, about 5 minutes. Serve warm, over the rice.

PER SERVING: Calories 455 • Protein 20g • Total Fat 8g • Sat. Fat 1g • Cholesterol 0mg • Carbohydrate 77g • Dietary Fiber 18g • Sodium 619mg

Thai Lettuce Wraps

MAKES 4 SERVINGS

These tasty grain-free wraps make a quick and easy weeknight supper if you use ready-shredded cabbage and carrots. Serve the filling in a shallow bowl surrounded by whole iceberg lettuce leaves (the very large outer leaves can be torn in half), and invite everyone to wrap his own. Deep-fried tofu or bean curd, often called *age*, is available in Asian markets and specialty stores. Small cubes of extra-firm tofu can be substituted, if desired.

1½ tablespoons peanut oil

2 shallots, thinly sliced

1 to 2 fresh red or green chilies, seeded and finely chopped

1 tablespoon chopped peeled fresh ginger

3 large cloves garlic, finely chopped

½ cup shredded carrot

½ cup shredded cabbage

3 scallions, white and green parts, thinly sliced

4 fresh shiitake or white mushrooms, thinly sliced

½ (2.9-ounce) package deep-fried tofu or bean curd (about 5 squares), cut into thin strips

3 tablespoons low-sodium tamari or soy sauce

2 tablespoons fresh lime juice

1 tablespoon toasted (dark) sesame oil

1 teaspoon Chinese chili paste, or to taste (optional)

2 cups bean sprouts

1 cup lightly packed fresh basil and/or cilantro, chopped

½ cup salted peanuts, coarsely chopped

About 16 large iceberg lettuce leaves (1 large head), rinsed and drained well

In a wok or large nonstick skillet, heat the peanut oil over medium-high heat. Add the shallots, chilies, ginger, and garlic; cook, stirring constantly, until fragrant, 1 minute. Add the carrot, cabbage, scallions, mushrooms, and tofu; cook, stirring constantly, 2 minutes. Add the tamari, lime juice, sesame oil, and chili paste (if using); cook, stirring constantly, 1 minute. Add the sprouts and toss to thoroughly combine. Remove from heat and add the basil and peanuts, tossing well to combine.

To assemble wraps, place about ¼ cup of the filling in the center of a lettuce leaf. Wrap up and serve at once.

PER SERVING: Calories 295 • Protein 13g • Total Fat 20g • Sat. Fat 3g • Cholesterol 0mg • Carbohydrate 22g • Dietary Fiber 7g • Sodium 488mg

Hot Mango Pilaf with Almonds

MAKES 4 TO 5 MAIN-COURSE OR 6 TO 8 SIDE-DISH SERVINGS

Fresh papaya and/or pineapple can replace all or part of the mango, if desired. For a milder yet equally delicious dish, omit the red pepper flakes and use only one fresh chili, such as a jalapeño, which is moderately hot.

2 tablespoons canola oil

½ cup chopped onion

½ tablespoon cumin seed

1½ cups long-grain white rice

½ teaspoon ground turmeric

¼ teaspoon crushed red pepper flakes

2¼ cups low-sodium vegetable broth, heated until hot

1 teaspoon salt

Freshly ground black pepper, to taste

2 medium mangoes, (about 12 ounces each), peeled, pitted, and chopped

¼ cup slivered almonds, toasted if desired (see Cook's Tip, page 130)

1 to 2 fresh green or red chilies, seeded and chopped

In a medium deep-sided skillet with a lid, heat the oil over medium heat. Add the onion and cook, stirring, 2 minutes. Add the cumin and cook, stirring, until the cumin is fragrant and the onion is softened but not browned, about 2 minutes. Add the rice, turmeric, and red pepper flakes; cook, stirring constantly, until the cumin is nicely toasted and the rice is beginning to brown, about 2 minutes. Carefully add the hot broth, salt, and black pepper, stirring well to combine; bring to a brisk simmer over medium-high heat. Reduce the heat to low, cover, and simmer until all the liquid has been absorbed, 16 to 18 minutes. Remove from the heat and let stand, covered, 5 minutes.

Uncover the skillet and fluff the rice with a fork. Add the mangoes, nuts, and chilies, tossing well with the fork to combine. Serve at once.

PER SERVING: Calories 467 • Protein 14g • Total Fat 12g • Sat. Fat 1g • Cholesterol 0mg • Carbohydrate 79g • Dietary Fiber 6g • Sodium 833mg

Vietnamese-Style Cellophane Noodles with Mixed Vegetables

MAKES 4 SERVINGS

In a nod to the French influence upon Vietnamese cuisine, shallots often replace standard yellow onions and vegetables are frequently julienned.

1 (7.75-ounce) package cellophane (mung bean) noodles

2 tablespoons peanut oil

4 shallots, thinly sliced

4 scallions, white and green parts separated, thinly sliced

4 large cloves garlic, finely chopped

1 tablespoon finely chopped fresh ginger

2 small carrots (about 2 ounces each), peeled and julienned

6 tablespoons low-sodium soy sauce or tamari, plus additional, to taste

¼ cup low-sodium vegetable broth

1 tablespoon toasted (dark) sesame oil

1 teaspoon light brown sugar, or more to taste

¼ teaspoon crushed red pepper flakes, or to taste (optional)

Salt and freshly ground black pepper, to taste

1 cup sliced fresh white mushrooms

2 small zucchini (about 4 ounces each), preferably 1 green and 1 yellow, julienned

¼ cup chopped peanuts or almonds (optional)

Soak the noodles in hot water according to package directions until translucent, about 15 minutes. Drain in a colander and rinse under cold-running water to cool; drain well. Cut into 6-inch bunches and set aside.

In a wok or large nonstick skillet, heat the oil over medium-high heat. Add the shallots, white parts of the scallions, garlic, and ginger; cook, stirring, 1 minute. Add the carrots, soy sauce, broth, sesame oil, sugar, red pepper flakes (if using), salt, and black pepper; cook, stirring, 1 minute. Add the mushrooms and cook, stirring, 1 minute. Add the zucchini and cook, stirring, 2 minutes. Add the noodles and cook, tossing and stirring constantly, until heated through, 1 to 2 minutes. Remove from heat and add the green parts of the scallions, tossing well to combine. Season with additional soy sauce, as needed. Let stand about 10 minutes to allow the noodles to absorb the flavors. Toss again and serve warm or at room temperature, garnished with the nuts (if using).

Fusion-Style Dragon Noodles with Asparagus

MAKES 5 TO 6 SERVINGS

This exotic fuchsia-hued pasta dish is an excellent choice for a buffet, as it can be served chilled or at room temperature. Dried dragon fruit from Thailand is available at Trader Joe's; unsweetened dried mango can be substituted, if necessary, but the linguine, of course, will not turn pink. Tiny thin green beans, or haricots vert, can replace the pencil-thin asparagus, if desired. If you don't have garlic-flavored olive oil, use a plain extra-virgin variety and garlic salt in lieu of the coarse variety.

12 ounces dry linguine (do not use fresh), broken in half

6 ounces pencil-thin asparagus, tough ends trimmed and discarded, tips trimmed from stalks, and stalks cut diagonally into 2-inch lengths

⅓ cup packed dried unsweetened dragon fruit, cut into thin strips with kitchen shears

1 bunch scallions (6 to 8), white and green parts, thinly sliced

4 tablespoons finely chopped cashews or peanuts

3 tablespoons low-sodium sauce soy or tamari

2 tablespoons garlic-flavored olive oil

2 tablespoons toasted (dark) sesame oil

2 tablespoons balsamic or red wine vinegar

1 tablespoon finely chopped pickled ginger

1 tablespoon sugar

1 to 2 teaspoons Chinese chili paste, or to taste

½ teaspoon salt, preferably the coarse variety, or to taste

Freshly ground black pepper, to taste

In a large stockpot filled with boiling salted water, cook the pasta according to package directions until just al dente, adding the asparagus and dried dragon fruit the last 2 to 3 minutes of cooking. Drain well. Return to the pot and add the remaining ingredients, tossing gently yet thoroughly to combine. Serve warm or at room temperature. Alternatively, cover and refrigerate up to 1 day and serve chilled or return to room temperature.

PER SERVING: Calories 456 • Protein 12g • Total Fat 15g • Sat. Fat 2g • Cholesterol 0mg • Carbohydrate 70g • Dietary Fiber 5g • Sodium 587mg

Malaysian Hot-and-Sour Noodles with Tofu and Baby Bok Choy

MAKES 4 TO 6 SERVINGS

Baby bok choy is available in Asian markets, specialty stores, and some well-stocked supermarkets. Because they are more tender and milder than their older counterparts, the entire plant can be used. While mature bok choy can be substituted in the recipe, do not use the stems, which require a longer cooking time.

12 ounces extra-firm tofu, well drained

4 tablespoons low-sodium soy sauce

3 tablespoons toasted (dark) sesame oil

1 tablespoon plain rice vinegar

1 pound baby bok choy, root ends trimmed about ¼ inch, coarsely chopped

1 bunch scallions, white and green parts separated, thinly sliced

3 tablespoons chopped peeled fresh ginger

2 tablespoons fresh lemon juice

1 tablespoon *sambal olek* or Chinese chili paste, or to taste

½ teaspoon turmeric

Salt and freshly ground black pepper, to taste

8 ounces egg-free Chinese noodles or other thin Asian pasta, cooked according to package directions until just al dente, rinsed under cold-running water, drained well

2 cups bean sprouts

Place the tofu on a deep-sided plate or shallow bowl. Top with a second plate and weight with a heavy can. Let stand for a minimum of 15 minutes (preferably 1 hour). Drain excess water. Cut into 1-inch cubes.

In a medium bowl, combine the tofu, soy sauce, 1 tablespoon of the oil, and the rice vinegar. Marinate 30 minutes at room temperature, or cover and refrigerate 1 hour or overnight.

In a wok or large nonstick skillet, heat 1 tablespoon of the remaining oil over medium-high heat. Using a slotted spoon, remove the tofu from the marinade, reserving marinade, and add the tofu to the wok; cook, stirring often, until crispy, 5 to 7 minutes.

Using a slotted spoon, transfer the tofu to a holding plate and add the remaining oil, bok choy, white parts of the scallions, and ginger; cook, stirring often, until the bok choy is crisp-tender, about 3 minutes. Add the scallion greens, reserved marinade, lemon juice, *sambal olek*, turmeric, salt, and pepper; cook, stirring, 30 seconds. Gradually add the noodles, tossing well after each addition. Add the tofu, tossing well to combine. Continue to cook, tossing

often, until mixture is heated through, about 2 minutes. Remove from heat and add the bean sprouts, tossing well to combine. Serve at once.

PER SERVING: Calories 404 • Protein 20g • Total Fat 15g • Sat. Fat 2g • Cholesterol 0mg • Carbohydrate 55g • Dietary Fiber 4g • Sodium 1,143mg

Thai-Style Fried Rice with Chili and Lime

MAKES 2 TO 3 MAIN-COURSE OR 4 SIDE-DISH SERVINGS

This fried rice recipe is a great way to use up a pint of leftover Chinese takeout rice. Omit the chili pepper for a milder yet equally delicious dish, if desired.

1½ tablespoons peanut oil

½ cup chopped onion

½ cup diced firm tofu

2 kaffir lime leaves, chopped, or about 1 to 1½ teaspoons chopped fresh lime peel

½ teaspoon finely chopped peeled fresh ginger

2 large cloves garlic, finely chopped

½ to 1 teaspoon finely chopped fresh red or green chili, or to taste

2 cups cooked white rice, cooled

2 scallions, white and green parts, thinly sliced

2 tablespoons low-sodium soy sauce or tamari

2 tablespoons light coconut milk

1 slice lime, cut into 8 pieces

Salt and freshly ground black pepper, to taste

In a medium deep-sided nonstick skillet, heat the oil over medium-high heat. Add the onion, tofu, lime leaves, ginger, garlic, and chili; cook, stirring constantly, 2 to 3 minutes. Add the rice and scallions; cook, stirring constantly, until the rice and tofu are beginning to brown, about 5 minutes. Stir in the soy sauce and coconut milk. Remove from heat and stir in the lime pieces. Season with salt and pepper and serve at once.

PER SERVING: Calories 426 • Protein 12g • Total Fat 16g • Sat. Fat 4g • Cholesterol 0mg • Carbohydrate 60g • Dietary Fiber 2g • Sodium 615mg

Bangkok-Style Rice Noodles

MAKES 4 TO 6 SERVINGS

Yellow bean sauce or paste is made from fermented soybeans, and is available in Asian markets and specialty stores. Black bean sauce or miso can be substituted, if necessary.

12 ounces thin (vermicelli-style) rice noodles, soaked according to package directions until almost al dente (see Cook's Tip, page 44)

1½ to 2 tablespoons yellow bean sauce or paste

1½ to 2 tablespoons fresh lime juice

1 tablespoon plain rice vinegar

1 to 2 tablespoons low-sodium soy sauce or tamari, or more to taste

1 to 1½ tablespoons light brown sugar

½ tablespoon toasted (dark) sesame oil

1 to 2 teaspoons Chinese chili paste

1½ tablespoons peanut oil

½ (15-ounce) package extra-firm tofu, cut into ½-inch cubes and drained well

2 shallots, thinly sliced

1 to 2 fresh red or green chilies, sliced in half lengthwise, seeded, and thinly sliced crosswise

2-inch piece peeled fresh ginger, thinly sliced

2 kaffir lime leaves, cut into thin strips with kitchen shears, or about 1 to 1½ teaspoons chopped fresh lime peel

1 stalk fresh lemongrass, tough outer leaves removed and stalk finely chopped, or 1 teaspoon grated fresh lemon peel

4 large cloves garlic, finely chopped

2 cups fresh broccoli florets

1 cup bean sprouts

1 cup cherry tomatoes, halved or quartered, depending on size

½ cup chopped fresh cilantro

½ cup chopped fresh basil

Drain the soaked noodles well and rinse under cold-running water 30 seconds. Set aside. In a small bowl, mix together the bean sauce, lime juice, vinegar, soy sauce, sugar, sesame oil, and chili paste until thoroughly blended. Set aside.

In a wok or large nonstick skillet, heat the peanut oil over medium-high heat. Add the tofu, shallots, chilies, ginger, lime leaves, lemongrass, and garlic; cook, stirring constantly, until fragrant, about 1 minute. Add the broccoli and cook, stirring constantly, until the broccoli turns bright green, about 1 minute. Stir in the reserved bean sauce mixture. Fold in the rice noodles and sprouts, tossing and turning until heated through and fully incorporated with the vegetables and sauce, about 2 minutes. Remove from heat and add the tomatoes, cilantro, and basil, tossing well to combine. Adjust the seasonings and serve at once.

PER SERVING: Calories 474 • Protein 8g • Total Fat 10g • Sat. Fat 2g • Cholesterol 0mg • Carbohydrate 90g • Dietary Fiber 4g • Sodium 253mg

Spicy Taiwanese-Style Black Sesame Noodles

MAKES 4 TO 5 SERVINGS

The heat of this fiery, tangy dish can be adjusted according to taste. Unlike the fresh variety, most packaged dry Chinese noodles are egg-free, but check the label carefully. Black sesame seeds, available in Asian markets and specialty stores, have a slightly stronger, earthier flavor than the regular variety, which can be substituted, if necessary.

2½ tablespoons low-sodium soy sauce or tamari
2½ tablespoons plain rice vinegar
2½ tablespoons sugar
2 tablespoons peanut oil
2 tablespoons toasted (dark) sesame oil
Juice of ½ lemon (about 1½ tablespoons)
1 tablespoon Chinese chili paste, or to taste
1 tablespoon chopped pickled ginger
1 teaspoon finely grated fresh lemon peel
½ teaspoon salt
4 scallions, white and green parts, thinly sliced
10 ounces curly egg-free Chinese noodles, cooked
    according to package directions until just al
    dente, rinsed under cold-running water, and
    drained well
2 tablespoons black sesame seeds, toasted (see
    Cook's Tip, page 153), plus additional, for
    garnish
Grated red radish, for garnish (optional)

In a large bowl, whisk together the soy sauce, vinegar, sugar, peanut oil, sesame oil, lemon juice, chili paste, ginger, lemon peel, and salt until thoroughly blended. Stir in the scallions and let stand about 5 minutes at room temperature. Stir again

and add the noodles and sesame seeds, tossing well to thoroughly combine. Serve at room temperature, garnished with additional sesame seeds and radish (if using). Alternatively, cover and refrigerate a minimum of 2 hours or up to 1 day and serve chilled or return to room temperature.

PER SERVING: Calories 431 • Protein 12g • Total Fat 16g • Sat. Fat 3g • Cholesterol 0mg • Carbohydrate 66g • Dietary Fiber 1g • Sodium 1,208mg

Thai Pumpkin Curry

MAKES 6 SERVINGS

This tropical curry is a breeze to prepare if you purchase ready-cubed butternut squash, available in the produce section of many major supermarkets.

Thai Red Curry Sauce (page 90)
1¼ pounds cubed, seeded, and peeled cooking
    pumpkin or butternut squash
1 medium sweet potato (about 6 ounces), peeled
    and cut into ¾-inch cubes
4 ounces baby carrots, cut lengthwise in half if thick
1 medium red bell pepper (about 6 ounces), cut into
    ½-inch cubes
1 (15-ounce) can chickpeas, rinsed and drained
1 tablespoon chopped fresh orange peel
4½ cups hot cooked jasmine rice (see Cook's Tip,
    page 79)
Fresh basil leaves, for garnish (optional)

In a large deep-sided skillet with a lid, bring the curry sauce, squash, potato, and carrots to a boil over medium-high heat, stirring occasionally.

Reduce the heat to medium, cover, and simmer until the vegetables have softened, about 10 minutes, stirring occasionally. Add the bell pepper, chickpeas, and orange peel; cook, covered, stirring occasionally, until all the vegetables are tender, about 5 minutes. Uncover and cook, stirring occasionally, until the mixture is slightly reduced, about 3 minutes. Serve warm, over the rice, garnished with the basil (if using).

PER SERVING: Calories 435 • Protein 12g • Total Fat 10g • Sat. Fat 7g • Cholesterol 0mg • Carbohydrate 77g • Dietary Fiber 6g • Sodium 450mg

Thai Red Curry Sauce

MAKES ABOUT 2 CUPS

Use this spicy Thai curry sauce to enliven countless vegetables and rice dishes.

1 (14-ounce) can light coconut milk

2 shallots, chopped

4 large cloves garlic, chopped

Juice of 1 medium orange

2 tablespoons low-sodium soy sauce or tamari

Juice of ½ lime

1 tablespoon plain rice vinegar

1 tablespoon ground cumin

2 teaspoons light brown sugar

1 teaspoon Thai red curry paste, or to taste

1 teaspoon coriander seed, crushed

1 teaspoon tamarind paste

½ teaspoon ground turmeric

½ teaspoon fennel seed, crushed

½ teaspoon salt

In a food processor fitted with the knife blade, or in a blender, process all ingredients until well blended. Use as directed in recipe. Mixture can be stored, covered, in refrigerator up to 3 days.

PER ¼ CUP: Calories 88 • Protein 2g • Total Fat 6g • Sat. Fat 5g • Cholesterol 0mg • Carbohydrate 8g • Dietary Fiber 0g • Sodium 324mg

Pad Thai Vegetarian Noodles

MAKES 4 TO 6 SERVINGS

This tasty vegetarian variation of Thailand's national rice noodle dish relies on deep-fried tofu or bean curd, often called *age*, and tamarind paste, also known as Thai fruit paste, for its distinctive flavor. Both products are available in Asian and international markets.

12 ounces dried flat (stir-fry or linguine-style) rice noodles, soaked according to package directions until almost al dente (see Cook's Tip, page 44)

½ tablespoon tamarind paste mixed with ½ cup water

¼ cup low-sodium soy sauce or tamari, plus additional, as necessary

3 tablespoons tomato ketchup

2 tablespoons fresh lime juice

1 tablespoon sugar

½ tablespoon dark (toasted) sesame oil

2 tablespoons peanut oil

3 shallots, thinly sliced

¼ to ½ teaspoon crushed red pepper flakes

½ (2.9-ounce) package deep-fried tofu or bean curd (about 5 squares), cut into small pieces

1 cup snow peas, trimmed

1 cup bean sprouts

1 cup fresh cilantro, chopped

3 scallions, white and green parts, thinly sliced

¼ cup finely chopped peanuts

Salt and freshly ground black pepper, to taste

Drain the soaked noodles well and rinse under cold-running water 30 seconds. Set aside.

In a small bowl, whisk together the tamarind paste mixture, soy sauce, ketchup, lime juice, sugar, and sesame oil. Set aside.

In a wok or large nonstick skillet, heat the peanut oil over medium-high heat. Add the shallots and red pepper flakes and cook, stirring, 1 minute. Add the tofu and cook, stirring, 1 minute. Add the snow peas and cook, stirring, until crisp-tender and bright green, 1 to 2 minutes. Reduce the heat to medium-low and add the tamarind sauce mixture and noodles, lifting and turning the noodles to combine all the ingredients, 2 to 3 minutes.

Remove the wok from the heat and add the remaining ingredients, tossing well to combine. Season with salt and pepper and additional soy sauce, as needed. Serve at once.

PER SERVING: Calories 529 • Protein 8g • Total Fat 15g • Sat. Fat 2g • Cholesterol 0mg • Carbohydrate 93g • Dietary Fiber 4g • Sodium 756mg

Spicy Thai-Style Pasta Twists

MAKES 4 TO 6 SERVINGS

This pasta dish is perfect for a buffet or potluck, as it can be served at room temperature. If you don't have Thai curry paste, substitute with two to three times the amount of Chinese chili paste, or crushed red pepper flakes, to taste.

1½ tablespoons peanut oil

1 medium red bell pepper (about 6 ounces), chopped

1 bunch scallions (6 to 8), white and green parts separated, thinly sliced

1 medium cucumber (about 10 ounces), seeded and chopped

½ tablespoon finely chopped peeled fresh ginger

2 large cloves garlic, finely chopped

¼ teaspoon Thai red curry paste, or more, to taste

3 to 4 tablespoons finely chopped fresh basil

2 to 3 tablespoons finely chopped fresh cilantro

Salt, preferably the coarse variety, and freshly ground black pepper, to taste

2 tablespoons low-sodium tamari or soy sauce

Juice of 1 lime

1 tablespoon toasted (dark) sesame oil

12 ounces rotelle or other twist pasta, cooked according to package directions until al dente, drained well

¼ cup chopped peanuts or whole pumpkin seeds

In a large nonstick skillet, heat the peanut oil over medium-high heat. Add the bell pepper and white parts of the scallions; cook, stirring constantly, 2 minutes. Reduce heat to medium and add the cucumber, green parts of scallions, ginger, garlic, and curry paste; cook, stirring often, 3 minutes.

Remove from heat and immediately stir in the basil, cilantro, salt, and pepper. Add the tamari, lime juice, and sesame oil, stirring well to combine. Add the pasta and peanuts, tossing well to thoroughly combine. Serve warm or at room temperature.

PER SERVING: Calories 484 • Protein 15g • Total Fat 15g • Sat. Fat 2g • Cholesterol 0mg • Carbohydrate 74g • Dietary Fiber 5g • Sodium 325mg

Caribbean-Style Potato-Vegetable Curry

MAKES 4 TO 6 SERVINGS

If you're like me and are partial to potatoes, you'll love this curry; feel free to vary the other vegetables, if desired.

¼ cup canola oil

1 small onion (about 4 ounces), chopped

4 large cloves garlic, finely chopped

2 teaspoons ground turmeric

1 teaspoon ground cumin

½ teaspoon ground allspice

½ teaspoon ground ginger

3 (4-ounce) white boiling potatoes, peeled and diced

1 medium sweet potato (about 6 ounces), peeled and diced

1 cup low-sodium vegetable broth

1 cup chopped fresh broccoli or cauliflower

1 cup rinsed, drained canned chickpeas

½ cup chopped red bell pepper

½ cup chopped green bell pepper

1 teaspoon salt

Freshly ground black pepper, to taste

3 to 4½ cups hot cooked rice (see Cook's Tip, page 79)

In a large nonstick skillet with a lid, heat the oil over medium heat. Add the onion and cook, stirring, until softened, about 3 minutes. Add the garlic, turmeric, cumin, allspice, and ginger; cook, stirring constantly, 1 minute. Add the white potatoes and cook, stirring, 1 minute. Add the sweet potato and cook, stirring, 2 minutes. Add the remaining ingredients, except the rice, and bring to a brisk simmer.

Cover, reduce the heat to medium-low, and cook until all the vegetables are tender, about 15 minutes, stirring occasionally. Serve warm, over the rice.

PER SERVING: Calories 511 • Protein 14g • Total Fat 16g • Sat. Fat 1g • Cholesterol 0mg • Carbohydrate 80g • Dietary Fiber 7g • Sodium 687mg

Jamaican Cook-Up Rice

MAKES 6 MAIN-COURSE OR 8 SIDE-DISH SERVINGS

This is a wonderful way to use up leftover vegetables—feel free to experiment with your favorites. Spinach can replace the kale, but add it when you stir in the beans.

1 tablespoon canola oil

1 medium onion (about 6 ounces), chopped

1 medium green bell pepper (about 6 ounces), chopped

1 to 2 jalapeño chilies, seeded and finely chopped

2 large cloves garlic, finely chopped

2 cups low-sodium vegetable broth

1 cup light coconut milk

1½ cups long-grain white rice

2 cups chopped, peeled sweet potatoes, preferably Garnet or Jewel

2 cups chopped fresh kale

2 tablespoons finely chopped fresh cilantro

2 tablespoons finely chopped fresh parsley

1 teaspoon dried thyme

1 teaspoon whole allspice, crushed

½ teaspoon salt

Freshly ground black pepper, to taste

1 (15-ounce) can red kidney beans or pigeon peas, rinsed and drained

In a large deep-sided nonstick skillet with a lid, heat the oil over medium heat. Add the onion, bell pepper, and chilies; cook, stirring, until softened, about 5 minutes. Add the garlic and cook, stirring, 2 minutes. Add the broth, coconut milk, rice, sweet potatoes, kale, cilantro, parsley, thyme, allspice, salt, and black pepper; bring to a boil over high heat. Reduce the heat to medium-low and cook, covered, 15 minutes. Stir in the beans and cook, covered, until all the liquid has been absorbed, about 5 minutes more. Remove from the heat and let stand, covered, 10 minutes. Fluff with a fork and serve at once.

PER SERVING: Calories 385 • Protein 14g • Total Fat 7g • Sat. Fat 4g • Cholesterol 0mg • Carbohydrate 68g • Dietary Fiber 7g • Sodium 387mg

Jackfruit and Spice Rice with Pistachios and Coconut

MAKES 5 TO 6 MAIN-COURSE OR 8 SIDE-DISH SERVINGS

While fresh jackfruit is difficult to come by in many Western markets (its tremendous size would be reason alone), both frozen and canned jackfruit are frequently available in international markets and specialty food stores everywhere. Fresh mango or papaya, though sweeter in taste, can be substituted, if desired; in this instance, opt for the unsweetened coconut.

2¼ cups low-sodium vegetable broth
¼ teaspoon saffron threads (optional)
2 tablespoons canola oil
3 to 4 whole cloves
1 to 2 cardamom pods
1 cinnamon stick
1½ cups basmati rice
½ teaspoon salt, or to taste
¼ teaspoon ground turmeric (if not using saffron)
Freshly ground black pepper, to taste
4 ounces thawed frozen or well-drained canned jackfruit, chopped
¼ cup chopped pistachios, cashews, or macadamia nuts
¼ cup shredded unsweetened or sweetened coconut
2 tablespoons golden raisins

In a small saucepan, combine the broth and saffron (if using); bring to a simmer over medium-high heat. Remove from heat, cover, and set aside.

In a medium deep-sided skillet with a lid, heat the oil over medium heat. Add the cloves, cardamom, and cinnamon; cook, stirring constantly, 2 minutes. Add the rice and cook, stirring constantly, until the rice is well-coated and fragrant, 1 to 2 minutes. Carefully add the hot broth mixture, salt, turmeric (if using), and pepper; bring to a brisk simmer over medium-high heat. Reduce the heat to low, cover, and simmer until all the liquid has been absorbed, 16 to 18 minutes. Remove from heat and stir in the jackfruit, nuts, coconut, and raisins. Cover and let stand 5 minutes. Toss with a fork and serve at once.

PER SERVING: Calories 365 • Protein 12g • Total Fat 12g • Sat. Fat 2g • Cholesterol 0mg • Carbohydrate 55g • Dietary Fiber 6g • Sodium 495mg

Thai Pineapple Fried Rice

MAKES 4 SERVINGS

Chopped fresh mango can replace the pineapple, if desired.

2 tablespoons peanut oil

3 cups cooked white rice, cooled

2 shallots, thinly sliced

3 large cloves garlic, finely chopped

1 fresh red or green fresh chili, seeded and finely chopped

½ cup frozen green peas, thawed

½ cup shredded carrot

¼ cup chopped cashews

2 tablespoons low-sodium soy sauce or tamari, plus additional, to taste

½ teaspoon mild curry powder

1 cup chopped fresh pineapple

¼ cup raisins or currants

3 scallions, white and green parts, finely sliced

¼ cup chopped fresh cilantro or basil

Salt and freshly ground black pepper, to taste

Mix ½ tablespoon of the oil with the rice, using your fingers to separate chunks; set aside.

In a large nonstick skillet or wok, heat the remaining oil over medium-high heat. Add the shallots, garlic, and chili; cook, stirring constantly, until fragrant, 1 to 2 minutes. Add the peas, carrot, cashews, soy sauce, and curry powder; cook, stirring constantly, 1 minute. Add the rice, pineapple, and raisins; cook, stirring constantly, until the rice begins to crackle and pop, 2 to 3 minutes. Remove from the heat and toss with the scallions and cilantro, adding additional soy sauce, if needed. Season with salt and pepper, and serve at once.

PER SERVING: Calories 382 • Protein 8g • Total Fat 12g • Sat. Fat 2g • Cholesterol 0mg • Carbohydrate 64g • Dietary Fiber 4g • Sodium 337mg

Thai Curried Peanut Butter Rice with Peas

MAKES 3 TO 4 SERVINGS

Chopped broccoli is also delicious here.

¼ cup smooth or chunky peanut butter

¼ cup low-sodium vegetable broth or water

1 tablespoon low-sodium soy sauce or tamari

1 teaspoon light brown sugar

½ to 1 teaspoon Thai red or green curry paste, or to taste

½ teaspoon salt, or to taste

¼ teaspoon ground ginger

3 cups hot cooked rice (see Cook's Tip, page 79)

1 cup frozen green peas, cooked according to package directions

In a medium deep-sided skillet, combine the peanut butter, broth, soy sauce, sugar, curry paste, salt, and ginger. Cook over low heat, stirring, until smooth and well combined, about 3 minutes. Add the rice and peas; cook, stirring, until heated through and well combined, 3 to 5 minutes. Serve warm.

PER SERVING: Calories 422 • Protein 14g • Total Fat 12g • Sat. Fat 2g • Cholesterol 0mg • Carbohydrate 65g • Dietary Fiber 5g • Sodium 784mg

Thai Fried Rice with Mixed Vegetables, Peanuts, and Basil

MAKES 4 SERVINGS

Though less authentic than white rice, cooked brown rice can be substituted for the white, if desired.

¼ cup low-sodium soy sauce or tamari
½ tablespoon toasted (dark) sesame oil
1 teaspoon sugar
2 tablespoons peanut oil
1 small onion (about 4 ounces), chopped
1 cup chopped red bell pepper
1 to 2 fresh red or green chilies, seeded and finely chopped
2 large cloves garlic, finely chopped
1 cup sliced fresh button mushrooms
3 cups cooked white rice, clumps separated with fingers
1 cup cooked tiny French green beans (haricots vert)
½ cup chopped salted peanuts
½ cup chopped fresh basil
Salt and freshly ground black pepper, to taste

In a small container, combine the soy sauce, sesame oil, and sugar; set aside.

In a wok or large nonstick skillet, heat the peanut oil over medium-high heat. Add the onion, bell pepper, chilies, and garlic; cook, stirring constantly, until beginning to brown, about 2 minutes. Add the mushrooms and cook, stirring, until the mushrooms begin to release their liquids, about 2 minutes. Add the cooked rice, green beans, peanuts, and soy sauce mixture; cook, stirring, until heated through, about 2 minutes. Add the basil and stir quickly to combine. Remove from heat

and season with salt and black pepper. Serve at once.

PER SERVING: Calories 410 • Protein 11g • Total Fat 18g • Sat. Fat 3g • Cholesterol 0mg • Carbohydrate 53g • Dietary Fiber 5g • Sodium 611mg

Curried Spinach and Peas in Coconut Milk over Basmati Rice

MAKES 4 SERVINGS

If you don't have shallots, substitute with about ¼ cup chopped red onion.

1 cup light coconut milk
1 tablespoon reduced-sodium soy sauce or tamari
1 teaspoon light brown sugar
¼ teaspoon mild curry powder
¼ teaspoon crushed red pepper flakes, or more to taste
Salt and freshly ground black pepper, to taste
2 large shallots, chopped
1¼ cups frozen green peas
1 (9-ounce) bag fresh spinach leaves
3 to 4 cups hot cooked basmati rice (see Cook's Tip, page 79)

In a large deep-sided skillet, bring the coconut milk, soy sauce, sugar, curry powder, red pepper flakes, salt, and black pepper to a gentle simmer over medium heat, stirring occasionally. Add the shallots and simmer 2 minutes, stirring occasionally. Add the peas and bring to a boil over medium-high heat, stirring occasionally. Reduce the heat to medium-low and add the spinach, tossing and stirring until wilted but not shriveled, about 3 minutes. Serve warm, over the rice.

PER SERVING: Calories 289 • Protein 10g • Total Fat 7g • Sat. Fat 5g • Cholesterol 0mg • Carbohydrate 50g • Dietary Fiber 4g • Sodium 279mg

medium heat, stirring often. Stir in the scallions and remove from the heat. Cover and keep warm.

To serve, make a 4-inch slit in the top of each sweet potato. Hold each potato with a pot holder and press upwards until filling "bursts" up through the slit. Top with equal portions (about ½ cup) of the bean mixture. Serve at once, garnished with the cilantro.

PER SERVING: Calories 350 • Protein 11g • Total Fat 2g • Sat. Fat 0g • Cholesterol 0mg • Carbohydrate 75g • Dietary Fiber 12g • Sodium 366mg

Caribbean-Style Baked Sweet Potatoes with Chili Black Beans

MAKES 4 SERVINGS

A tossed green salad rounds out these yummy baked sweet potatoes for a delicious and nutritious dinner.

4 (8-ounce) sweet potatoes

¾ cup rinsed and drained canned black beans

¾ cup vegetarian refried pinto beans

¾ cup mild or medium salsa or picante sauce

1 teaspoon mild chili powder, or more to taste

½ teaspoon ground cumin

Salt and freshly ground black pepper, to taste

3 scallions, white and green parts, thinly sliced

4 teaspoons chopped fresh cilantro

Preheat oven to 400F (205C). Line a baking sheet with foil.

Pierce each sweet potato several times with the tines of a fork and place on prepared baking sheet. Bake until tender, about 45 minutes.

Meanwhile, in a small saucepan, combine the black beans, refried beans, salsa, chili powder, cumin, salt, and pepper. Bring to a simmer over

Sweet Potato and Black Bean Quesadillas

MAKES 3 MAIN-COURSE, 6 SNACK-SIZE, OR 12 APPETIZER SERVINGS

You can make these nutritious quesadillas even healthier by using whole wheat flour tortillas. They make an especially delicious appetizer offered with Kiwifruit Salsa (page 19) and Tomatillo Guacamole (page 29)

1 (8-ounce) sweet potato, peeled and cut into small pieces

½ tablespoon extra-virgin olive oil

1 teaspoon fresh lime juice

¼ teaspoon garlic salt

¼ teaspoon ground cumin

Freshly ground black pepper, to taste

½ tablespoon diced canned mild green chilies, drained

6 (8-inch) flour tortillas

¾ cup rinsed and drained canned black beans

Salsa and/or guacamole, to serve

In a small saucepan, bring the sweet potato and enough salted water to cover to a boil over high heat. Reduce the heat to medium-high and cook until very soft, about 10 minutes. Drain and return to the saucepan. Add the oil, lime juice, garlic salt, cumin, and black pepper; mash well with a potato masher or fork. Stir in the chilies and mix well to thoroughly combine.

Lay out one tortilla. Cover with one-third of the mashed sweet potato (about ¼ cup), then top with ¼ cup of the black beans. Cover with a tortilla. Repeat with remaining ingredients.

Heat a 10-inch nonstick skillet over medium-high heat. Place 1 quesadilla in the skillet and press down lightly with a spatula. Cook until lightly browned on the bottom, 1 to 2 minutes. Turn over and cook until opposite side is lightly browned, another 1 to 2 minutes. Repeat with remaining tortillas and toppings. Cut each quesadilla into wedges and serve at once, with the salsa and/or guacamole passed separately.

PER SERVING: Calories 386 • Protein 11g • Total Fat 8g • Sat. Fat 1g • Cholesterol 0mg • Carbohydrate 68g • Dietary Fiber 6g • Sodium 516mg

1 to 2 teaspoons Thai red curry paste

2 medium sweet potatoes (about 6 ounces each), peeled and cubed

1 (14-ounce) can light coconut milk

1 tablespoon low-sodium sauce soy or tamari

½ teaspoon salt

3 to 4½ cups hot cooked jasmine rice (see Cook's Tip, page 79)

¼ cup chopped peanuts

2 scallions, mostly green parts, thinly sliced

In a medium deep-sided skillet with a lid, heat the oil over medium heat. Add the onion and cook, stirring, until softened, about 3 minutes. Add the garlic and cook, stirring, 1 minute. Add the curry paste and cook, stirring, 30 seconds. Add the sweet potatoes and cook, stirring, 3 minutes. Add the coconut milk, soy sauce, and salt; bring to a simmer over medium-high heat. Reduce the heat to medium-low, cover, and simmer until potatoes are tender, about 15 minutes. Serve warm, over the rice, sprinkled with the peanuts and scallions.

PER SERVING: Calories 506 • Protein 12g • Total Fat 20g • Sat. Fat 11g • Cholesterol 0mg • Carbohydrate 72g • Dietary Fiber 5g • Sodium 510mg

Thai Sweet Potato Curry

MAKES 4 TO 6 SERVINGS

You can also serve this spicy-sweet potato curry over rice noodles, if desired.

1 tablespoon canola oil

1 medium onion (about 6 ounces), finely chopped

1 large clove garlic, finely chopped

Grilled Tofu with Mango Slaw

MAKES 4 SERVINGS

Crispy grilled tofu atop a bed of hot-and-sour mango slaw is a delightful combination of tastes and textures.

1 pound extra-firm tofu, drained

1 tablespoon toasted (dark) sesame oil

½ teaspoon freshly ground black pepper

2 tablespoons reduced-sodium soy sauce or
    tamari

Mango Slaw (below), at room temperature

Place the tofu on a deep-sided plate or shallow bowl. Top with a second plate and weight with a heavy can. Let stand for a minimum of 15 minutes (preferably 1 hour). Drain excess water. Slice lengthwise into quarters.

Brush the tofu slices on all sides with the oil and arrange along the bottom of a shallow dish just large enough to hold them in a single layer. Rub with half of the pepper, and then brush with half of the soy sauce. Turn the slices over and repeat with remaining pepper and soy sauce. Cover with plastic wrap and refrigerate 8 hours, or overnight.

Prepare a medium-hot charcoal grill or gas grill, or preheat a broiler. Position the grill or oven rack 4 to 6 inches from heat source. If broiling, lightly oil a large baking sheet and set aside. Or heat a large nonstick stovetop grilling pan with ridges over medium-high heat.

Grill or broil the tofu slices until browned, 3 to 4 minutes each side. Serve at once, over equal portions of the slaw.

PER SERVING: Calories 240 • Protein 11g • Total Fat 9g • Sat. Fat 1g • Cholesterol 0mg • Carbohydrate 33g • Dietary Fiber 4g • Sodium 762mg

Mango Slaw

MAKES 4 TO 6 SIDE-DISH SERVINGS

This virtually fat-free, hot-and-sour slaw is a refreshing and tasty accompaniment to any variety of dishes. For a sweeter slaw, use half the amount of *sambal olek*.

⅓ cup plain rice vinegar

3 tablespoons low-sodium soy sauce or tamari

3 tablespoons sugar

1 tablespoon *sambal olek* or Chinese chili paste
    (see Cook's Tip, below)

1 teaspoon mirin

2 large semi-ripe mangoes (about 14 ounces each),
    peeled and julienned

¼ cup finely chopped fresh cilantro

In a medium bowl, whisk together the vinegar, soy sauce, sugar, *sambal olek*, and mirin until thoroughly blended. Let stand about 5 minutes to allow the flavors to blend; whisk again. Add the mango and cilantro, tossing well to combine. Let stand 30 minutes at room temperature to allow the flavors to blend. Toss and serve at room temperature. Alternatively, cover and refrigerate a minimum of 2 hours or up to 1 day and serve chilled or return to room temperature.

PER SERVING: Calories 119 • Protein 2g • Total Fat 0g • Sat. Fat 0g • Cholesterol 0mg • Carbohydrate 30g • Dietary Fiber 3g • Sodium 454mg

COOK'S TIP: *Sambal olek is a hot chili paste popular in Indonesian and various Asian cuisines. It is available in Asian markets, specialty stores, and some well-stocked supermarkets. Chinese chili paste can be substituted; however, unlike the Chinese paste, sambal olek contains no garlic.*

Hawaiian-Style Vegetable Stir-Fry with Green Mango

MAKES 5 TO 6 SERVINGS

In Hawaii, green, semi-ripe mangoes add an incomparable depth of flavor to many dishes. Here, they are combined with fresh vegetables for a flavorful stir-fry that is tossed with lo mein. If you'd rather, serve the stir-fry over rice.

2 tablespoons canola oil

8 ounces sliced button mushrooms

1 medium onion (about 6 ounces), chopped

1 medium red bell pepper (about 6 ounces), cut into thin strips

2 large cloves garlic, finely chopped

2 cups fresh broccoli florets

1 large semi-ripe mango (about 14 ounces), peeled, pitted, and cubed

½ cup low-sodium vegetable broth

¼ cup fresh pineapple juice

3 tablespoons low-sodium soy sauce or tamari

1 tablespoon toasted (dark) sesame oil

Salt and freshly ground black pepper, to taste

2 tablespoon creamy peanut butter

12 ounces lo mein noodles, cooked according to package directions and drained

In a wok or large nonstick skillet, heat the oil over medium-high heat. Add the mushrooms, onion, and bell pepper; cook, stirring constantly, until softened, about 2 minutes. Add the garlic and cook, stirring constantly, 2 minutes. Add the broccoli and mango and cook, stirring constantly, until the broccoli is bright green and crisp-tender, about 3 minutes. Add the broth, pineapple juice, soy sauce, sesame oil, and salt and black pepper, and bring to a simmer. Reduce the heat to medium and cook, stirring often, until the sauce is slightly reduced, 4 to 5 minutes. Reduce heat to low and add the peanut butter, stirring until thoroughly incorporated. Add the noodles and toss until well combined. Serve at once.

PER SERVING: Calories 427 • Protein 16g • Total Fat 12g • Sat. Fat 2g • Cholesterol 0mg • Carbohydrate 71g • Dietary Fiber 5g • Sodium 991mg

Coconut Tofu with Spicy Pineapple Chutney over Rice

MAKES 4 TO 6 SERVINGS

You can serve this tasty tofu and spicy sauce without the rice for a delicious appetizer or first course, if desired.

15 ounces extra-firm tofu, drained

1 cup pineapple juice

¼ cup plus 1 tablespoon low-sodium tamari or soy sauce

3 tablespoons crushed canned pineapple

2 tablespoons mango chutney

1 teaspoon plain rice vinegar

½ teaspoon Chinese chili paste, or to taste

1 cup unsweetened shredded coconut

2 tablespoons canola oil

3 to 4½ cups hot cooked rice (see Cook's Tip, page 79)

Place the tofu on a deep-sided plate or shallow bowl. Top with a second plate and weight with a heavy can. Let stand for a minimum of 15 minutes (preferably 1 hour). Drain excess water. Place tofu on cutting board. Starting on the short side of the block, cut the tofu into 12 slices, about ½ inch thick.

In a shallow casserole large enough to hold the tofu in a single layer, combine ¾ cup of the pineapple juice and ¼ cup tamari sauce. Add the tofu and turn gently to coat. Let marinate 30 minutes at room temperature, or cover and refrigerate 1 hour or overnight.

Meanwhile, mix together the remaining pineapple juice and tamari with the crushed pineapple, chutney, vinegar, and chili paste until thoroughly blended. Set aside.

Spread the coconut evenly on a flat dinner plate. Coat the tofu slices on all sides with coconut, patting it on with your fingers as necessary to help it stick.

In a large nonstick skillet, heat 1 tablespoon of the oil over medium heat. Place half the tofu in the skillet and cook until lightly browned, 2 to 3 minutes per side, carefully turning with a spatula. Transfer to a covered baking dish and keep warm. Repeat with remaining tofu, browning in the remaining oil.

To serve, divide the rice evenly among 4 to 6 serving plates. Top each with 2 (or 3) tofu slices. Spoon equal amounts of the pineapple-chutney mixture over the tofu. Serve at once.

PER SERVING: Calories 466 • Protein 14g • Total Fat 19g • Sat. Fat 7g • Cholesterol 0mg • Carbohydrate 61g • Dietary Fiber 4g • Sodium 767mg

Thai-Style Stir-Fry with Crispy Tofu and Hoisin Sauce

MAKES 4 SERVINGS

This is one of my favorite ways to enjoy tofu. Serve over rice noodles, if desired.

12 ounces extra-firm tofu, drained

¼ cup fresh lime juice

3 tablespoons hoisin sauce

1 tablespoon toasted (dark) sesame oil

½ tablespoon low-sodium tamari or soy sauce

1 teaspoon light brown sugar

½ teaspoon crushed red pepper flakes, or to taste

1 tablespoon plus 1 teaspoon peanut oil

1 medium red or yellow bell pepper (about 6 ounces), cut into thin strips

1 medium green bell pepper (about 6 ounces), cut into thin strips

1 medium onion (about 6 ounces), thinly sliced into half-rings

8 ounces cultivated white and/or wild mushrooms, sliced

1 tablespoon chopped peeled fresh ginger

2 large cloves garlic, finely chopped

¼ cup chopped fresh cilantro

3 to 4 cups hot cooked rice (see Cook's Tip, page 79)

¼ cup chopped fresh basil

1 to 2 fresh red or green chilies, seeded and thinly sliced crosswise (optional)

Place the tofu on a deep-sided plate or shallow bowl. Top with a second plate and weight with a heavy can. Let stand for a minimum of 15 minutes (preferably 1 hour). Drain excess water. Cut into 1½-inch cubes.

In a medium bowl, combine the tofu, lime juice, hoisin sauce, sesame oil, tamari, sugar, and red pepper flakes. Marinate 30 minutes at room temperature, or cover and refrigerate 1 hour or overnight.

In a wok or large nonstick skillet, heat 1 tablespoon peanut oil over medium-high heat. Using a slotted spoon, remove the tofu from the marinade, reserving marinade. Add the tofu to the wok; cook, stirring often, until crispy, 5 to 7 minutes. Transfer the tofu to a holding plate and add the remaining peanut oil, bell peppers, and onion to the skillet; cook, stirring often, 2 minutes. Add the mushrooms, ginger, and garlic; cook, stirring often, until the mushrooms release their juices, 4 to 5 minutes. Reduce the heat to low and stir in the reserved tofu, reserved marinade, and cilantro; cook, stirring, until heated through, about 5 minutes. Serve at once, over the rice, garnished with the basil and the fresh chilies (if using).

PER SERVING: Calories 415 • Protein 14g • Total Fat 13g • Sat. Fat 2g • Cholesterol 0mg • Carbohydrate 63g • Dietary Fiber 6g • Sodium 286mg

Hawaiian-Style Pineapple-Teriyaki Baked Tofu with Rice

MAKES 4 SERVINGS

Mirin is a sweet rice wine available in Asian markets, specialty stores, and many well-stocked supermarkets. A medium-dry or sweet sherry can be substituted, if necessary.

1 pound extra-firm tofu, drained

¼ cup low-sodium tamari or soy sauce

2 tablespoons light brown sugar

2 tablespoons orange-pineapple juice

2 tablespoons pineapple preserves

2 teaspoons plain rice vinegar

½ tablespoon toasted (dark) sesame oil

1 teaspoon mirin

1 teaspoon finely chopped peeled fresh ginger

3 to 4 cups hot cooked rice (see Cook's Tip, page 79)

Preheat oven to 350F (175C). Lightly oil an 8-inch-square baking pan and set aside.

Place the tofu on a deep-sided plate or shallow bowl. Top with a second plate and weight with a heavy can. Let stand for a minimum of 15 minutes (preferably up to 1 hour). Drain excess water. Slice lengthwise into quarters.

In a small saucepan, combine the tamari, sugar, juice, preserves, vinegar, oil, mirin, and ginger. Heat over medium heat, stirring often, until the preserves are dissolved. Spoon about one-third of the sauce into the prepared pan. Place the tofu on the sauce and top with remaining sauce.

Bake, uncovered, 30 minutes. Carefully turn the tofu over and bake another 30 minutes, basting occasionally, until the tofu is nicely glazed and the sauce is reduced and syrupy. Serve at once, over the rice.

PER SERVING: Calories 348 • Protein 14g • Total Fat 8g • Sat. Fat 1g • Cholesterol 0mg • Carbohydrate 57g • Dietary Fiber 3g • Sodium 619mg

Thai Red Curry with Tofu, Mango, and Snow Peas

MAKES 4 TO 6 SERVINGS

Fresh sugar snap peas can be substituted for the snow peas, if desired, but increase their initial cooking time to 1 minute. Also, frozen mango cubes, thawed, can be used in lieu of the fresh, if necessary. The dish will still be delicious.

1 (15-ounce) package extra-firm tofu, drained

2 tablespoons canola oil

Salt, to taste

1 medium red onion (about 6 ounces), sliced into thin half-rings

2 large cloves garlic, finely chopped

2 cups snow peas, trimmed

½ cup light coconut milk

1 to 2 teaspoons Thai red curry paste, or to taste

1 teaspoon light brown sugar

1 medium mango (about 12 ounces), peeled, pitted, and cut into bite-size cubes

¼ cup coarsely chopped salted peanuts

¼ cup chopped fresh cilantro

1 to 2 tablespoons fresh lime juice

3 to 4½ cups hot cooked jasmine rice (see Cook's Tip, page 79)

Place the tofu on a deep-sided plate or shallow bowl. Top with a second plate and weight with a heavy can. Let stand for a minimum of 15 minutes (preferably up to 1 hour). Drain excess water. Cut into ½-inch cubes.

In a wok or large nonstick skillet, heat 1½ tablespoons of the oil over medium-high heat. Add the tofu and cook without stirring until golden brown on the bottom, 4 to 5 minutes. Season well with salt and, using a wide spatula, turn the cubes over; cook until golden brown on opposite side, another 4 to 5 minutes. Transfer the tofu to a holding plate. Add the remaining oil, onion, and garlic to the skillet; cook, stirring constantly, 1 minute. Add the snow peas and cook, stirring constantly, 30 seconds. Add the coconut milk, curry paste, and sugar, stirring well to thoroughly incorporate; bring to a brisk simmer. Cook, stirring and tossing occasionally, until the snow peas are crisp-tender, about 2 minutes. Reduce the heat to low and add the tofu, mango, peanuts, cilantro, and lime juice, stirring until heated through. Serve at once, over the rice.

PER SERVING: Calories 491 • Protein 18g • Total Fat 20g • Sat. Fat 4g • Cholesterol 0mg • Carbohydrate 62g • Dietary Fiber 6g • Sodium 66mg

Hawaiian Sweet-and-Sour Vegetables over Rice

MAKES 4 MAIN-COURSE SERVINGS

These yummy vegetables can also be served over couscous, or on their own as a side dish. Feel free to substitute with your own favorite veggie combinations.

1 cup unsweetened pineapple juice

6 tablespoons light brown sugar

2 tablespoons plain rice vinegar

½ tablespoon cornstarch

½ teaspoon ground ginger

1 tablespoon peanut oil

1 cup sliced red onion

1 cup sliced fresh green bell pepper

2 large cloves garlic, finely chopped

2 cups fresh broccoli florets

1 cup sliced fresh carrots

1 cup fresh snow peas, trimmed

½ teaspoon salt, or to taste

Freshly ground black pepper, to taste

1 cup fresh cubed pineapple

3 to 4 cups hot cooked white or brown rice (see Cook's Tip, page 79)

In a small bowl, whisk together the juice, sugar, vinegar, cornstarch, and ginger until thoroughly blended. Set aside.

In a wok or large nonstick skillet, heat the oil over medium-high heat. Add the onion, bell pepper, and garlic; cook, stirring, 1 minute. Add the broccoli and carrots and cook, stirring, 2 minutes. Add the snow peas and cook, stirring, 1 minute. Add the reserved liquid mixture, salt, and black pepper; bring to a brisk simmer, stirring constantly. Add the pineapple cubes and reduce the heat to medium-low. Cook, stirring, until thickened, about 3 minutes. Serve at once, over the rice.

PER SERVING: Calories 409 • Protein 7g • Total Fat 4g • Sat. Fat 1g • Cholesterol 0mg • Carbohydrate 87g • Dietary Fiber 5g • Sodium 303mg

Thai Stir-Fried Mixed Vegetables over Jasmine Rice

MAKES 4 SERVINGS

One of the few Thai-style dishes in the book without hot chilies or curry paste, this fragrant and colorful stir-fry is a delicious way to get children to eat their vegetables.

¼ cup water

2½ tablespoons low-sodium tamari or soy sauce, plus additional, to taste

1½ teaspoons cornstarch

1 tablespoon fresh lime juice

½ tablespoon toasted (dark) sesame oil

½ teaspoon sugar, or more to taste

2 tablespoons peanut oil

6 medium-size cultivated white mushrooms, cut into eighths

4 ounces baby carrots, sliced lengthwise in half

2 tablespoons chopped peeled fresh ginger

4 to 6 large cloves garlic, finely chopped

1 large red bell pepper (about 8 ounces) cut into thin strips

6 scallions, cut into 1-inch lengths

8 ounces fresh broccoli florets, halved if large

8 ounces fresh snow peas, trimmed

Salt and freshly ground black pepper, to taste

2 tablespoons chopped fresh basil

3 to 4 cups hot cooked jasmine rice (see Cook's Tip, page 79)

4 tablespoons chopped unsalted peanuts or cashews (optional)

In a small container with a lid, combine the water, tamari, cornstarch, lime juice, sesame oil, and sugar; cover and shake until well combined. Set aside.

In a wok or large nonstick skillet, heat the oil over medium-high heat. Add the mushrooms, carrots, ginger, and garlic; cook, stirring, 1 minute. Add the bell pepper and scallions and cook, stirring, 1 minute. Add the broccoli and cook, stirring, 2 minutes. Add the snow peas and cook until the snow peas are just tender, stirring, 2 minutes. Stir in the reserved liquid mixture and season with salt and pepper; bring to a brisk simmer. Reduce the heat to medium-low and add the basil; cook, stirring, until sauce is slightly thickened, 2 to 3 minutes. Season with additional tamari, as necessary.

Serve at once, over rice, garnished with the peanuts (if using).

Thai-Style Spicy Mixed Vegetables in Coconut Milk over Rice

MAKES 4 SERVINGS

These tasty Thai-style vegetables are delicious served over rice noodles, as well.

1 cup light coconut milk

3 kaffir lime leaves, shredded, or about ½ tablespoon chopped fresh lime peel

1 shallot, finely chopped

1 tablespoon light brown sugar

1 tablespoon low-sodium soy sauce

½ teaspoon green peppercorns

½ teaspoon crushed red pepper flakes, or to taste

½ teaspoon salt, or to taste

1 cup sliced button mushrooms

1 cup frozen green peas

1 cup shredded cabbage

1 cup (2-inch-long) diagonally cut fresh green beans

½ cup shredded carrot

3 to 4 cups hot cooked jasmine rice (see Cook's Tip, page 79)

In a large saucepan, bring the coconut milk, lime leaves, shallot, sugar, soy sauce, peppercorns, red pepper flakes, and salt to a gentle simmer over medium-high heat. Add the remaining ingredients, except the rice, and return to a gentle simmer. Reduce the heat to medium-low and simmer until the vegetables are tender, stirring occasionally, about 5 minutes. Serve warm, over the rice.

Roasted Vegetables in African Peanut Sauce with Fufu

MAKES 6 SERVINGS

This spicy, creamy peanut sauce is delicious served with sautéed or steamed vegetables, as well. Though it would be less authentic, rice or couscous can replace the fufu.

1 large eggplant (about 1 pound), unpeeled, cut into 1-inch cubes

1 medium zucchini (about 8 ounces), cut into 1-inch cubes

1 medium red bell pepper (about 6 ounces), cut into 1-inch pieces

1 medium green bell pepper (about 6 ounces), cut into 1-inch pieces

1 medium carrot (about 4 ounces), cut into ½-inch-thick rounds

3 tablespoons peanut oil

Salt and freshly ground black pepper, to taste

1 medium red onion (about 6 ounces), finely chopped

4 large cloves garlic, finely chopped

1 cup low-sodium vegetable broth

½ cup creamy or chunky peanut butter

2 tablespoons tomato paste

½ teaspoon crushed red pepper flakes, or to taste

1 bay leaf

Fufu (page 45)

Hot pepper sauce (optional)

Preheat oven to 450F (230C). In a 15 × 10-inch shallow casserole, preferably glass (or a large baking sheet with sides), place the eggplant, zucchini, bell peppers, and carrot. Add 2 tablespoons of the oil and toss well to thoroughly coat. Sprinkle with salt and pepper and toss again. Bake 15 minutes, until the vegetables are beginning to char. Remove from oven and stir and turn the vegetables. Bake 10 to 15 minutes, until lightly charred.

Meanwhile, in a large deep-sided nonstick skillet, heat the remaining oil over medium heat. Add the onion and cook, stirring, until softened, about 3 minutes. Add the garlic and cook, stirring, 1 minute. Add the broth, peanut butter, tomato paste, red pepper flakes, bay leaf, and salt; bring to a simmer over medium-high heat. Reduce the heat and simmer gently, stirring occasionally, until thickened, about 5 minutes. Add the roasted vegetables and cook, stirring occasionally, until heated through, about 5 minutes. Discard the bay leaf. Serve warm, with the fufu, and pass the hot pepper sauce (if using).

PER SERVING (without Fufu): Calories 257 • Protein 9g • Total Fat 18g • Sat. Fat 3g • Cholesterol 0mg • Carbohydrate 19g • Dietary Fiber 6g • Sodium 245mg

Sweet Potato Patties with Green Mango Relish

MAKES 6 SERVINGS

These tasty patties are also delicious with Caribbean-Style Creole Sauce (page 80), Papaya Ketchup (page 127), store-bought chili sauce, or on their own.

2 pounds sweet potatoes, preferably Garnet or
  Jewel, peeled and cut into small cubes

1 teaspoon ground cumin

½ teaspoon salt

Freshly ground black pepper, to taste

2 scallions, white and green parts, finely chopped

1 tablespoon finely chopped fresh parsley (optional)

About ½ cup all-purpose flour

2 tablespoons peanut oil

Green Mango Relish, to taste (page 106)

In a large saucepan or medium stockpot, bring the sweet potatoes and enough salted water to cover to a boil over high heat. Reduce the heat slightly and boil until tender, about 15 minutes. Drain well and return to pan. Add the cumin, salt, and pepper, and mash well with a potato masher. Add the scallions and parsley (if using), stirring well to evenly distribute.

Place the flour on a small plate. Shape the potato mixture into 6 flattened patties. Dredge lightly in the flour, shaking off any excess.

In a large nonstick skillet, heat the oil over medium heat. Add the patties and cook until browned, 4 to 5 minutes per side. Serve at once, with Green Mango Relish passed separately.

PER SERVING (without relish): Calories 240 • Protein 3g • Total Fat 5g • Sat. Fat 1g • Cholesterol 0mg • Carbohydrate 47g • Dietary Fiber 6g • Sodium 192mg

Green Mango Relish

Serve this tasty fat-free relish as a topping for grilled vegetables, particularly eggplant and zucchini, grilled tofu, or veggie burgers.

- 2 medium very green mangoes (about 12 ounces each), peeled, pitted, and finely chopped
- 2 teaspoons finely chopped fresh cilantro
- ½ tablespoon tomato ketchup
- 1½ to 3 teaspoons finely chopped red onion
- ½ teaspoon soy sauce
- ½ teaspoon light brown sugar
- ¼ teaspoon salt, or to taste
- ⅛ teaspoon prepared yellow mustard
- 1 or 2 pinches freshly ground black pepper
- 1 or 2 pinches cayenne pepper (optional)

In a small bowl, mix together all the ingredients until thoroughly combined. Cover and refrigerate a minimum of 3 hours, or overnight. Serve chilled.

PER ABOUT ¼ CUP (⅙ of recipe): Calories 48 • Protein 0g • Total Fat 0g • Sat. Fat 0g • Cholesterol 0mg • Carbohydrate 13g • Dietary Fiber 2g • Sodium 135mg

Side Dishes

Side dishes have always been superstars in the tropics. Now's the time for them to shine in kitchens across the globe, as health experts continue telling us to move those all-important vegetables, legumes, and fruits to center stage. If straight-up veggies are what you're looking for, choose from dishes such as Vietnamese-Style Cauliflower, Cambodian-Style Hot-and-Sour Eggplant, Brazilian-Style Braised Pumpkin, or Thai-Style Barbecued Vegetables. If it's legumes, check out the Cuban-Style Black-Eyed Pea Fritters or Caribbean-Style Black Beans. For fruits, do try the Costa Rican–Style Roasted Plantains or Aussie-Style Green Mango Sauce. But if it's those comforting sides you're really craving, treat yourself to Trinidad-Style Curried Mashed Potatoes, Jamaican-Style Sweet Potato Casserole, Bangkok-Style Basil-Sesame Noodles, Indonesian-Style Fried Rice, or Mexican Sweet Corn Cakes—yum.

Caribbean-Style Black Beans

MAKES 6 SERVINGS

Serve these versatile beans as a hot dip for tortilla chips, or filling for tacos and burritos, as well.

1 tablespoon extra-virgin olive oil

1 bunch scallions (6 to 8), white and green parts, thinly sliced

4 large cloves garlic, finely chopped

1 to 2 jalapeño chilies, seeded and finely chopped

2 (15-ounce) cans black beans, rinsed and drained

1 cup low-sodium vegetable broth

1 teaspoon ground cumin

½ teaspoon dried oregano

¼ teaspoon dried thyme leaves

⅛ teaspoon ground allspice

Salt and freshly ground black pepper, to taste

Cayenne pepper, to taste (optional)

¼ cup chopped fresh cilantro

In a medium deep-sided nonstick skillet, heat the oil over medium-high heat. Add the scallions, garlic, and chilies; cook, stirring constantly, 1 minute. Add the beans, broth, cumin, oregano, thyme, allspice, salt, black pepper, and cayenne (if using); bring to a boil over high heat, stirring occasionally. Reduce the heat to medium and simmer, uncovered, 5 minutes, stirring occasionally. Transfer half of the bean mixture to a food processor fitted with the knife blade, or to a blender; process until smooth and pureed. Return pureed mixture to the skillet and add the cilantro, stirring well to combine. Cook over medium-low heat, stirring occasionally, until the mixture is hot and slightly thickened, about 5 minutes (simmer longer if a thicker consistency is desired). Serve warm.

PER SERVING: Calories 155 • Protein 10g • Total Fat 3g • Sat. Fat 0g • Cholesterol 0mg • Carbohydrate 24g • Dietary Fiber 5g • Sodium 92mg

Cuban-Style Black-Eyed Pea Fritters

MAKES 4 SERVINGS; ABOUT 12 FRITTERS

These tasty fritters are delicious on their own, or wrapped in flour tortillas with some salsa or guacamole.

1 (16-ounce) can black-eyed peas, rinsed and drained

3 large cloves garlic, finely chopped

½ teaspoon table salt

¼ teaspoon freshly ground black pepper

2 to 4 tablespoons water

2 tablespoons peanut oil

Coarse salt, to taste

Fresh lime juice, to taste

Line a baking sheet with several layers of paper towels and set aside.

In a food processor fitted with the knife blade, or in a blender, place the peas, garlic, table salt, and pepper. Process or blend until smooth and pureed, adding water as necessary to achieve desired consistency.

In a large nonstick skillet, heat the oil over medium-high heat until hot (oil should sizzle when a tiny amount of pea mixture is dropped into the skillet). Drop the pea mixture by heaping spoonfuls into the hot oil to make 2-inch mounds and fry until golden brown, about 2 minutes per side (if oil seems too hot, reduce heat slightly). Transfer to the prepared baking sheet. Serve at once, sprinkled with coarse salt and lime juice.

PER SERVING: Calories 138 • Protein 5g • Total Fat 7g • Sat. Fat 1g • Cholesterol 0mg • Carbohydrate 14g • Dietary Fiber 6g • Sodium 269mg

Thai-Style Cabbage Slaw

MAKES 8 SERVINGS

This exotic coleslaw always gets rave reviews at picnics and potlucks.

1 (16-ounce) bag shredded coleslaw mix
½ cup thinly sliced red onion, soaked in cold water to cover 10 minutes, drained well
½ cup chopped fresh mint or basil leaves
½ cup chopped fresh cilantro
3 tablespoons fresh lime juice
2 tablespoons low-sodium soy sauce or tamari
2 tablespoons peanut oil
2 tablespoons toasted (dark) sesame oil
2 tablespoons sugar
½ teaspoon crushed red pepper flakes, or more to taste
Salt and freshly ground black pepper, to taste
½ cup chopped salted peanuts

Mix all ingredients, except the peanuts, until well combined. Cover and refrigerate a minimum of 3 hours or up to 1 day. Just before serving, toss with the peanuts. Serve chilled or return to room temperature.

PER SERVING: Calories 147 • Protein 4g • Total Fat 12g • Sat. Fat 2g • Cholesterol 0mg • Carbohydrate 10g • Dietary Fiber 2g • Sodium 163mg

Hawaiian Orange-Ginger Carrots

MAKES 4 SERVINGS

Blanched or steamed asparagus is also delicious tossed with this delicate orange-ginger sauce.

1 pound baby carrots
¼ cup fresh orange juice
1 tablespoon sugar
1 teaspoon cornstarch
½ teaspoon salt
¼ teaspoon ground ginger
Freshly ground black pepper, to taste

In a large saucepan, bring the carrots and enough salted water to cover to a boil over high heat. Reduce the heat to medium and simmer until tender, 5 to 10 minutes, depending on thickness. Drain and return to saucepan; cover and keep warm.

Meanwhile, in a small saucepan, combine the orange juice, sugar, cornstarch, salt, and ginger. Bring to a simmer over medium-low heat, whisking constantly. Pour over the hot carrots and season with pepper, tossing to thoroughly coat. Serve warm.

PER SERVING: Calories 65 • Protein 1g • Total Fat 1g • Sat. Fat 0g • Cholesterol 0mg • Carbohydrate 15g • Dietary Fiber 3g • Sodium 306mg

Vietnamese-Style Cauliflower

MAKES 4 TO 6 SERVINGS

This flavorful recipe is a delightful way to enjoy an important cruciferous vegetable.

2 tablespoons peanut oil

3 shallots, thinly sliced

3 large cloves garlic, finely chopped

3 medium tomatoes (about 6 ounces each), seeded and chopped

1 to 2 tablespoons low-sodium soy sauce or tamari

1 large head cauliflower, cut into small florets

4 scallions, white and green parts, thinly sliced

2/3 cup low-sodium vegetable broth

1/2 teaspoon fresh lemon juice

1/2 teaspoon light brown sugar

Salt and freshly ground black pepper, to taste

Cayenne pepper, to taste (optional)

1/4 cup chopped fresh cilantro

In a wok or large nonstick skillet with a lid, heat the oil over medium-high heat. Add the shallots and garlic and cook, stirring, 1 minute. Add the tomatoes and soy sauce and cook, stirring, 3 minutes.

Add the cauliflower, scallions, broth, lemon juice, sugar, salt, black pepper, and cayenne (if using); bring to a simmer. Reduce the heat to medium-low and cook, partially covered, until the cauliflower is crisp-tender, 7 to 10 minutes, stirring occasionally. Remove from the heat and toss with the cilantro. Serve warm.

PER SERVING: Calories 157 • Protein 7g • Total Fat 8g • Sat. Fat 1g • Cholesterol 0mg • Carbohydrate 20g • Dietary Fiber 6g • Sodium 296mg

Cambodian-Style Grilled Corn

MAKES 4 SERVINGS

This is awesome corn. If you don't have time to grill, the corn can be boiled instead, and then placed under the broiler a few minutes to brown.

1/4 cup canola oil

2 scallions, white and green parts, thinly sliced

2 tablespoons sugar

1/2 teaspoon salt

4 ears fresh corn, in husks, soaked in water to cover 1 hour, drained

Freshly ground black pepper, to taste

Prepare a medium-hot charcoal grill or gas grill. Position the grill rack 4 to 6 inches from heat source.

In a small saucepan, heat the oil over medium heat. Add the scallions and cook, stirring constantly, until lightly browned and fragrant, about 3 minutes. Remove from heat and stir in the sugar and salt. Set aside.

Grill the corn (in husks) until tender and slightly charred, 15 to 20 minutes, turning occasionally. When cool enough to handle, remove and discard the husks. Return the corn briefly to the grill, turning a few times, until golden. Transfer to a platter or individual serving plates and spread evenly with the oil mixture. Season with pepper and serve at once.

PER SERVING: Calories 268 • Protein 5g • Total Fat 15g • Sat. Fat 1g • Cholesterol 0mg • Carbohydrate 34g • Dietary Fiber 4g • Sodium 289mg

Mexican-Style Corn

MAKES 4 TO 6 SERVINGS

This is a simple yet delicious way to spruce up frozen corn. For a milder dish, replace the jalapeño chili with minced pimiento.

16 ounces frozen corn, cooked according to
    package directions, well drained
1 jalapeño chili, seeded and finely chopped
¼ cup chopped fresh cilantro
1 tablespoon canola oil
½ teaspoon garlic salt
Freshly ground black pepper, to taste

Place the corn in a medium bowl and add the remaining ingredients; toss well to combine. Serve warm.

PER SERVING: Calories 135 • Protein 4g • Total Fat 4g • Sat. Fat 0g • Cholesterol 0mg • Carbohydrate 25g • Dietary Fiber 3g • Sodium 261mg

2 cups fresh or frozen yellow corn kernels, cooked
    and drained
1 cup chopped red bell pepper
¼ cup chopped fresh cilantro
1 tablespoon fresh lime juice
1 tablespoon drained canned diced mild green
    chilies
1 teaspoon sugar
½ teaspoon salt
Freshly ground black pepper, to taste

In a medium nonstick skillet, heat the oil over medium heat. Add the onion and cook, stirring, until softened but not browned, about 3 minutes. Add the corn and bell pepper and toss to combine. Remove the skillet from heat and add the remaining ingredients, tossing well to combine. Transfer to a serving bowl and serve at room temperature. The relish can be stored, covered, in refrigerator up to 3 days before returning to room temperature and using.

PER SERVING: Calories 83 • Protein 2g • Total Fat 3g • Sat. Fat 0g • Cholesterol 0mg • Carbohydrate 14g • Dietary Fiber 2g • Sodium 187mg

Mexican Corn Relish

MAKES 6 SERVINGS

This perennial favorite goes well with just about any Mexican-style entrée, namely the Black Bean and Avocado Enchiladas with Chipotle Sauce (page 76) and Sweet Potato and Black Bean Quesadillas (page 96).

1 tablespoon canola oil
1 cup chopped onion

Mexican Sweet Corn Cake

MAKES 8 TO 12 SERVINGS

Primarily used for making tortillas, tamales, and many other dishes from Mexico, Central America, and South America, *masa harina* is flour made from dried masa. Masa is dough prepared from special lime-processed corn (hominy). It can be found in Latin markets as well as the international aisle of many well-stocked supermarkets. For a softer consistency, you can bake this scrumptiously sweet corn cake in a *bain-marie*, or water bath, and serve with an ice cream scoop.

⅓ cup sugar

3 tablespoons yellow cornmeal

¼ teaspoon baking powder

¼ teaspoon salt

¼ cup vegetable shortening

2 tablespoons canola oil

½ cup masa harina

¼ cup cold water

10 ounces frozen yellow corn kernels, thawed and coarsely chopped

Preheat oven to 350F (175C). Lightly grease an 8-inch-square baking dish and set aside.

In a small bowl, whisk together the sugar, cornmeal, baking powder, and salt; set aside.

In a medium mixing bowl, using an electric beater on low speed, beat the shortening and oil until creamy. Gradually beat in the masa harina, then the water, mixing until thoroughly combined. Stir in the cornmeal mixture, mixing until thoroughly combined. Stir in the corn, mixing until evenly distributed. Transfer to the prepared baking dish and cover with foil. (If desired, place in a larger baking pan; fill the larger pan with very hot water reaching halfway up the sides of the smaller pan.)

Bake 40 to 50 minutes, until set and firm to the touch. Let stand at room temperature 10 minutes (remove from the water bath, if used). Cut into squares (or scoop with an ice cream scoop) and serve warm.

PER SERVING: Calories 189 • Protein 2g • Total Fat 10g • Sat. Fat 3g • Cholesterol 0mg • Carbohydrate 24g • Dietary Fiber 2g • Sodium 80mg

Cucumber and Chayote Slaw

MAKES 4 TO 6 SERVINGS

This unusual slaw is a delicious accompaniment to any Mexican- or Southwestern-style entrée.

2 tablespoons canola oil

2 tablespoons unsweetened pineapple juice

½ tablespoon sugar

1 teaspoon chipotle puree (see Cook's Tip, below)

1 teaspoon Dijon mustard

Salt and freshly ground black pepper, to taste

1 large cucumber (about 12 ounces), peeled, seeded, quartered lengthwise, and thinly sliced crosswise

1 large chayote, peeled under cold-running water to remove stickiness, pitted, quartered lengthwise, and thinly sliced crosswise

2 cups cubed fresh pineapple

In a large bowl, whisk together the oil, juice, sugar, chipotle puree, mustard, salt, and pepper. Add the remaining ingredients, tossing well to combine. Refrigerate, covered, a minimum of 1 hour, or overnight. Serve chilled.

PER SERVING: Calories 133 • Protein 1g • Total Fat 8g • Sat. Fat 1g • Cholesterol 0mg • Carbohydrate 17g • Dietary Fiber 3g • Sodium 20mg

COOK'S TIP: *To make chipotle puree, place 1 (7-ounce) can chipotle chilies in adobo sauce in a food processor fitted with the knife blade, or in a blender; process or blend until smooth and pureed. Store, covered, in the refrigerator for several weeks.*

Cambodian-Style Hot-and-Sour Eggplant

MAKES 6 SIDE-DISH SERVINGS

Serve this tasty eggplant dish over rice and garnish with chopped peanuts for a complete meal.

1 large eggplant (about 1 pound), unpeeled, cut into 1-inch cubes, sprinkled with salt, and set in a colander to drain 30 minutes (salting is optional)

½ cup plus 2 tablespoons water

1 tablespoon dry sherry

1 tablespoon cornstarch

1 tablespoon peanut oil

2 large cloves garlic, finely chopped

1 tablespoon chopped peeled fresh ginger

4 scallions, white and green parts, thinly sliced

¼ cup low-sodium soy or tamari sauce

¼ cup distilled white vinegar

3 tablespoons sugar

½ teaspoon crushed red pepper flakes, or to taste

¼ cup finely chopped fresh basil (optional)

Rinse the drained eggplant under cold-running water. Dry between paper towels.

In a small container, mix together the 2 table-spoons of the water and sherry with the cornstarch until thoroughly blended; set aside.

In a large nonstick skillet, heat the oil over medium-high heat. Add the eggplant and cook, stirring and tossing constantly, until softened, about 4 minutes. Add the garlic, ginger, and scallions; cook, stirring constantly, 2 minutes. Add the soy sauce, vinegar, ¼ cup of the remaining water, sugar, and red pepper flakes; cook, stirring, until most of the liquids have evaporated, about 5 minutes. Reduce the heat to medium and add the corn-starch mixture and remaining water; cook, stirring, until thickened, about 3 minutes. Remove from heat and toss with the basil (if using). Serve warm or at room temperature.

PER SERVING: Calories 83 • Protein 2g • Total Fat 2g • Sat. Fat 0g • Cholesterol 0mg • Carbohydrate 14g • Dietary Fiber 2g • Sodium 405mg

COOK'S TIP: *Salting helps draw out the eggplant's bitter juices. However, if you are short on time, the step can be omitted here and in other recipes where the eggplant is to be cooked with several ingredients, as any bitterness is typically masked by the other flavors.*

Eggplant in Cuban-Style Mojo Sauce

MAKES 8 SERVINGS

Serve this citrus- and garlic-infused eggplant dish with lots of crusty bread to sop up the delicious mojo sauce.

2 medium eggplants (about ¾ pound each), unpeeled, sliced into ¼-inch-thick rounds, sprinkled with salt, and set in a colander to drain 30 minutes (salting is optional)

Cuban-Style Mojo Sauce (page 114)

Preheat oven to 400F (205C). Lightly oil a 13×9-inch baking dish and set aside.

Rinse the drained eggplant under cold-running water. Dry between paper towels.

Arrange half the eggplant in the prepared baking dish. Cover with half of the sauce. Top with remaining eggplant, followed by the remaining sauce. Cover with foil (lightly oil underside if foil will touch eggplant) and bake 40 minutes. Remove the baking dish from the oven and turn the eggplant slices over in the sauce. Continue baking, covered, another 20 minutes, or until eggplant is very tender. Serve warm.

PER SERVING: Calories 109 • Protein 1g • Total Fat 9g • Sat. Fat 1g • Cholesterol 0mg • Carbohydrate 7g • Dietary Fiber 2g • Sodium 269mg

Cuban-Style Mojo Sauce

MAKES ABOUT 1 CUP

Originating in the Canary Islands, mojo is a hot sauce and marinade that is also immensely popular throughout the Caribbean, especially Cuba, where it is considered the national sauce. While there are many variations among Cuban cooks, mojo always contains lots of garlic, olive oil, and a citrus juice, primarily orange or lime, and is seasoned with cumin and, sometimes, hot chilies. Use mojo as a marinade for tofu, seitan, or grilled portobello mushrooms, to dress numerous vegetables and potatoes, or as a tasty dip for bread.

⅓ cup extra-virgin olive oil

6 large cloves garlic, finely chopped

⅓ cup fresh orange juice

⅓ cup fresh lime juice

1 teaspoon salt

½ teaspoon ground cumin

½ teaspoon freshly ground black pepper

¼ teaspoon crushed red pepper flakes (optional)

In a medium deep-sided saucepan, heat the oil over medium heat. Add the garlic and cook, stirring constantly, until fragrant and lightly browned, about 1 minute. Carefully add the remaining ingredients.

Bring to a rapid boil over high heat. Immediately remove from heat. Let cool slightly before using in recipes requiring further cooking. If using as a marinade, let cool to room temperature before using. Completely cooled sauce can be stored, covered, in refrigerator up to 5 days. Reheat over low heat or bring to room temperature before using.

PER TABLESPOON: Calories 46 • Protein 0g • Total Fat 5g • Sat. Fat 1g • Cholesterol 0mg • Carbohydrate 1g • Dietary Fiber 0g • Sodium 134mg

Sri Lankan–Style Curried Green Beans with Cashews

MAKES 4 SERVINGS

The Indian influence upon the cuisine of Sri Lanka is evident in this delicious curried green bean dish.

1 pound fresh green beans, trimmed

1½ tablespoons extra-virgin olive oil

½ small red onion (about 2 ounces), chopped

1 large clove garlic, finely chopped

¼ cup unsalted chopped cashews or peanuts

¼ cup golden raisins

2 tablespoons water

½ teaspoon salt, or to taste

¼ teaspoon mild curry powder

¼ teaspoon ground turmeric

Freshly ground black pepper, to taste

In a large stockpot filled with boiling salted water, cook the green beans until barely tender, about 3 minutes. Drain well.

In a large nonstick skillet, heat the oil over medium heat. Add the onion and cook, stirring, until softened, about 3 minutes. Add the garlic and cook, stirring, 1 minute. Add the green beans, cashews, raisins, water, salt, curry powder, turmeric, and pepper; cook, stirring, until the beans are crisp-tender, about 3 minutes. Serve at once.

PER SERVING: Calories 165 • Protein 4g • Total Fat 9g • Sat. Fat 2g • Cholesterol 0mg • Carbohydrate 20g • Dietary Fiber 5g • Sodium 277mg

Spicy Thai Green Beans and Tofu

MAKES 4 SERVINGS

You can serve this spicy green bean side dish over hot cooked rice for a complete meal.

1 tablespoon peanut oil

2 to 3 kaffir lime leaves, torn into 3 or 4 pieces, or 1 to 2 teaspoons chopped fresh lime peel

½ to 1 teaspoon Thai red curry paste

¾ pound fresh green beans, trimmed and cut into 1-inch lengths

½ cup low-sodium vegetable broth

1 to 2 tablespoons low-sodium tamari or soy sauce, plus additional, to taste

1 teaspoon toasted (dark) sesame oil

1 teaspoon palm sugar or light brown sugar

Salt and freshly ground black pepper, to taste

1 cup cubed firm tofu

In a medium deep-sided skillet with a lid, heat the peanut oil over medium heat. Add the lime leaves

and curry paste; cook, stirring until fragrant, 1 minute. Add the green beans, broth, tamari, sesame oil, sugar, salt, and pepper; bring to a boil over medium-high heat. Reduce the heat to medium-low and cook, covered, until the beans are just tender, about 5 minutes, stirring occasionally. Add the tofu and cook, covered, until the beans are soft and tender, 5 to 10 minutes more, stirring a few times. Serve at once.

PER SERVING: Calories 130 • Protein 8g • Total Fat 8g • Sat. Fat 1g • Cholesterol 0mg • Carbohydrate 9g • Dietary Fiber 4g • Sodium 243mg

Bangkok-Style Basil Sesame Noodles

MAKES 5 TO 6 SIDE-DISH OR 3 MAIN-COURSE SERVINGS

The basil-sesame sauce that coats the noodles here is delicious tossed with any pasta, as well as rice or steamed vegetables, particularly green beans. Fresh cilantro can replace the basil, if desired.

1 cup loosely packed fresh basil

2 tablespoons sesame seeds

1 tablespoon canola oil

1 tablespoon toasted (dark) sesame oil

1 tablespoon low-sodium soy sauce or tamari

1 tablespoon fresh lime juice

4 large cloves garlic, finely chopped

¼ teaspoon crushed red pepper flakes, or to taste

Salt and freshly ground black pepper, to taste

8 ounces soba or somen noodles, cooked according to package directions until al dente, drained, and rinsed briefly under cold-running water

In a food processor fitted with the knife blade, process the basil, sesame seeds, canola oil, sesame oil, soy sauce, lime juice, garlic, red pepper flakes, salt, and black pepper until smooth.

In a large bowl, toss together the noodles and basil mixture until well combined. Serve at room temperature. Alternatively, refrigerate a minimum of 2 hours or up to 2 days and serve chilled.

PER SERVING: Calories 260 • Protein 9g • Total Fat 8g • Sat. Fat 1g • Cholesterol 0mg • Carbohydrate 44g • Dietary Fiber 3g • Sodium 371mg

Aussie-Style Green Mango Sauce

MAKES 8 SERVINGS

Use this delicious side dish or relish as you would applesauce.

3 cups bite-size semi-ripe mango pieces
1 cup sugar
1 cup water

In a medium saucepan, combine all the ingredients. Cook over medium heat, stirring often, until the consistency of applesauce, about 15 minutes. Serve warm or at room temperature. Alternatively, cover and refrigerate completely cooled sauce a minimum of 2 hours or up to 3 days, and serve chilled or return to room temperature.

PER SERVING: Calories 137 • Protein 0g • Total Fat 0g • Sat. Fat 0g • Cholesterol 0mg • Carbohydrate 36g • Dietary Fiber 1g • Sodium 1mg

Costa Rican–Style Roasted Plantains

MAKES 4 TO 5 SERVINGS

Serve this tasty plantain side dish as you would roasted potato wedges or fries. It's especially delicious accompanied by Papaya Ketchup (page 127) or Green Mango Relish (page 106). Fully ripe plantains have black peels; you can buy the plantains a week before roasting and let them ripen at room temperature.

1½ pounds fully ripe plantains (about 3 large), peeled and sliced diagonally into ¼-inch-thick pieces
1 tablespoon canola oil
¼ teaspoon salt, plus additional, to taste

Preheat oven to 400F (205C).

On a baking sheet with a rim, toss the plantains and oil until thoroughly coated. Sprinkle with the salt and toss. Bake 15 to 20 minutes, turning occasionally with a spatula, until lightly browned and tender. Season with additional salt, if desired, and serve warm.

PER SERVING: Calories 165 • Protein 1g • Total Fat 4g • Sat. Fat 0g • Cholesterol 0mg • Carbohydrate 35g • Dietary Fiber 3g • Sodium 138mg

Trinidad-Style Curried Mashed Potatoes

MAKES 4 SIDE-DISH OR 8 APPETIZER SERVINGS

The East Indian influence upon the cuisine of Trinidad is apparent in these curried mashed potatoes, also known as potato *choka*. They make a terrific side dish or appetizer, rolled into bite-size balls and accompanied by toothpicks.

1 pound medium round red or white potatoes, peeled and quartered

1½ tablespoons canola oil

4 ounces finely chopped red onion

1 jalapeño chili, seeded and finely chopped

3 large cloves garlic, finely chopped

½ teaspoon coarse salt

¼ teaspoon mild curry powder

Freshly ground black pepper, to taste

In a large saucepan or medium stockpot, bring the potatoes and enough salted water to cover to a boil over high heat. Reduce the heat slightly and boil gently until tender, 15 to 20 minutes. Drain and return to the pot; add ½ tablespoon of the oil and mash well.

Meanwhile, in a small nonstick skillet, heat the remaining oil over medium heat. Add the onion and chili and cook, stirring, until softened but not browned, 3 to 4 minutes. Add the garlic, salt, curry powder, and pepper; cook, stirring constantly, 1 to 2 minutes. Remove the skillet from the heat and add the onion mixture to the mashed potatoes, mixing well to thoroughly combine. Serve at once. Alternatively, using your fingers, form into small balls and serve at room temperature, accompanied by toothpicks.

PER SERVING: Calories 131 • Protein 3g • Total Fat 5g • Sat. Fat 0g • Cholesterol 0mg • Carbohydrate 20g • Dietary Fiber 2g • Sodium 242mg

Costa Rican–Style Tortillas with Potatoes

MAKES 4 SERVINGS

Called *gallitos* in Costa Rica, these open-faced corn tortillas topped with potatoes are also delicious garnished with a bit of salsa.

4 corn tortillas

2 tablespoons extra-virgin olive oil

1 cup chopped onion

1 pound boiling potatoes, peeled and chopped

1 teaspoon garlic salt

2 tablespoons, water, plus additional as needed

1 teaspoon sugar

½ teaspoon sweet paprika

Freshly ground black pepper, to taste

2 to 4 teaspoons chopped fresh cilantro

Preheat oven to 200F (95C).

Arrange the tortillas on an ungreased baking sheet. Heat until softened and warmed, about 10 minutes.

Meanwhile, in a large nonstick skillet with a lid, heat the oil over medium heat. Add the onion and cook, stirring, until softened, about 3 minutes. Add the potatoes and garlic salt and cook, stirring, until the onion is translucent, about 5 minutes. Stir in the water, sugar, paprika, and pepper; cover the skillet and reduce the heat to low. Cook, stirring occasionally, until the potatoes are tender, about

15 minutes, adding more water as necessary to prevent the mixture from drying out. To serve, top the warm tortillas with equal amounts of the potato mixture. Sprinkle evenly with the cilantro and serve at once.

PER SERVING: Calories 203 • Protein 4g • Total Fat 8g • Sat. Fat 1g • Cholesterol 0mg • Carbohydrate 32g • Dietary Fiber 4g • Sodium 559mg

Venezuelan-Style Baked Potato Casserole

MAKES 6 SERVINGS

In a pinch, this rustic potato casserole can be made using two (15-ounce) cans sliced white potatoes, rinsed and drained, in lieu of the fresh.

2 pounds small round red or white potatoes, left whole

2 tablespoons extra-virgin olive oil

1 large onion (about 8 ounces), thinly sliced into half-rings

2 large cloves garlic, finely chopped

4 medium tomatoes (about 6 ounces each), seeded and coarsely chopped

¾ cup low-sodium vegetable broth

4 tablespoons finely chopped fresh parsley or cilantro

1 tablespoon ground cumin

½ tablespoon all-purpose flour

½ teaspoon sweet paprika

½ teaspoon salt, or to taste

Freshly ground black pepper, to taste

Cayenne pepper, to taste (optional)

Preheat oven to 350F (175C). Lightly grease a 10-inch ceramic pie or quiche dish and set aside.

In a medium stockpot, combine the potatoes and enough salted water to cover by 2 inches. Bring to a boil over high heat. Reduce the heat slightly and boil until the potatoes are just tender, 10 minutes. Drain well and let cool slightly. When cool enough to handle, cut the potatoes into ¼-inch-thick slices.

Meanwhile, in a large nonstick skillet, heat the oil over medium heat. Add the onion and cook, stirring, until translucent and just beginning to brown, about 8 minutes, adding the garlic the last few minutes of cooking. Add the tomatoes, broth, half of the parsley, cumin, flour, paprika, salt, black pepper, and cayenne (if using); bring to a brisk simmer over medium-high heat. Reduce the heat to medium-low and simmer, uncovered, stirring occasionally, until a thick and chunky sauce is formed, about 15 minutes.

Arrange one-third of the potatoes in the bottom of the prepared dish, then top with one-third of the sauce. Repeat layers two more times, ending with sauce. Bake uncovered 25 to 30 minutes, or until most of the liquids have been absorbed and top is lightly browned. Let stand about 5 minutes before serving. Garnish with the remaining parsley and serve warm.

PER SERVING: Calories 183 • Protein 6g • Total Fat 5g • Sat. Fat 1g • Cholesterol 0mg • Carbohydrate 31g • Dietary Fiber 4g • Sodium 264mg

Brazilian-Style Braised Pumpkin

MAKES 4 SERVINGS

Here is a simple yet delicious method of preparing an important vitamin A–rich vegetable.

2 tablespoons extra-virgin olive oil

3 scallions, white and green parts, thinly sliced

1 large clove garlic, finely chopped

2½ cups cubed pumpkin or butternut squash (about 1 pound)

¼ cup low-sodium vegetable broth, plus additional, as necessary

½ teaspoon salt, or to taste

Freshly ground black pepper, to taste

In a medium deep-sided skillet with a lid, heat the oil over medium heat. Add the scallions and garlic and cook, stirring, 2 minutes. Add the pumpkin, broth, salt, and pepper; cover, and reduce the heat to medium-low. Cook, stirring occasionally, until the pumpkin is fork-tender, about 15 minutes, adding additional broth as necessary to prevent the pumpkin from sticking. Serve warm.

PER SERVING: Calories 88 • Protein 2g • Total Fat 7g • Sat. Fat 1g • Cholesterol 0mg • Carbohydrate 6g • Dietary Fiber 2g • Sodium 302mg

Thai-Style Basil Rice

MAKES 4 TO 6 SERVINGS

Perfume your kitchen with the wonderful aroma of this delicious basil-scented rice. For a less spicy dish, omit the crushed red pepper flakes.

2 tablespoons canola oil

2 shallots, finely chopped

1 scallion, white and green parts, thinly sliced

3 cloves garlic, finely chopped

1 cup long-grain white rice

½ cup chopped fresh basil

2 cups low-sodium vegetable broth

1 tablespoon unsweetened flaked coconut, or to taste (optional)

¼ teaspoon crushed red pepper flakes, or to taste

Salt and freshly ground black pepper, to taste

In a medium deep-sided skillet with a lid, heat the oil over medium heat. Add the shallots and cook, stirring, until softened but not browned, about 3 minutes. Add the scallion and garlic and cook, stirring, 1 minute. Add the rice and half of the basil and cook, stirring, 2 minutes. Add the broth, coconut (if using), red pepper flakes, salt, and black pepper; bring to a boil over high heat. Reduce the heat to low, cover, and simmer until all the liquid has been absorbed, about 20 minutes. Fluff with a fork and toss with the remaining basil. Serve at once.

PER SERVING: Calories 270 • Protein 10g • Total Fat 7g • Sat. Fat 1g • Cholesterol 0mg • Carbohydrate 41g • Dietary Fiber 2g • Sodium 264mg

Puerto Rican–Style Green Rice with Tomatillos

MAKES 6 SERVINGS

If you like tomatillos, you'll love this unusual rice dish. To turn it into a main course for three or four, add about 1½ cups of cooked black beans when you stir in the salsa.

6 large tomatillos (about ¾ pound), husked, stemmed, and rinsed under warm water to remove stickiness

About 1 cup water

¼ cup finely chopped fresh cilantro

1 tablespoon finely chopped jalapeño chili (optional)

1 tablespoon extra-virgin olive oil

2 large cloves garlic, finely chopped

½ teaspoon salt, plus additional, to taste

1¼ cups long-grain white rice

¼ cup mild or medium tomato salsa, preferably chunky style

In a medium stockpot or large saucepan filled with boiling water, add the tomatillos and cook until soft, about 5 minutes. Drain.

Transfer the tomatillos to a food processor fitted with the knife blade, or to a blender; process until smooth and pureed. Add enough water to the tomatillos to measure 2½ cups total.

In a medium deep-sided skillet with a lid, combine the tomatillo mixture, cilantro, chili (if using), oil, garlic, and salt; bring to a boil over high heat. Stir in the rice, cover, and reduce heat to low; simmer until all the liquid is absorbed, about 20 minutes. Remove from heat and stir in the salsa and additional salt, if necessary. Let stand, covered, 5 minutes; fluff with a fork and serve.

PER SERVING: Calories 183 • Protein 4g • Total Fat 3g • Sat. Fat 0g • Cholesterol 0mg • Carbohydrate 35g • Dietary Fiber 2g • Sodium 208mg

Indonesian-Style Fried Rice

MAKES 4 TO 6 SIDE DISH OR 2 TO 3 MAIN COURSE SERVINGS

Indonesian-style fried rice, or *nasi goreng*, makes a delicious meal garnished with lightly steamed or stir-fried vegetables, and tofu. While you can use left-over rice, this dish is better prepared with freshly cooked rice that has been allowed to cool for about two hours at room temperature before using. Chopped red onion can replace the shallots, if desired.

1 tablespoon canola oil

4 medium shallots (about 1 ounce each), finely chopped

1 large clove garlic, finely chopped (optional)

1 tablespoon reduced-sodium soy sauce or tamari

1 tablespoon tomato ketchup

1 teaspoon *sambal olek* or Chinese chili paste, or to taste

3 cups cooked long-grain white rice, cooled to room temperature (see Cook's Tip, page 79)

½ teaspoon salt, or to taste

Assorted stir-fried or steamed vegetables and/or stir-fried cubed tofu, for garnish (optional)

In a large nonstick skillet, heat the oil over medium heat. Add the shallots and cook, stirring, until softened but not browned, about 3 minutes. Add the garlic (if using), soy sauce, ketchup, and *sambal olek*; cook, stirring, 30 seconds. Add the rice and salt; toss until combined. Increase the heat to medium-high and cook, tossing and stirring constantly, until just beginning to brown, about 3 minutes. Remove from heat and serve at once, with the vegetables and/or tofu (if using).

PER SERVING: Calories 235 • Protein 5g • Total Fat 4g • Sat. Fat 0g • Cholesterol 0mg • Carbohydrate 45g • Dietary Fiber 1g • Sodium 467mg

Mango Rice

MAKES 4 TO 6 SERVINGS

Mango nectar is available in Latin and Caribbean markets, as well as the international aisle of many well-stocked supermarkets.

    1 tablespoon canola oil
    2 tablespoons finely chopped red onion
    1 jalapeño chili, seeded and finely chopped
    1¼ cups water
    ¾ cup mango nectar
    ¼ cup finely chopped fresh cilantro
    Juice of half a lime
    1 teaspoon salt, plus additional, to taste
    Freshly ground black pepper, to taste
    1 cup long-grain white rice
    Mango chunks, for garnish (optional)

In a medium deep-sided skillet with a tight-fitting lid, heat the oil over medium heat. Add the onion and chili and cook, stirring, until softened and fragrant, about 3 minutes. Add the water, nectar, half of the cilantro, lime juice, 1 teaspoon salt, and black pepper; bring to a boil over high heat. Add the rice and bring to a brisk simmer. Reduce the heat to low, cover, and simmer until the rice has

absorbed all the liquids, 17 to 20 minutes. Remove from the heat and let stand, covered, 5 minutes. Uncover and stir in the remaining cilantro and additional salt and pepper, if needed. Fluff with a fork and serve at once, garnished with the mango chunks (if using).

PER SERVING: Calories 232 • Protein 4g • Total Fat 4g • Sat. Fat 0g • Cholesterol 0mg • Carbohydrate 45g • Dietary Fiber 1g • Sodium 540mg

Chili-Roasted Sweet Potato Fries

MAKES 6 SERVINGS

These tasty sweet potatoes are a delicious accompaniment to Island Bean Burgers (page 79).

    3 (8-ounce) sweet potatoes, scrubbed, cut lengthwise into 8 wedges
    2 tablespoons peanut oil
    Juice of half a lime
    ½ teaspoon chili powder
    ½ teaspoon garlic salt, plus additional, to taste
    ¼ teaspoon freshly ground black pepper

Preheat oven to 425F (220C).

Place the potatoes on a large baking sheet with a rim and drizzle with the oil and lime juice. Using a wide spatula, toss well to thoroughly coat. In a small container, combine the remaining ingredients. Sprinkle over the potatoes, then toss well to evenly coat. Arrange the potatoes in a single layer. Bake in the upper third of the oven until browned and tender, 15 to 20 minutes, turning halfway through cooking time. Season with additional garlic salt, if desired, and serve at once.

PER SERVING: Calories 161 • Protein 2g • Total Fat 5g • Sat. Fat 1g • Cholesterol 0mg • Carbohydrate 28g • Dietary Fiber 4g • Sodium 188mg

Caribbean Tomato Brown Rice

MAKES 6 SERVINGS

This is a good recipe to save for overripe or blemished tomatoes. To turn this dish into a complete meal serving four, add 1½ cups rinsed and drained canned black beans, or other beans, the last 10 minutes or so of simmering.

1 tablespoon extra-virgin olive oil

½ cup finely chopped onion

3 cloves garlic, finely chopped

2½ cups low-sodium vegetable broth

½ teaspoon salt

¼ teaspoon dried thyme

⅛ teaspoon crushed red pepper flakes

Freshly ground black pepper, to taste

1 cup brown rice

2 medium ripe tomatoes (about 6 ounces each), peeled, seeded, and coarsely chopped

In a medium deep-sided skillet with a lid, heat the oil over medium heat. Add the onion and cook, stirring, until softened but not browned, about 3 minutes. Add the garlic and cook, stirring, 1 minute. Add the broth, salt, thyme, red pepper flakes, and black pepper; bring to a boil over high heat. Stir in the rice and tomatoes, cover, and reduce the heat to between low and medium-low. Simmer gently until the liquids have been absorbed and the rice is tender, about 45 minutes. Remove from the heat and let stand, covered, 5 minutes. Fluff with a fork and serve warm.

PER SERVING: Calories 174 • Protein 8g • Total Fat 3g • Sat. Fat 1g • Cholesterol 0mg • Carbohydrate 29g • Dietary Fiber 3g • Sodium 400mg

African-Style Spinach and Zucchini Sauté with Pumpkin Seeds and Dried Pineapple

MAKES 4 SERVINGS

Serve this delicious and nutritious dish over brown rice for a complete meal. Any dried tropical fruit, as well as raisins, currants, or apricots, can replace the pineapple, if desired.

2 tablespoons canola oil or peanut oil

½ medium red onion (about 3 ounces), coarsely chopped

2 medium zucchini (about 6 ounces each), coarsely chopped

4 scallions, white and green parts, thinly sliced

¼ cup unsalted raw pumpkin seeds, coarsely chopped

Salt and freshly ground black pepper, to taste

¼ cup low-sodium vegetable broth

¼ cup chopped dried unsweetened pineapple

1 (6-ounce) bag baby spinach

In a large nonstick skillet with a lid, heat the oil over medium heat. Add the onion and cook, stirring, until softened and fragrant, about 5 minutes. Add the zucchini, scallions, pumpkin seeds, salt, and pepper; cook, stirring, 3 minutes. Add the broth and pineapple, stirring to combine. Add the spinach, tossing well to combine. Cover, reduce the heat to low, and cook, stirring a few times, until the spinach is wilted (but not shriveled) and the zucchini is tender, about 5 minutes. Serve warm.

PER SERVING: Calories 154 • Protein 5g • Total Fat 8g • Sat. Fat 1g • Cholesterol 0mg • Carbohydrate 19g • Dietary Fiber 6g • Sodium 74mg

Gingered Sugar Snap Peas

MAKES 4 SERVINGS

You can prepare snow peas in the same fashion, but cook for about half the time.

1 tablespoon peanut oil

1 pound sugar snap peas, strings removed

1 tablespoon finely chopped peeled fresh ginger

¼ cup water

Salt and freshly ground black pepper, to taste

In a large nonstick skillet, heat the oil over medium-high heat. Add the peas and ginger and cook, stirring occasionally, until the peas begin to brown, about 3 minutes.

Add the water and reduce heat to medium. Sea-son with salt and pepper and cook, stirring and scraping up ginger from bottom of skillet with a wooden spoon, until the peas are crisp-tender, about 2 minutes. Serve at once.

PER SERVING: Calories 66 • Protein 2g • Total Fat 4g • Sat. Fat 1g • Cholesterol 0mg • Carbohydrate 8g • Dietary Fiber 4g • Sodium 7mg

Orange-Glazed Snow Peas with Cardamom

MAKES 4 SERVINGS

Cloves and cardamom lend these scrumptious glazed snow peas a subtly enticing flavor.

½ cup fresh orange juice

2 tablespoons orange marmalade

1 tablespoon canola oil

½ teaspoon salt

¼ teaspoon ground cardamom

⅛ teaspoon ground cloves

1 teaspoon toasted (dark) sesame oil

1 pound snow peas, strings removed

Freshly ground black pepper, to taste

In a small saucepan, bring the juice, marmalade, canola oil, salt, cardamom, and cloves to a boil over medium heat, stirring occasionally. Boil without stirring until mixture is reduced by about half (5 tablespoons), 5 to 8 minutes. Remove from heat and stir in the sesame oil. Cover and keep warm.

Meanwhile, in a large stockpot filled with boiling salted water, blanch the snow peas until just softened, 30 seconds to 1 minute. Drain well and immediately transfer to a serving dish. Add orange juice mixture and black pepper; toss well to thoroughly coat. Serve at once.

mixture, tossing well to thoroughly coat. Bake about 40 minutes, turning and stirring halfway through cooking time, or until potatoes are tender through the center. Serve warm.

Aussie-Style Roasted Sweet Potatoes with Guava Jelly

MAKES 6 SERVINGS

These yummy sweet potatoes are a delicious accompaniment to roast Tofurky at Thanksgiving. Guava jelly is available in Latin markets and in the international aisle of many well-stocked supermarkets. Pineapple jelly or mango chutney can be substituted, if desired.

    6 tablespoons guava jelly or jam
    1 tablespoon water
    ½ tablespoon canola oil
    Salt and freshly ground black pepper, to taste
    2 large sweet potatoes (about 12 ounces each),
        peeled, cut into 1-inch cubes

Preheat oven to 375F (190C). Lightly oil a shallow baking dish large enough to hold the sweet potatoes in a single layer and set aside.

In a small saucepan, heat the jelly, water, oil, salt, and pepper over medium-low heat until the jelly is dissolved, stirring often. Place the sweet potatoes in the prepared dish and add the guava

Jamaican-Style Sweet Potato Casserole with Banana and Coconut

MAKES 6 SERVINGS

This quick and easy casserole can be made with freshly boiled or baked sweet potatoes, if desired.

    2 (15-ounce) cans cut sweet potatoes in light syrup,
        rinsed and drained well
    1 medium very ripe banana, cut into bite-size
        chunks
    ⅓ cup fresh orange juice
    1 tablespoon canola oil
    Salt and freshly ground black pepper, to taste
    1 jalapeño chili, seeded and finely chopped
        (optional)
    ¼ cup pecans or walnuts, coarsely chopped
    ¼ cup sweetened flaked coconut

Preheat oven to 350F (175C). Lightly oil an 8-inch-square baking dish and set aside.

In a medium bowl, mash together the sweet potatoes and banana until smooth but still slightly chunky. Add the orange juice, oil, salt, and pepper and mash until smooth. Stir in the chili (if using).

Transfer the mixture to the prepared baking dish. Top with the pecans and coconut. Cover with foil and bake 25 minutes. Uncover and bake an additional 5 minutes, or until the coconut is lightly toasted. Serve at once.

PER SERVING: Calories 194 • Protein 2g • Total Fat 7g • Sat. Fat 1g • Cholesterol 0mg • Carbohydrate 33g • Dietary Fiber 4g • Sodium 46mg

salt, ginger, and pepper. Mash well with a potato masher until very smooth. Stir in the scallions and serve at once. The mixture will become sticky as it cools.

PER SERVING: Calories 201 • Protein 4g • Total Fat 5g • Sat. Fat 4g • Cholesterol 0mg • Carbohydrate 39g • Dietary Fiber 6g • Sodium 248mg

Hawaiian-Style Mashed Taro with Ginger and Coconut

MAKES 5 TO 6 SERVINGS

Used to make the standard Hawaiian dish known as poi, taro is toxic in its raw state and must always be eaten fully cooked. Plastic gloves are recommended for sensitive individuals when handling the rough, hairy-like skins. Sweet potatoes or white potatoes can replace the taro, if desired, but cook for about half the amount of time.

1½ pounds taro, peeled and cubed
1 cup light coconut milk, heated
½ teaspoon salt, or to taste
¼ teaspoon ground ginger
Freshly ground black pepper, to taste
2 scallions, white and green parts, thinly sliced

In a large saucepan, bring the taro and enough salted water to cover by 2 inches to a boil over high heat. Reduce the heat slightly and boil, uncovered, until tender, about 40 minutes. Drain well. Return to the pan and add the coconut milk,

Thai-Style Barbecued Vegetables

MAKES 4 SERVINGS

Feel free to substitute your favorite veggies here—medium-thick asparagus, red onion, or parboiled new potatoes are especially tasty.

1 medium eggplant (about 12 ounces), unpeeled, cut into ½-inch-thick rounds, sprinkled with salt, and set in a colander to drain 30 minutes
1 cup fresh cilantro
6 large cloves garlic, peeled
Juice of 1 lime (about 2 tablespoons)
1 tablespoon low-sodium tamari or soy sauce
1 tablespoon toasted (dark) sesame oil
½ tablespoon salt
1 medium red or green bell pepper (about 6 ounces), cut lengthwise into 8 pieces
2 small zucchini (about 4 ounces each), preferably 1 green and 1 yellow, cut into ½-inch-thick rounds
Fresh cilantro leaves, for garnish (optional)

Rinse the drained eggplant under cold-running water. Drain well.

Place the cilantro, garlic, lime juice, tamari, oil,

and salt in a food processor fitted with the knife blade; process until smooth.

Place the eggplant, bell pepper, and zucchini in a large bowl. Add the cilantro mixture, tossing well to combine. Using your fingers, rub the marinade over all sides of the vegetables to thoroughly coat. Let stand 30 minutes at room temperature, or cover and refrigerate up to 1 day, turning a few times.

Meanwhile, prepare a medium-hot charcoal grill or gas grill, or preheat a broiler. Position the grill or oven rack 4 to 6 inches from heat source. If broiling, lightly oil a large baking sheet and set aside. Or heat a large nonstick stovetop grilling pan with ridges over medium-high heat.

Remove the vegetables from the marinade (discard any remaining marinade, or see Cook's Tip, below) and grill or broil the vegetables until browned and tender, 3 to 4 minutes per side for the bell pepper, and 2 to 3 minutes per side for the eggplant and zucchini, working in batches as necessary. Serve warm or at room temperature, garnished with fresh cilantro leaves (if using).

PER SERVING: Calories 79 • Protein 2g • Total Fat 4g • Sat. Fat 1g • Cholesterol 0mg • Carbohydrate 11g • Dietary Fiber 4g • Sodium 956mg

COOK'S TIP: *Cook 8 ounces somen, soba, lo mein, or rice noodles according to package instructions and toss the hot noodles with 1 teaspoon toasted (dark) sesame oil and remaining marinade. Serve warm or at room temperature, with the barbecued vegetables.*

Thai-Style Sweet-and-Sour Vegetables with Turmeric

MAKES 6 SERVINGS

Not surprisingly, this delicious vegetable dish is wonderful over jasmine rice. You can substitute broccoli for half or all of the cauliflower, if desired.

2 tablespoons canola oil

2 shallots, thinly sliced

2 large cloves garlic, finely chopped

¼ teaspoon crushed red pepper flakes, or more to taste

4 ounces baby carrots, cut lengthwise in half

½ pound cauliflower (about half a small head), separated into small florets

1 small cucumber (about 6 ounces), seeded and cut into 2-inch-long strips

1 small red bell pepper (about 4 ounces), cut into 2-inch-long strips

1 teaspoon ground turmeric

¼ cup distilled white vinegar

¼ cup water

1½ tablespoons sugar

Salt and freshly ground black pepper, to taste

½ cup salted roasted peanuts, crushed

In a large nonstick skillet or wok, heat the oil over medium heat. Add the shallots and cook, stirring often, until golden, 6 to 8 minutes. Transfer with a slotted spoon to paper towels to drain and reduce the heat to medium-low. Add the garlic and crushed red pepper flakes and cook, stirring constantly, 2 minutes. Add the carrots and cauliflower; cook, stirring, 3 minutes. Add the cucumber, bell pepper, and turmeric; cook, stirring, 2 minutes. Add the vinegar, water, sugar, salt, and black pepper and bring to a boil over high heat, stirring often; cook, stirring constantly, until vegetables are crisp-tender, 2 to 3 minutes. Serve hot, warm, or at room temperature, sprinkled with the reserved shallots and peanuts.

PER SERVING: Calories 159 • Protein 5g • Total Fat 11g • Sat. Fat 1g • Cholesterol 0mg • Carbohydrate 14g • Dietary Fiber 3g • Sodium 119mg

Baked "French-Fried" Yucca

MAKES 4 SERVINGS

Also known as cassava or tapioca, yucca root makes a tasty alternative to French-fried potatoes in this low-fat recipe. If you don't have time to prepare Papaya Ketchup, standard tomato ketchup can be substituted.

1 pound fresh yucca root, cut into 3-inch sections and peeled

1 tablespoon canola oil

½ tablespoon coarse salt, plus additional, to taste

Papaya Ketchup, to taste (opposite)

Preheat oven to 350F (175C). Lightly oil a baking sheet and set aside.

In a medium stockpot, bring the yucca and enough salted water to cover by 1 inch to a boil over high heat. Reduce the heat slightly and simmer, uncovered, until tender through the center, 20 to 25 minutes. With a slotted spoon, transfer the yucca to a cutting board to cool.

When cool enough to handle, cut the yucca lengthwise into ½-inch-wide strips, discarding the thin woody core. Transfer to the prepared baking sheet and toss with the oil and salt, arranging in a single layer. Cover with foil and bake in the center of the oven 8 minutes. Remove the baking sheet from the oven. Increase the oven temperature to 425F (220C).

Remove the foil and place the baking sheet on the upper oven rack. Bake 10 to 12 minutes, or until lightly browned. Serve at once, sprinkled with additional coarse salt, to taste.

PER SERVING (without Papaya Ketchup): Calories 166 • Protein 4g • Total Fat 4g • Sat. Fat 0g • Cholesterol 0mg • Carbohydrate 31g • Dietary Fiber 0g • Sodium 714mg

Papaya Ketchup

MAKES ABOUT 1 CUP

Use this tasty tropical ketchup as you would tomato ketchup. Mango can replace the papaya, if desired.

1½ tablespoons canola oil

½ cup chopped red onion

½ tablespoon chopped peeled fresh ginger

2 cloves garlic, finely chopped

1 small ripe papaya (about 1 pound), peeled, seeded, and chopped

½ cup water, plus additional, as needed

¼ cup sugar

¼ cup cider vinegar

¼ teaspoon salt, or to taste

¼ teaspoon hot pepper sauce

⅛ teaspoon ground allspice

Pinch ground cloves

In a medium saucepan, heat the oil over medium heat. Add the onion and ginger and cook, stirring, until the onion is softened, about 3 minutes. Add the garlic and cook, stirring constantly, 2 minutes. Add the papaya and cook, stirring constantly, about 3 minutes. Add the remaining ingredients and bring to a boil over medium-high heat, stirring and scraping the bottom to loosen any brown bits. Reduce the heat and simmer, uncovered, stirring occasionally, until thickened, about 20 minutes.

Transfer mixture to a food processor fitted with the knife blade, or to a blender; process until smooth and pureed, adding additional water as needed to achieve desired consistency. Let cool to room temperature before using. The ketchup can be stored, covered, in refrigerator up to 5 days before using.

PER TABLESPOON, OR ¹⁄₁₆ OF RECIPE:
Calories 34 • Protein 0g • Total Fat 1g • Sat. Fat 0g • Cholesterol 0mg • Carbohydrate 6g • Dietary Fiber 0g • Sodium 35mg

Desserts and Other Sweets

The luscious fruits and produce from the tropics are ripe for decadent desserts. With ingredients like sweet pineapple and coconut, tart lime and lemon, aromatic mango and papaya, tangy star fruit and orange, rich macadamias and chocolate, tropical desserts are deliciously exotic to the eye as well as to the palate. Consider a scrumptious Papaya-Pineapple Strudel, or a silken Kiwifruit-Lime Sorbet. If you're nuts about macadamias, crazy for bananas, and wild over chocolate, don't miss the Hawaiian Chocolate-Coated Frozen Bananas. If simple yet elegant is in order for your next dinner party, the Fresh Mango with Cointreau and Mint from Australia is a must. Wish you had a little treat to accompany a cup of tea or coffee? A slice of Trinidad Coconut Tea Bread or a Tropical Whole-Grain Muffin is sure to satisfy. If these recipes tempt you to get into the kitchen, feel free to experiment with different fruit-and-nut combinations, and create some irresistible tropical desserts of your own.

Java-Almond "Fudge"

MAKES ABOUT 20 PIECES

These Indonesian treats can also be made with cashews or pecans. Palm sugar is a coarse brown sugar with a distinct caramel flavor made from the sap of coconut palms. It can be located at Asian and international markets, typically in packages of individual sugar cakes. To make it easier to measure, microwave on low power about 10 seconds and crumble into smaller pieces. Light or dark brown sugar can be substituted.

¾ cup granulated white sugar

¼ cup packed palm sugar or packed light brown sugar

¼ cup water

½ teaspoon ground cinnamon

¼ teaspoon ground ginger

¼ teaspoon salt

1 teaspoon pure vanilla extract

½ cup slivered almonds, toasted (see Cook's Tip, opposite)

Line a baking sheet with waxed paper and set aside.

In a small heavy-bottomed saucepan, combine white sugar, palm sugar, water, cinnamon, ginger, and salt; bring to a brisk simmer over medium heat, stirring until the sugars are dissolved. Boil until the mixture forms a soft ball when dropped into cold water, or reaches 235F to 240F (118C to 120C) on a candy thermometer. Remove from heat and, working quickly, stir in the vanilla. Quickly add the almonds and stir about 10 seconds. Quickly drop by the heaping teaspoonfuls onto prepared baking sheet, making about 20 clusters. Let cool to room temperature. Transfer to an airtight container and store at room temperature for up to 5 days, or refrigerate for a few weeks.

PER PIECE: Calories 57 • Protein 1g • Total Fat 2g • Sat. Fat 0g • Cholesterol 0mg • Carbohydrate 11g • Dietary Fiber 0g • Sodium 28mg

COOK'S TIP: *To toast slivered almonds, chopped macadamia nuts, or other small nut shapes or pieces in the oven: Preheat the oven to 350F (175C). Spread the nuts in a single layer on an ungreased light-colored baking sheet. Bake until lightly golden, about 5 minutes, stirring halfway through the cooking time. Immediately remove from the baking sheet and set aside to cool. To toast on the stovetop: Heat a small skillet over medium heat. Add the nuts and cook, stirring constantly, until lightly golden, 3 to 5 minutes. Immediately remove from the skillet and set aside to cool. For larger whole nuts and nut pieces, increase the cooking time by a few minutes.*

Fuji Apples with Toasted Sesame Seeds

MAKES 4 TO 6 SERVINGS

The apple is the most heavily consumed imported fruit in Taiwan, and the Fuji variety, with its sweet taste and firm texture, is by far the favored variety. Brown rice syrup, a mild-flavored, naturally processed sweetener derived by culturing rice with enzymes to break down the starches, is available in health food stores and specialty markets. Although not authentic to the recipe, pure maple syrup is a delightful substitute.

3 medium Fuji apples (about 6 ounces each), unpeeled, cored, and cut into eighths

Juice of half a lemon (about 1½ tablespoons)

½ cup brown rice syrup or pure maple syrup

½ cup sesame seeds, toasted (see Cook's Tip, page 153)

Fresh mint, for garnish (optional)

In a small bowl, toss the apples with the lemon juice. Add the syrup and toss well to coat. Add half the sesame seeds and toss again. Transfer to a small platter and arrange in a circular manner. Sprinkle with the remaining sesame seeds and serve at once, garnished with mint (if using).

PER SERVING: Calories 226 • Protein 3g • Total Fat 8g • Sat. Fat 1g • Cholesterol 0mg • Carbohydrate 40g • Dietary Fiber 6g • Sodium 80mg

Brazilian Avocado Cream with Grapes

MAKES 6 SERVINGS

In Brazil, the avocado is glorified in desserts as well as savory dishes. If desired, omit the grapes and serve with apple or pear wedges.

    3 very ripe avocados, peeled, pitted, and quartered
    ¼ cup white grape, apple, or pear juice
    2 tablespoons granulated white sugar
    1 tablespoon palm sugar or light brown sugar
    1 tablespoon fresh lime juice
    24 to 36 seedless white grapes

In a food processor fitted with the knife blade, or in a blender, puree the avocados, juice, white sugar, half of the palm sugar, and lime juice until smooth. Transfer to 6 (4-ounce) ramekins or cus-

tard dishes and garnish each with 4 to 6 grapes. Sprinkle evenly with the remaining palm sugar (¼ teaspoon each). Cover and chill 1 to 4 hours (but no longer, as mixture will begin to brown). Serve chilled.

PER SERVING: Calories 204 • Protein 2g • Total Fat 16g • Sat. Fat 3g • Cholesterol 0mg • Carbohydrate 19g • Dietary Fiber 3g • Sodium 12mg

Banana Crepes with Tropical Fruit and Coconut Syrup

MAKES 4 (8-INCH) CREPES

Of course, you can have these delectable crepes for dessert, but why not for breakfast? Pure maple syrup can be used in lieu of the coconut syrup.

    1 cup all-purpose flour
    2 tablespoons sugar
    2 teaspoons baking powder
    ¼ teaspoon salt
    1 medium very ripe banana
    1¼ cups light coconut milk
    2 tablespoons water
    ½ teaspoon pure vanilla extract
    Assorted sliced fruit such as banana, mango, papaya, kiwifruit, and pineapple
    Coconut Syrup (page 132)

In a large bowl, whisk together the flour, sugar, baking powder, and salt.

In a small bowl, mash the banana with a fork and add ¼ cup of the coconut milk, mixing together until there are almost no lumps (some small lumps are okay). Stir in the remaining coconut milk, water, and vanilla. Add the banana mixture to the flour mixture and stir until smooth and combined.

Heat a 10-inch nonstick skillet over medium heat. Making one crepe at a time, drop one-fourth of the batter (about ⅔ cup) onto the hot skillet and swirl slightly to make a crepe about 8 inches in diameter; cook until several bubbles form on the surface, 2 to 3 minutes. Turn the crepe over and cook until underside is golden brown, about 2 more minutes. Repeat with remaining batter. To serve, place desired amount of fruit to one side of each crepe and fold over. Drizzle with syrup and serve at once, with additional syrup passed separately, if desired.

PER ONE CREPE (without fruit or syrup): Calories 252 • Protein 6g • Total Fat 8g • Sat. Fat 7g • Cholesterol 0mg • Carbohydrate 41g • Dietary Fiber 2g • Sodium 344mg

Coconut Syrup

MAKES ABOUT 1¼ CUPS

Use this scrumptious syrup as a topping for pancakes, crepes, waffles, cakes, fruits, sorbets, and nondairy frozen desserts. Thin with a touch of water, if desired.

1 (14-ounce) can light coconut milk

½ cup confectioners' sugar

1 teaspoon water, or more, if necessary

In a medium saucepan, combine the coconut milk and sugar. On a back burner (mixture tends to sputter), bring to a boil over medium-high heat, stirring constantly with a long-handled wooden spoon. Reduce the heat to medium-low and simmer, stirring frequently, until reduced to about

1¼ cups, 10 to 15 minutes. Remove from heat and let cool to lukewarm or room temperature before using. For a thinner consistency, stir in 1 teaspoon, or more, of water. Completely cooled syrup can be refrigerated, covered, up to one week. For best results, warm slightly before using.

PER TABLESPOON: Calories 37 • Protein 1g • Total Fat 2g • Sat. Fat 2g • Cholesterol 0mg • Carbohydrate 4g • Dietary Fiber 0g • Sodium 8mg

VARIATION: *To make Chocolate-Coconut Syrup, use chocolate confectioners' sugar in lieu of the regular variety.*

Banana-Chocolate-Coconut "Sushi Rolls"

MAKES 16 PIECES

Delight your guests with these delicious mock sushi desserts at your next party. Though optional, the kiwifruit and crystallized ginger nicely mimic green wasabi and pickled ginger, standard sushi condiments. Make sure the coconut is free of any clumps before using in the recipe.

1½ cups sweetened coconut flakes, plus additional, as necessary

4 ounces (¼ pound) bittersweet chocolate

2 large ripe bananas

Slices of fresh kiwifruit and/or chopped crystallized ginger (optional)

Divide the coconut between 2 shallow bowls or plates each large enough to hold one banana comfortably. Line a dinner-size plate with waxed paper.

Place chocolate in an 8½- or 9-inch microwave-safe pie dish. Microwave on 50 percent power for about 4 minutes, stirring halfway through cooking, or until most of the chocolate is melted.

Roll a banana in the chocolate to completely cover and immediately transfer to one of the bowls of coconut; turn to completely cover with flakes. Transfer to waxed paper, sprinkling with additional coconut to cover any exposed areas. Repeat with remaining banana, chocolate, and coconut. Refrigerate a minimum of 1 hour, or overnight (if refrigerating longer than 1 hour, cover loosely with waxed paper).

Just before serving, cut each banana into 8 pieces and arrange on a plate, garnished with sliced kiwi fruit and crystallized ginger (if using).

PER PIECE (without fruit or ginger): Calories 83 • Protein 1g • Total Fat 6g • Sat. Fat 4g • Cholesterol 0mg • Carbohydrate 9g • Dietary Fiber 2g • Sodium 19mg

Thai-Style Fried Banana Rolls

MAKES 8 BANANA ROLLS; 8 SERVINGS

This Thai recipe transforms the ordinary banana into something extraordinary. Just make sure that you use low-smoking oil such as peanut oil, and a wok or other high-sided pot or pan as the hot oil will spatter when you add the banana rolls.

8 (8-inch) round rice papers
4 medium ripe bananas, halved crosswise
Peanut oil, for frying

Confectioners' sugar
Coconut Syrup (opposite page) or pure maple syrup (optional)

Prepare a bowl of warm water large enough in which to dip the rice papers.

Working with one at a time, dip the rice paper in the water until it just begins to soften, 6 or 7 seconds. Transfer to a flat work surface. Working quickly, place a banana half on each wrapper. Fold the bottom of the wrapper up over the banana, and then fold each side toward the center. Roll from the bottom to the top of each roll, as tightly as you can without ripping the wrapper. Repeat with remaining papers and bananas.

Line a baking sheet or dinner plate with several layers of paper towels and set aside.

In a wok, medium stockpot, or other high-sided pot or pan, heat between 1 and 1½ inches of oil over medium-high heat. To test when oil is hot enough, using tongs, dip a corner of a roll in the oil; if oil begins to sizzle, the oil is ready. Working with 2 or 3 at a time, carefully place the rolls in the oil. Fry the rolls until golden brown, anywhere from a few seconds to 1 minute on each side, depending on the heat of the oil (oil will become hotter with each batch; if necessary, reduce the heat to medium). Transfer to the prepared baking sheet to absorb the excess oil. Repeat with remaining rolls. Serve hot, sprinkled with confectioners' sugar and accompanied by syrup (if using).

PER ROLL (without sugar or syrup, based on ¼ cup total peanut oil absorbed by fried rolls after draining): Calories 135 • Protein 1g • Total Fat 7g • Sat. Fat 1g • Cholesterol 0mg • Carbohydrate 18g • Dietary Fiber 1g • Sodium 46mg

Indonesian Sweet Banana Compote

MAKES 6 SERVINGS

From Java, this decadently sweet dessert is also a wonderful topping for Hawaiian Beer Cake (page 137).

½ cup light coconut milk
1 tablespoon cornstarch
1 cup water
1 cup packed light brown sugar
1 teaspoon ground cardamom
1 teaspoon ground cloves
½ teaspoon pure vanilla extract
6 medium ripe bananas, cut into 1-inch slices

In a small bowl, whisk together the coconut milk and cornstarch until thoroughly blended. Set aside.

In a medium saucepan, bring the water, sugar, cardamom, and cloves to a boil over medium heat, stirring often. Boil, stirring often, until thick and syrupy, 8 to 10 minutes.

Remove from heat and slowly add the coconut milk mixture, stirring constantly. Return to medium-low heat and stir in the vanilla. Add the bananas and simmer gently, stirring occasionally, until the liquid is the consistency of thin custard, about 8 minutes. Serve warm.

PER SERVING: Calories 273 • Protein 2g • Total Fat 3g • Sat. Fat 2g • Cholesterol 0mg • Carbohydrate 65g • Dietary Fiber 3g • Sodium 24mg

Mini Banana-Guava Pies

MAKES 9 SERVINGS

Individual ready-made graham cracker piecrusts make quick work of these extremely simple yet seriously delicious banana pies. Guava nectar is available in Latin and Caribbean markets, as well as the international aisle of many well-stocked supermarkets.

3 tablespoons cornstarch
3 tablespoons water
1¼ cups guava nectar
½ cup sugar
1 tablespoon fresh lemon juice
¼ teaspoon salt
2 medium ripe yet firm bananas
1½ (6-count) packages graham cracker piecrusts (9 crusts)
Sweetened coconut flakes (optional)

In a small container, mix together the cornstarch and water until thoroughly blended. Set aside.

In a small saucepan over medium heat, bring the guava nectar, sugar, lemon juice, and salt to a brisk simmer, stirring often. Stir in the cornstarch mixture and reduce the heat to medium-low; cook, stirring constantly, until thickened and glossy, about 2 minutes. Remove from heat and let cool to room temperature.

Peel and slice the bananas and add to the cooled guava mixture and stir to thoroughly combine. Spoon evenly into the piecrusts. Sprinkle evenly with coconut (if using), and serve at once. Or cover and refrigerate up to 1 day (but no longer, as the crusts may grow soggy), and serve chilled.

Aussie-Style Hurricane Finger Bananas

MAKES 4 SERVINGS

Though not quite as cute, four medium-size regular bananas, halved crosswise, can be used in lieu of the finger variety; the dish will still taste quite delicious.

- ⅓ cup guava nectar
- 2 tablespoons canola oil
- 2 tablespoons golden raisins
- 1 tablespoon cider vinegar
- 1 tablespoon molasses
- 1 tablespoon light brown sugar
- 1 tablespoon chopped peeled fresh ginger
- 1 tablespoon freshly grated orange peel
- 4 whole cloves
- 1 cinnamon stick
- 8 small ripe finger bananas (each 3 to 4 inches in length), peeled

In a skillet large enough to hold the bananas comfortably in a single layer, bring all the ingredients, except the bananas, to a boil over medium heat, stirring occasionally. Boil until the mixture is reduced by about one-third, 2 to 3 minutes. Reduce the heat to low and add the bananas, turning gently to evenly coat. Remove and discard the cloves and cinnamon. Serve warm, with equal portions of the sauce spooned over the bananas.

Hawaiian Chocolate-Coated Frozen Bananas

MAKES 4 GENEROUS OR 8 SNACK-SIZE SERVINGS

Although macadamia nuts and crystallized ginger lend this classic banana dessert a distinctly Hawaiian flavor, feel free to substitute with your other favorite combinations. Finely chopped almonds and grated coconut are equally delicious. To ensure that the chocolate coating sticks, the bananas must be frozen, so don't rush this step.

You will need eight flat wooden skewers.

- 4 medium ripe yet firm bananas
- 3 ounces bittersweet chocolate, chopped
- 1½ tablespoons vegetable shortening
- 2 tablespoons finely chopped macadamia nuts
- 1 to 2 tablespoons finely chopped crystallized ginger

Line a baking sheet with waxed paper. Peel the bananas and cut crosswise in half; insert skewers halfway through cut ends. Place on the prepared baking sheet and freeze about 3 hours, or until frozen.

Just before serving, place chocolate and shortening in a small, shallow microwave-safe bowl. Microwave on 50 percent power for about 3 minutes, stirring halfway through cooking, until most of the chocolate is melted. Add the nuts and ginger and mix well. Immediately dip each frozen banana half into chocolate mixture, turning to evenly coat (use a small spoon, if necessary, to completely coat). Place directly on serving plates or waxed-paper lined serving platter and serve within 15 minutes. Alternatively, wrap in waxed paper, place in self-sealing freezer bags, and store in the freezer up to 2 days.

PER SERVING: Calories 297 • Protein 4g • Total Fat 20g • Sat. Fat 9g • Cholesterol 0mg • Carbohydrate 33g • Dietary Fiber 6g • Sodium 6mg

Banana-Orange Brown-Rice Pudding

MAKES 6 SERVINGS

If serving this healthy whole grain rice pudding chilled, a garnish of shredded coconut is a nice touch.

- 1 large banana, cut into ¼-inch-thick slices
- 1 (11-ounce) can mandarin orange segments, drained well
- ¼ cup water
- 1 tablespoon molasses
- 1 tablespoon brown rice syrup or light corn syrup
- ½ teaspoon pure vanilla extract
- ½ teaspoon ground cinnamon
- ¼ teaspoon ground nutmeg
- ¼ teaspoon salt
- 2 cups cooked brown rice (see Cook's Tip, page 79)
- ⅔ cup light coconut milk
- Sweetened shredded coconut (optional)

In a medium saucepan, combine the banana, oranges, water, molasses, rice syrup, vanilla, cinnamon, nutmeg, and salt. Bring to a simmer over medium heat, stirring occasionally. Add the rice and coconut milk and return to a simmer, stirring occasionally. Reduce the heat to medium-low and simmer, uncovered, until the mixture is thickened, stirring often from the bottom to prevent sticking, 5 to 10 minutes. Serve warm, chilled, or at room temperature, garnished with the shredded coconut (if using).

PER SERVING: Calories 168 • Protein 3g • Total Fat 4g • Sat. Fat 3g • Cholesterol 0mg • Carbohydrate 31g • Dietary Fiber 2g • Sodium 105mg

Taiwanese Bananas and Star Fruit with Cinnamon–Coconut Cream Sauce

MAKES 6 SERVINGS

The cream sauce can also be used as a delicious topping for countless fruits, cakes, pies, and crepes.

- 1 (14-ounce) can light coconut milk
- 1 tablespoon cornstarch
- ½ cup cream of coconut, such as Coco López
- 2 tablespoons sugar
- ½ teaspoon ground cinnamon, or to taste
- 6 medium ripe yet firm bananas, quartered
- 1 star fruit, trimmed and thinly sliced (see Cook's Tip, page 55)
- Fresh mint (optional)

In a small container, mix together 3 tablespoons of the coconut milk and the cornstarch until thoroughly blended. Set aside.

In a small saucepan, bring the remaining coconut milk, cream of coconut, sugar, and cinnamon to a boil over medium heat, whisking often. Add the cornstarch mixture and cook, whisking constantly, until thickened, about 2 minutes. Remove from heat and let cool slightly.

Peel the bananas, cut in half crosswise, and cut the halves into quarters. Divide the bananas evenly among 6 bowls and cover with equal amounts of sauce. Top with equal amounts of the star fruit and garnish with the mint (if using). Serve at once.

PER SERVING: Calories 283 • Protein 4g • Total Fat 15g • Sat. Fat 13g • Cholesterol 0mg • Carbohydrate 39g • Dietary Fiber 4g • Sodium 28mg

Hawaiian Beer Cake

MAKES 12 SERVINGS

This makes a nice and light fruitcake for the holidays. Any beer can be used with success, as long as it is at room temperature. If you can't locate a tropical dried fruit blend, make your own or use all raisins. For an extra-special dessert, serve with the optional Hawaiian Coconut Sauce. Your guests will thank you.

1½ cups beer, preferably a Hawaiian brew such as
    Kona, at room temperature

1 cup molasses

½ cup canola oil

1 cup dried tropical fruit blend (mango, papaya,
    pineapple)

½ cup golden raisins

3 cups all-purpose flour

1 tablespoon baking powder

1 teaspoon salt

1 teaspoon ground cinnamon

¼ teaspoon baking soda

¼ teaspoon ground nutmeg

¼ teaspoon ground ginger

¼ teaspoon ground cloves

½ cup chopped macadamia nuts or walnuts

Confectioners' sugar

Hawaiian Coconut Sauce (page 138, optional)

Preheat oven to 375F (190C). Liberally grease an 8-cup fluted tube pan with shortening and dust lightly with flour, shaking out excess. Set aside.

In a large bowl, whisk together the beer, molasses, and canola oil. Stir in the tropical fruit blend and raisins and let stand about 10 minutes to allow the fruit to soften. Stir again.

In another large bowl, whisk together the flour, baking powder, salt, cinnamon, baking soda, nutmeg, ginger, and cloves until thoroughly combined. Gradually add the beer mixture, mixing well to thoroughly combine. Stir in the nuts and transfer the batter to the prepared pan. Bake in the center of the oven 40 to 50 minutes, or until a toothpick inserted in the center comes out clean. (If cake appears to be browning too quickly after about 30 minutes, cover loosely with foil.) Cool on a wire rack 15 minutes before inverting onto a plate. Let cool completely before dusting with confectioners' sugar. Serve with the sauce (if using).

PER SERVING (without confectioners' sugar or sauce): Calories 362 • Protein 4g • Total Fat 14g • Sat. Fat 1g • Cholesterol 0mg • Carbohydrate 56g • Dietary Fiber 2g • Sodium 310mg

Hawaiian Coconut Sauce

This versatile coconut sauce, also known as *haupia* sauce, makes a delicious topping for countless fruits, cakes, pies, and crepes. You can add ½ teaspoon vanilla extract and/or ¼ teaspoon almond extract, if desired.

- 1¼ cups light coconut milk
- ¼ cup water
- ¼ cup sugar
- 1 tablespoon cornstarch

In a small saucepan, whisk together all the ingredients. Bring to a boil over medium heat, whisking frequently; boil 15 seconds, whisking constantly. Remove from heat and let cool to room temperature. Serve at room temperature, stirring just before serving. Or cover and refrigerate a minimum of 2 hours, or up to 2 days, and serve chilled or return to room temperature.

PER TABLESPOON: Calories 24 • Protein 0g • Total Fat 1g • Sat. Fat 1g • Cholesterol 0mg • Carbohydrate 3g • Dietary Fiber 0g • Sodium 5mg

Baked Churros

This baked version is not only healthier than the traditional deep-fried churros, but easier to make with the help of ready-made flour tortillas. Top with Coconut Sorbet (page 140) for an extra-special dessert.

- 2 tablespoons sugar
- ¼ teaspoon ground cinnamon
- 6 (6-inch) snack-size flour tortillas
- 3 tablespoons canola oil

Preheat oven to 450F (230C). In a small bowl, combine the sugar and cinnamon and set aside.

Place tortillas on an ungreased large baking sheet and brush both sides evenly with the oil. Sprinkle the tops evenly with the sugar mixture. Bake in the center of the oven until golden and puffed in spots, about 5 minutes, taking care not to burn. Serve at once.

PER SERVING: Calories 190 • Protein 3g • Total Fat 9g • Sat. Fat 1g • Cholesterol 0mg • Carbohydrate 24g • Dietary Fiber 1g • Sodium 167mg

Caribbean Cocoa Ice

A cross between a sorbet and granita, this refreshing tropical chocolate ice can be enjoyed year-round. For a special summertime presentation, scoop on top of fresh pineapple rings.

- ⅔ cup sugar
- 3 tablespoons unsweetened cocoa powder, preferably Dutch processed
- 1¾ cups water
- 3 tablespoons frozen pineapple juice concentrate, thawed
- 1 tablespoon dark rum

In a small saucepan, combine the sugar and cocoa powder. Add the water and bring to a boil over medium heat, stirring until the sugar is dissolved. Reduce the heat and simmer gently, 3 minutes. Remove from heat and let cool to room temperature. Stir in the pineapple juice concentrate and rum. Cover and refrigerate a minimum of 1 hour.

Transfer the chilled mixture to a shallow metal pan, such as a cake pan. Place in the freezer until almost frozen solid, 4 to 6 hours, stirring from the outside toward the center every couple hours, if possible. (At this point, the mixture can be stored, covered, in freezer up to 5 days.) If too hard to scoop, let thaw about 30 minutes in the refrigerator, or break up into chunks and process with on/off motions in a food processor fitted with the knife blade until fairly smooth.

To serve, scoop the mixture into chilled dessert bowls or goblets. Serve at once.

PER SERVING: Calories 167 • Protein 1g • Total Fat 1g • Sat. Fat 0g • Cholesterol 0mg • Carbohydrate 41g • Dietary Fiber 2g • Sodium 2mg

Hawaiian Coconut Pudding

MAKES 8 SERVINGS

This traditional luau favorite, known as *haupia* pudding in Hawaii, is best made with full-fat coconut milk. Thin slices of kiwifruit can replace the banana, or, if you'd rather, omit the fruit altogether.

1 medium ripe banana, thinly sliced

1 teaspoon fresh lemon or lime juice

1½ cups coconut milk

1½ cups water

¼ teaspoon almond extract

½ cup plus 2 tablespoons sugar

½ cup plus 2 tablespoons cornstarch

⅓ cup sweetened coconut flakes, toasted if desired

Lightly oil an 8-inch-square baking dish and set aside.

In a small bowl, toss the banana slices with the lemon juice and set aside.

In a medium saucepan, bring the coconut milk, water, almond extract, sugar, and cornstarch to a gentle simmer over medium heat, whisking almost constantly, about 8 minutes. Reduce heat to low and cook, whisking constantly, until mixture is thick and can easily stick to the whisk, about 2 more minutes. Pour half the pudding mixture into the prepared dish and top with the banana slices, pressing down gently with your fingers to partially immerse. Cover with remaining pudding mixture. Sprinkle evenly with the coconut flakes. Let cool to room temperature. Cover with plastic wrap and refrigerate until set, about 4 to 6 hours, or up to 1 day. Cut into 8 squares and serve chilled.

PER SERVING: Calories 230 • Protein 1g • Total Fat 12g • Sat. Fat 10g • Cholesterol 0mg • Carbohydrate 32g • Dietary Fiber 1g • Sodium 16mg

VARIATION: *Pour the hot pudding into a lightly oiled 5-cup ring mold. Omit the banana and reserve the coconut flakes. Allow pudding to set as otherwise directed in the recipe. Unmold and fill the center with cubes of tropical fruit, sprinkling with the reserved coconut flakes.*

Coconut Sorbet

MAKES 6 SERVINGS

Coconut water is available in Latin markets and the international aisle of many well-stocked supermarkets. For a creamier sorbet, use all full-fat coconut milk.

1 cup coconut water

¾ cup sugar

1 cup regular coconut milk

1 cup light coconut milk

½ teaspoon coconut-flavored rum (optional)

In a small saucepan, combine coconut water with sugar and cook over low heat until sugar is dissolved. Stir in the coconut milks and rum (if using). Transfer to a covered container and refrigerate until well chilled, 2 to 3 hours.

Freeze in an ice cream maker according to manufacturer's instructions. Alternatively, pour into 2 (16-cube) ice cube trays and freeze until solid, 4 to 6 hours. Transfer to a food processor fitted with the metal blade; process until smooth, working in batches, if necessary. If not serving immediately, transfer to a covered plastic container and store in the freezer up to 3 days. If too hard to scoop, let thaw about 30 minutes in the refrigerator, or break up into chunks and process with on/off motions in a food processor fitted with the knife blade until fairly smooth.

To serve, scoop the mixture into chilled dessert bowls or goblets. Serve at once.

PER SERVING: Calories 237 • Protein 3g • Total Fat 13g • Sat. Fat 11g • Cholesterol 0mg • Carbohydrate 31g • Dietary Fiber 0g • Sodium 23mg

COOK'S TIP: *To remove the frozen sorbet cubes more easily, dip the bottom of the ice cube tray briefly in tepid water.*

Trinidad Coconut Tea Bread

MAKES 1 LOAF; 12 SLICES

You can add ½ cup chopped macadamia or walnuts to this delicious tea bread for added crunch and protein, if desired.

1½ cups all-purpose flour

½ cup sugar, plus additional for sprinkling

½ tablespoon baking powder

½ teaspoon salt

1 very ripe banana, mashed well

¾ cup sweetened flaked coconut

½ cup light coconut milk

¼ cup canola oil

½ teaspoon pure vanilla extract

Preheat oven to 350F (175C). Lightly oil a 9×5-inch loaf pan and set aside.

In a large bowl, using a wire whisk, combine the flour, ½ cup sugar, baking powder, and salt. In a medium bowl, mix together the banana, flaked coconut, coconut milk, oil, and vanilla until thoroughly blended. Gradually stir the banana mixture into the flour mixture until moistened and combined.

Transfer the batter to the prepared pan. Sprinkle the top lightly with sugar. Bake on the center rack about 40 minutes, until a toothpick inserted in the center comes out clean. Let cool 10 minutes before removing from the pan to a wire rack to cool to room temperature. Completely cooled bread can be stored in an airtight container up to 2 days at room temperature, or frozen up to 1 month.

PER SLICE: Calories 172 • Protein 2g • Total Fat 7g • Sat. Fat 3g • Cholesterol 0mg • Carbohydrate 25g • Dietary Fiber 1g • Sodium 150mg

with the remaining sugar mixture (do not toss). Cover and refrigerate a minimum of 3 hours, or overnight. Just before serving, toss gently and serve chilled.

PER SERVING: Calories 132 • Protein 1g • Total Fat 1g • Sat. Fat 0g • Cholesterol 0mg • Carbohydrate 34g • Dietary Fiber 4g • Sodium 5mg

Taiwanese Fruit Salad with Five-Spice

MAKE 4 SERVINGS

The island of Taiwan is world-renowned for its high-quality fruits, tropical and nontropical alike. Feel free to substitute with your favorites.

    2 tablespoons granulated white sugar
    1 tablespoon palm or light brown sugar
    ¼ teaspoon Chinese five-spice powder
    ¼ teaspoon almond extract
    1 large mango (about 14 ounces), peeled, pitted, and sliced
    1 large banana, peeled and sliced
    2 kiwifruit, peeled and sliced
    ½ cup sliced fresh strawberries
    2 tablespoons fresh lime juice

In a small bowl, mix together the white sugar, palm sugar, and five-spice powder. Sprinkle with the almond extract and mix again. Set aside.

In a medium bowl, toss the fruit and lime juice gently until combined. Sprinkle with half the sugar mixture and toss again. Sprinkle the top

Kiwifruit-Lime Sorbet

MAKES 4 TO 6 SERVINGS

Impress your guests with this luscious and refreshing sorbet at your next dinner party.

    1 cup water
    ½ cup sugar
    ½ cup light corn syrup
    About 3 kiwifruits, peeled
    5 teaspoons fresh lime juice
    ½ teaspoon finely grated fresh lime peel

In a small saucepan, combine the water, sugar, and corn syrup. Cook over medium heat, stirring constantly, just until the sugar is dissolved. Remove from heat and let cool to room temperature.

In a food processor fitted with the knife blade, or in a blender, process enough kiwifruit to equal ¾ cup puree. Add cooled sugar mixture, lime juice, and lime peel; process until combined. Transfer to a shallow metal pan, such as a cake pan.

Place the pan in the freezer for 1 to 2 hours, or until mixture is firm but not solid. Using a wire whisk, whisk until well combined. Return to the freezer and freeze 2 to 3 more hours, or until firm enough to scoop. (At this point, the sorbet can be stored, covered, in freezer up to 5 days.) If too hard to scoop, let thaw about 30 minutes in the refrigerator, or break up into chunks and process with on/off motions in a food processor fitted with the knife blade until fairly smooth.

To serve, scoop the mixture into chilled dessert bowls or goblets. Serve at once.

PER SERVING: Calories 254 • Protein 1g • Total Fat 0g • Sat. Fat 0g • Cholesterol 0mg • Carbohydrate 67g • Dietary Fiber 2g • Sodium 32mg

Mixed Tropical Fruit Salad with Coconut Cream

MAKES 6 TO 8 SERVINGS

Perfect for a party, this delicious tropical fruit salad can be prepared with just about any fruit, so feel free to substitute the suggested ones with your own favorites. If using bananas, add them just before serving.

½ cup cream of coconut, such as Coco López
1 tablespoon fresh lime juice
2 cups cubed fresh pineapple
2 cups cubed fresh mango
2 cups cubed seedless watermelon
2 cups cubed honeydew
2 cups cubed cantaloupe
Sweetened flaked coconut (optional)

In a large bowl, whisk together the cream of coconut and lime juice until thoroughly blended. Add the remaining ingredients, except the flaked coco-nut, and toss gently yet thoroughly to combine. Cover and refrigerate a minimum of 2 hours, or overnight. Toss just before serving. Serve chilled, sprinkled with the flaked coconut (if using).

PER SERVING: Calories 186 • Protein 2g • Total Fat 8g • Sat. Fat 6g • Cholesterol 0mg • Carbohydrate 32g • Dietary Fiber 3g • Sodium 14mg

Thai Tropical Fruit Salad with Basil

MAKES 4 SERVINGS

A member of the mint family, basil is an ideal garnish here. Feel free to vary the tropical fruit according to what's available at the market.

2 cups cubed fresh pineapple
1 banana, peeled and sliced
1 kiwifruit, peeled and sliced
1 cup sliced strawberry papaya, regular papaya, or mango
2 tablespoons light brown sugar, or more, to taste
Juice of 1 lime, or more, to taste
4 large basil or mint leaves, cut into thin strips
Sweetened shredded coconut (optional)

Place the fruit in a medium bowl and sprinkle with the sugar and lime juice; toss gently yet thoroughly to combine. Let stand about 10 minutes before tossing gently again, adding additional sugar or lime juice, if desired. Serve at once, garnished with the basil and coconut (if using). Alternatively, cover and refrigerate up to 12 hours and serve chilled.

Guava Ice

MAKES 6 SERVINGS

Guava nectar can be found in Latin markets and the international aisle of many well-stocked supermarkets. Any fruit nectar can replace the guava.

    3 cups guava nectar
    ⅔ cup light corn syrup
    ¼ cup superfine sugar
    2 tablespoons fresh lime or lemon juice

In a medium bowl, mix together all the ingredients until thoroughly blended. Let stand about 5 minutes to allow the sugar to dissolve; mix briefly again. Cover and refrigerate a minimum of 1 hour.

Transfer the chilled mixture to a shallow metal pan, such as a cake pan. Place in the freezer until almost frozen solid, 4 to 6 hours, stirring from the outside toward the center every hour, if possible. (At this point, the ice can be stored, covered, in freezer up to 5 days.) If too hard to scoop, let thaw about 30 minutes in the refrigerator, or break up into chunks and process with on/off motions in a food processor fitted with the knife blade until fairly smooth.

To serve, scoop the mixture into chilled dessert bowls or goblets. Serve at once.

Florida Key Lime Ice

MAKES 5 SERVINGS

The Key lime is smaller and seedier than the more common Tahitian or Persian lime, and its juice is considered to be more flavorful. If you don't have access to fresh Key limes, substitute with equal parts regular lime juice and lemon juice.

    1 cup water
    ¼ cup sugar
    ⅓ cup fresh Key lime juice, or equal parts fresh
        Persian lime and lemon juice

In a small saucepan, heat the water and sugar over low heat, stirring until the sugar dissolves. Remove from heat and let cool to room temperature. Stir in the lime juice. Divide evenly among 5 (3-ounce) paper cups. Place in freezer until partially frozen, 1 to 2 hours. Insert a small wooden or plastic spoon into center of each cup and return to the freezer until frozen solid, 2 to 3 hours. Serve frozen.

Lychee Sorbet

MAKES 6 TO 8 SERVINGS

This exotic, pale sorbet looks lovely in colorful dishes, or garnished with fresh tropical fruit, such as pineapple or kiwifruit.

2 (20-ounce) cans lychees packed in light syrup,
   1 drained, 1 undrained
¼ cup light corn syrup
1 tablespoon fresh lemon juice
¼ teaspoon ground cinnamon
⅛ teaspoon ground ginger
Pinch ground cloves

In a food processor fitted with the knife blade, or in a blender, process or blend all ingredients until smooth and pureed.

Freeze in an ice-cream maker according to the manufacturer's directions. Alternatively, pour into 2 (16-cube) ice cube trays and freeze until solid, 4 to 6 hours. Transfer to a food processor fitted with the metal blade; process until smooth, working in batches, if necessary. If not serving immediately, transfer to a covered plastic container and store in the freezer up to 3 days. If too hard to scoop, let thaw about 30 minutes in the refrigerator, or break up into chunks and process with on/off motions in a food processor fitted with the knife blade until fairly smooth.

To serve, scoop the mixture into chilled dessert bowls or goblets. Serve at once.

PER SERVING: Calories 189 • Protein 1g • Total Fat 0g • Sat. Fat 0g • Cholesterol 0mg • Carbohydrate 49g • Dietary Fiber 1g • Sodium 12mg

Lychee Compote in Puff Pastry Cups

MAKES 6 SERVINGS

This unusual and delicious compote also makes a fine topping for Coconut Sorbet (page 140). The dried cherries, though not tropical, lend the pale lychees pretty flecks of color.

1 (10-ounce) package frozen puff pastry shells
   (6 shells)
½ tablespoon cornstarch
½ cup water
1 (15-ounce) can lychees in light syrup, well drained
   and halved
½ cup sugar
¼ cup sweetened dried tiny cherries or cranberries
1 tablespoon fresh lemon juice

Bake the pastry according to package directions. (If not serving immediately, let cool completely and store in an airtight container at room temperature up to 24 hours. Reheat in a low oven to crisp just before serving.) In a small container, stir the cornstarch into 1 tablespoon of the water until smooth.

In a small saucepan, bring the lychees, sugar, remaining water, dried cherries, and lemon juice to a gentle simmer over medium heat, stirring occasionally. Add the cornstarch mixture and bring to a boil, stirring gently and constantly. Reduce heat to between low and medium-low and simmer gently, stirring occasionally, until thickened, about 5 minutes. Remove from heat and let cool about 15 minutes. (At this point, the compote can be brought to room temperature and refrigerated, covered, up to 3 days before reheating gently and proceeding with the following recipe, or using chilled or at room temperature in other recipes.)

To serve, place a pastry shell on each of 6 dessert plates and fill with equal amounts of the compote (some will overflow). Serve warm.

PER SERVING: Calories 384 • Protein 4g • Total Fat 18g • Sat. Fat 3g • Cholesterol 0mg • Carbohydrate 53g • Dietary Fiber 0g • Sodium 119mg

Hawaiian Macadamia Lace Cookies

MAKES ABOUT 2 DOZEN COOKIES

Thin, crispy, and sweet, these melt-in-your mouth cookies are wonderful with a cup of coffee, or crumbled over frozen desserts and puddings. For lacy edges, bake only one sheet of cookies at a time.

- 1 cup all-purpose flour
- ½ cup macadamia nuts, very finely chopped
- 4 teaspoons unsweetened cocoa powder
- ½ teaspoon ground cinnamon
- ¼ teaspoon salt
- ½ cup vegetable shortening
- ½ cup light corn syrup
- ½ cup packed light brown sugar

Preheat the oven to 375F (190C). Lightly oil 2 large baking sheets and set aside.

In a medium bowl, whisk together the flour, nuts, cocoa powder, cinnamon, and salt. Set aside.

In a medium saucepan, bring the shortening, corn syrup, and brown sugar to a boil over medium heat, stirring constantly. Remove from heat and gradually stir in the flour mixture.

Drop the dough by level tablespoons, about 3 inches apart, onto the prepared baking sheets. Working with 1 sheet at a time, bake 5 to 7 minutes, until bubbling and edges look crisp. Let cool on the baking sheet about 1 to 2 minutes (separate cookies, if necessary, with the edge of a spatula), then transfer with a spatula to a wire rack to cool. Completely cooled cookies can be stored in airtight containers up to 1 week.

PER COOKIE: Calories 114 • Protein 1g • Total Fat 6g • Sat. Fat 2g • Cholesterol 0mg • Carbohydrate 14g • Dietary Fiber 1g • Sodium 29mg

Fresh Mango with Cointreau and Mint

MAKES 4 SERVINGS

This simply elegant recipe comes from Australia, where the Western world's influence is apparent in many of the tropical dishes.

- 2 large mangoes (about 14 ounces each), peeled, pitted, and sliced
- Juice of 1 to 2 limes
- ½ tablespoon sugar
- 4 tablespoons Cointreau, Grand Marnier, or other orange liqueur
- Chopped fresh mint, for garnish

In a medium bowl, toss the mangoes with the lime juice and sugar. Let stand about 10 minutes at room temperature, and then toss again. (At this point, the mixture can be refrigerated, covered, up to 12 hours before continuing with the recipe.)

Transfer to individual serving bowls and drizzle each serving with 1 tablespoon of the orange liqueur. Sprinkle with the mint and serve at once.

PER SERVING: Calories 121 • Protein 1g • Total Fat 0g • Sat. Fat 0g • Cholesterol 0mg • Carbohydrate 24g • Dietary Fiber 2g • Sodium 2mg

Remove from the heat and serve warm or at room temperature, garnished with the coconut and mint (if using). Alternatively, cover and refrigerate up to 1 day and serve chilled.

PER SERVING: Calories 110 • Protein 1g • Total Fat 0g • Sat. Fat 0g • Cholesterol 0mg • Carbohydrate 26g • Dietary Fiber 2g • Sodium 6mg

Hot Gingered Mango

MAKES 4 SERVINGS

This virtually fat-free dessert is also delicious served chilled.

2½ cups cubed fresh mango
⅓ cup mango-peach-orange juice blend, or other mango combination
2 tablespoons sugar
1 tablespoon fresh lime juice
1 teaspoon freshly grated orange peel
Pinch ground cinnamon, or more to taste
1 tablespoon chopped crystallized ginger
Shredded sweetened coconut, for garnish (optional)
Fresh mint, for garnish (optional)

In a food processor fitted with the knife blade, or in a blender, process ½ cup of the mango until smooth and pureed. Set aside.

In a medium saucepan, combine the juice blend, sugar, lime juice, orange peel, and cinnamon; bring to a boil over medium heat, stirring occasionally. Boil until mixture is slightly reduced, about 1 minute. Reduce the heat to low and add the pureed mango and ginger; cook, stirring, 1 minute. Add the remaining cubed mango and cook, stirring, until just warmed, about 1 minute.

Australian Mango and Lychee Fruit Salad with Passion Fruit Syrup

MAKES 6 SERVINGS

You can also serve this exotic fruit salad with Papaya Coulis (page 151), if desired.

4 large mangoes (about 14 ounce each), peeled, pitted, and sliced
1 (20-ounce) can lychees in light syrup, drained
½ recipe Passion Fruit Syrup (opposite page), plus additional, to serve
¼ cup fresh mint leaves, coarsely chopped

Arrange mango slices and lychees on 6 deep-rimmed dessert plates. Drizzle each serving with about 2 tablespoons of the syrup and garnish with the mint. Serve at once, with additional syrup passed separately.

PER SERVING: Calories 246 • Protein 2g • Total Fat 1g • Sat. Fat 0g • Cholesterol 0mg • Carbohydrate 63g • Dietary Fiber 5g • Sodium 8mg

Passion Fruit Syrup

MAKES ABOUT 1½ CUPS

Use this delicious syrup on pancakes, crepes, and waffles, as well as countless fruits, cakes, puddings, and sorbets. The following recipe retains the edible seeds, which are loaded with fiber and are a pretty addition to the fruit salad to boot; if desired, you can strain them out before using the syrup. Ripe passion fruit appears dry and very wrinkled. If necessary, use the frozen pulp, available in Latin markets and other specialty stores, as well as some well-stocked supermarkets.

- 1 cup sugar
- ½ cup passion fruit pulp with seeds (from about 7 ripe passion fruits)
- ½ cup fresh orange juice
- ¼ cup fresh lemon juice
- ¼ cup water

In a small heavy-bottomed saucepan, bring all the ingredients to a boil over medium-high heat, stirring constantly until the sugar dissolves. Reduce the heat to medium-low and simmer, stirring occasionally, until reduced to about 1½ cups, 10 to 15 minutes. Remove from heat and let cool completely to room temperature (syrup will thicken as it cools). The syrup can be refrigerated, covered, up to 2 days before using. For best results, serve slightly chilled or return to room temperature.

PER ¼ CUP: Calories 160 • Protein 1g • Total Fat 0g • Sat. Fat 0g • Cholesterol 0mg • Carbohydrate 41g • Dietary Fiber 2g • Sodium 6mg

Hawaiian Mango-Nut Sweet Bread

MAKES 1 LOAF; 12 SLICES

This sweet bread is wonderful with a cup of tea. Select a ripe mango whose flesh is still firm, not mushy.

- 1 cup all-purpose flour
- ¾ cup sugar
- ½ teaspoon baking soda
- ¼ teaspoon salt
- ¼ teaspoon ground cinnamon
- 1 very ripe banana, mashed well
- ¼ cup canola oil
- ½ teaspoon pure vanilla extract
- 1 cup chopped mango (about 1 medium)
- ¼ cup chopped dates or raisins
- ¼ cup chopped macadamia nuts or walnuts

Preheat oven to 350F (175C). Lightly oil a 9×5-inch loaf pan and set aside.

In a large bowl, using a wire whisk, combine the flour, sugar, baking soda, salt, and cinnamon. In a medium bowl, mix together the banana, oil, and vanilla until thoroughly blended. Gradually stir the banana mixture into the flour mixture until moistened and combined (batter will be stiff). Stir in the mango, dates, and nuts. Transfer to the prepared pan. Bake on the center rack 40 to 55 minutes, until a toothpick inserted in the center comes out clean. Let cool 10 minutes before removing from the pan to a wire rack. Cool to room temperature. Completely cooled bread can be stored in an airtight container up to 2 days at room temperature, or frozen up to 1 month.

PER SLICE: Calories 177 • Protein 2g • Total Fat 7g • Sat. Fat 1g • Cholesterol 0mg • Carbohydrate 29g • Dietary Fiber 2g • Sodium 98mg

Mango Sorbet

MAKES 4 TO 6 SERVINGS

Thawed frozen mango chunks can be used in lieu of the fresh, if desired.

3 cups fresh mango chunks

⅔ cup light corn syrup

¼ cup fresh lemon or lime juice

2 tablespoons superfine sugar

In a food processor fitted with the knife blade, or in a blender, process or blend all the ingredients until very smooth. Let stand about 5 minutes to allow the sugar to dissolve; process briefly again.

Freeze in an ice-cream maker according to the manufacturer's directions. Or transfer to a shallow metal pan, such as a cake pan. Place the pan in the freezer for 1 to 1½ hours, or until mixture is firm but not solid. Using a wire whisk, whisk until well combined. Return to the freezer and freeze 2 more hours, or until firm enough to scoop. (At this point, the sorbet can be stored, covered, in freezer up to 5 days.) If too hard to scoop, let thaw about 30 minutes in the refrigerator, or break up into chunks and process with on/off motions in a food processor fitted with the knife blade until fairly smooth.

To serve, scoop the mixture into chilled dessert bowls or goblets. Serve at once.

PER SERVING: Calories 263 • Protein 1g • Total Fat 0g • Sat. Fat 0g • Cholesterol 0mg • Carbohydrate 71g • Dietary Fiber 2g • Sodium 40mg

Tropical Whole-Grain Muffins

MAKES 12 MUFFINS

These healthy whole-grain muffins freeze well. Pineapple can replace the kiwi or mango, if desired.

¾ cup all-purpose flour

½ cup whole wheat flour

½ cup stone-ground cornmeal

½ cup sugar

1 tablespoon baking powder

½ teaspoon salt

½ cup canola oil

½ cup light coconut milk

1 very ripe banana, mashed

2 tablespoons pineapple preserves

½ cup chopped kiwifruit (about 1 medium)

½ cup chopped mango

½ cup sweetened flaked coconut

Preheat oven to 400F (205C). Line a 12-cup muffin pan with paper liners and set aside.

In a medium bowl, whisk together the flours, cornmeal, sugar, baking powder, and salt until well combined. Set aside.

In a large bowl, whisk together the oil, coconut milk, banana, and preserves until thoroughly blended. Stir in kiwifruit, mango, and flaked coconut, mixing well to combine.

Add the dry ingredients to the fruit mixture, stirring until combined.

Spoon the batter into the prepared muffin pan. Bake 15 to 20 minutes, or until a toothpick inserted in the center of a muffin comes out clean. Serve warm or at room temperature. Completely cooled muffins can be stored at room temperature in an airtight container up to 2 days, or frozen up to 1 month.

PER MUFFIN: Calories 228 • Protein 3g • Total Fat 11g • Sat. Fat 2g • Cholesterol 0mg • Carbohydrate 31g • Dietary Fiber 3g • Sodium 196mg

Caramel-Lime Oranges

MAKES 4 TO 6 SERVINGS

This is a great make-ahead, fat-free dessert to serve company. It also makes a wonderful topping for Coconut Sorbet (page 140).

½ cup sugar
¼ cup water
4 large navel oranges, peeled and segmented
Juice of half a lime

In a small saucepan, combine the sugar and water. Cook over low heat, stirring gently just until the sugar dissolves. Increase the heat to medium-high and bring to a boil. Reduce the heat to medium and simmer briskly without stirring until mixture is a light caramel color, about 10 minutes, shaking the saucepan a few times to promote even heating. Remove from heat and let cool 1 minute (but no longer, as mixture will harden).

Meanwhile, place the orange segments in a shallow, nonreactive bowl. Add the lime juice and toss gently to combine. Drizzle the caramel mixture evenly over the orange segments; let cool 5 minutes (caramel will harden). Cover and refrigerate a minimum of 8 hours or up to 1 day and serve chilled, stirring gently to coat the orange segments in the sauce (most of the caramel will have become a sauce).

PER SERVING: Calories 163 • Protein 2g • Total Fat 0g • Sat. Fat 0g • Cholesterol 0mg • Carbohydrate 42g • Dietary Fiber 2g • Sodium 2mg

Baked Papaya

MAKES 6 SERVINGS

These are delicious served with Hawaiian Coconut Sauce (page 138).

3 ripe yet firm papayas (about 1 pound each), peeled, cut lengthwise in half, and seeds removed
12 teaspoons palm sugar or light brown sugar
1 vanilla bean, cut into 6 pieces

Preheat the oven to 350F (175C).

Arrange the papaya halves, cut sides up, in a shallow baking dish large enough to comfortably hold them in a single layer. Add about ½ inch of water to the dish. Sprinkle 2 teaspoons of the sugar in the center of each papaya half and top with a piece of vanilla bean. Bake, uncovered, 45 minutes, or until tender. Serve warm.

PER SERVING: Calories 94 • Protein 1g • Total Fat 0g • Sat. Fat 0g • Cholesterol 0mg • Carbohydrate 24g • Dietary Fiber 3g • Sodium 9mg

Papaya-Pineapple Strudel

MAKES 6 SERVINGS

Fresh mango can be used in lieu of the papaya, if desired.

1 sheet frozen puff pastry, thawed according to
    package directions
½ cup pineapple preserves
1 cup chopped ripe fresh papaya (from about
    1 small papaya)
¼ cup chopped macadamia nuts, walnuts, almonds,
    or pecans (optional)
¼ cup sweetened shredded coconut (optional)

Preheat oven to 375F (190C).

Unfold pastry onto an ungreased baking sheet. Spread evenly with the preserves. Arrange half the papaya along the middle third of pastry. Sprinkle evenly with half the nuts (if using) and half the coconut (if using). Fold the third of the pastry to your left over the papaya; top pastry with the remaining papaya. Sprinkle evenly with remaining nuts and coconut (if using). Fold the third of the pastry to your right as far over to the other side as it will comfortably stretch, pressing the dough together where it meets to seal. (Do not seal the ends.) Cut about 6 1-inch-long slits across the top.

Bake in center of oven about 25 minutes, until golden. Cool on baking sheet on a wire rack 30 minutes, loosening edges with a spatula after about 15 minutes. Cut into 6 slices and serve warm or at room temperature. Completely cooled strudel can be stored, covered, in refrigerator up to 1 day. For the best flavor, reheat strudel in a low oven and serve slightly warm.

PER SERVING (without nuts or coconut): Calories 289 • Protein 3g • Total Fat 11g • Sat. Fat 3g • Cholesterol 0mg • Carbohydrate 46g • Dietary Fiber 4g • Sodium 146mg

African-Style Caramelized Ripe Plantains

MAKES 6 SERVINGS

Select plantains with black peels for this popular tropical African dessert. To prevent excessive sticking, use a nonstick skillet.

2 tablespoons canola oil
4 ripe plantains, peeled and sliced into ½-inch-thick
    rounds
1 tablespoon granulated sugar
Confectioners' sugar, Coconut Syrup (page 132),
    or pure maple syrup, to taste (optional)

In a large nonstick skillet, heat the oil over medium heat. Add the plantains and cook, stirring and turning occasionally, until lightly browned and slightly caramelized, 5 to 8 minutes. Sprinkle with the granulated sugar and allow the sugar to caramelize slightly, 1 to 2 minutes. Remove the skillet from the heat and serve at once, sprinkled with the confectioners' sugar (if using).

PER SERVING: Calories 194 • Protein 2g • Total Fat 5g • Sat. Fat 1g • Cholesterol 0mg • Carbohydrate 40g • Dietary Fiber 3g • Sodium 5mg

Pomegranate-Currant Salad with Almonds and Papaya Coulis

MAKES 6 SERVINGS

You will need about two large pomegranates to obtain 2 cups of seeds. To remove seeds from pomegranates, cut the fruit into quarters and pull them off the rind and inner membrane with your fingers.

    2 cups pomegranate seeds
    ¾ cup dried currants
    ½ cup slivered almonds
    Papaya Coulis (below)
    Fresh mint leaves, for garnish (optional)

In a small bowl, mix together the seeds, currants, and almonds. Divide equally among 6 dessert bowls. Pour equal amounts of the coulis (about ¼ cup) over each serving and garnish with a mint leaf (if using). Serve at once.

PER SERVING: Calories 173 • Protein 4g • Total Fat 5g • Sat. Fat 1g • Cholesterol 0mg • Carbohydrate 32g • Dietary Fiber 3g • Sodium 5mg

Papaya Coulis

MAKES ABOUT 1½ CUPS

This delightful tropical coulis can also be made with ripe mango, if desired.

    2¼ cups cubed papaya
    3 tablespoons fresh lemon juice
    1½ tablespoons fresh orange juice
    1½ tablespoons sugar, or more to taste

Combine all the ingredients in a food processor fitted with a knife blade, or in a blender; process until smooth and pureed. Serve at once.

PER ¼ CUP: Calories 36 • Protein 0g • Total Fat 0g • Sat. Fat 0g • Cholesterol 0mg • Carbohydrate 9g • Dietary Fiber 1g • Sodium 2mg

Pumpkin Empanadas

MAKES 8 EMPANADAS; 8 GENEROUS OR 16 SMALL SERVINGS

These dessert empanadas are always a festive ending to any Mexican-style meal. They freeze well, and reheat nicely in the microwave for a quick and easy dessert.

    1 (15-ounce) can pumpkin puree
    ½ cup sugar
    ½ teaspoon ground cinnamon
    ¼ teaspoon salt
    ¼ teaspoon ground ginger
    ⅛ teaspoon ground cloves
    Empanada Dough (page 152)
    Confectioners' sugar, to taste

Preheat oven to 350F (175C). Lightly grease a large baking sheet and set aside.

In a medium bowl, mix together the pumpkin, sugar, cinnamon, salt, ginger, and cloves until thoroughly blended. Set aside.

Divide dough into 2 equal pieces. Divide each piece into 4 equal balls, for a total of 8 dough balls. Flatten each ball between floured palms. On a lightly floured work surface, roll out each flattened ball into a 6-inch circle. Place about 2 heaping tablespoons of pumpkin filling on the center of each circle. Fold the dough over the filling and seal edges by pressing lightly with a fork on both sides. Transfer to prepared baking sheet.

Bake in the center of the oven 15 to 20 minutes, until golden brown, taking care not to burn. Cut in half, if desired, and serve warm or at room temperature, sprinkled with confectioners' sugar.

PER EMPANADA: Calories 440 • Protein 6g • Total Fat 20g • Sat. Fat 8g • Cholesterol 0mg • Carbohydrate 60g • Dietary Fiber 3g • Sodium 344mg

VARIATION: *To make Philippine-Style Pumpkin Empanadas, omit the cinnamon, ginger, and cloves and replace with 3/4 teaspoon Chinese five-spice powder.*

Empanada Dough

Use this recipe to make any of your favorite empanadas. For savory fillings, reduce the sugar by half and omit the cinnamon, if desired.

⅓ cup water
¼ cup sugar
2 (¼-ounce) packages active dry yeast
1 teaspoon salt
⅛ teaspoon baking powder
2 generous pinches cinnamon
3 cups all-purpose flour
¾ cup vegetable shortening

In a medium bowl, combine the water, sugar, yeast, salt, baking powder, and cinnamon. Using an electric mixer, gradually blend in half of the flour on low speed. Add the shortening and thoroughly blend. Gradually blend in remaining flour. Use immediately (within 15 minutes), as directed in recipe.

PER SERVING (per ⅛ of recipe): Calories 373 • Protein 6g • Total Fat 20g • Sat. Fat 8g • Cholesterol 0mg • Carbohydrate 43g • Dietary Fiber 2g • Sodium 274mg

Pineapple Sorbet

MAKES 4 TO 6 SERVINGS

This naturally creamy sorbet can be enjoyed any time of year with thawed frozen pineapple chunks or tidbits.

3 cups fresh pineapple chunks
⅓ cup light corn syrup
¼ cup superfine sugar
2 tablespoons fresh lemon juice

In a food processor fitted with the knife blade, or in a blender, process all the ingredients until very smooth. Let stand about 5 minutes to allow the sugar to dissolve; process briefly again.

Freeze in an ice-cream maker according to the manufacturer's directions. Or transfer to a shallow metal pan, such as a cake pan. Place the pan in the freezer for 1 to 1½ hours, or until mixture is firm but not solid. Using a wire whisk, whisk until well combined. Return to the freezer and freeze about 2 more hours, until firm enough to scoop. (At this point, the sorbet can be stored, covered, in freezer up to 5 days.). If too hard to scoop, let thaw about 30 minutes in the refrigerator, or break up into chunks and process with on/off motions in a food processor fitted with the knife blade until fairly smooth.

To serve, scoop the mixture into chilled dessert bowls or goblets. Serve at once.

PER SERVING: Calories 184 • Protein 1g • Total Fat 1g • Sat. Fat 0g • Cholesterol 0mg • Carbohydrate 49g • Dietary Fiber 1g • Sodium 20mg

Sticky Rice with Sesame Seeds

MAKES 12 SERVINGS

Sesame sticky rice is one of Southeast Asia's most famous tasty treats. It's very easy to make. Full-fat coconut milk is recommended for the best texture.

2 cups sushi-style (glutinous or sticky) white rice

1 cup water

1 (14-ounce) can regular coconut milk

1 cup sugar

2 tablespoons pure vanilla extract

½ teaspoon salt

½ cup sesame seeds, toasted (see Cook's Tip, opposite)

Rinse the rice in a fine-meshed sieve under cold-running water until the water runs clear. Drain well. Lightly oil an 8-inch-square baking dish and set aside.

Place the rice and water in a medium saucepan and cover with a tight-fitting lid. Bring to a boil over high heat; immediately reduce the heat to medium and cook 5 minutes. Reduce the heat to low and cook 15 minutes. Remove from heat and let stand, covered, 10 minutes. Uncover and toss with a fork to break up. Set aside.

In a large saucepan, bring the coconut milk, sugar, vanilla, and salt to a simmer over medium heat, stirring occasionally; cook, stirring often, until thickened, 10 to 15 minutes. Add the rice and stir well to combine. Remove from heat and transfer to prepared baking dish. Sprinkle the top with the sesame seeds, pressing down lightly with a spatula. Let stand at room temperature 2 to 3 hours, or until set (mixture will harden as it cools). Cut into squares and serve at room temperature. Alternatively, cover and refrigerate a minimum of 2 hours or up to 1 day (but no longer, as rice will become too hardened) and serve chilled.

PER SERVING: Calories 292 • Protein 4g • Total Fat 11g • Sat. Fat 7g • Cholesterol 0mg • Carbohydrate 46g • Dietary Fiber 2g • Sodium 97mg

VARIATION: *To make Sticky Rice with Black Sesame Seeds, substitute black sesame seeds, available in Asian markets and some well-stocked supermarkets, for the regular variety; toast as directed below.*

COOK'S TIP: *To toast sesame seeds, heat a small, heavy-bottomed skillet over medium heat. Add the sesame seeds and cook without stirring 30 seconds. Begin shaking the skillet occasionally until toasted and fragrant, about 2 minutes. Immediately transfer to a small plate and let cool to room temperature. Use as directed in recipe.*

Malaysian Tapioca Cake

MAKES 12 SERVINGS

This puddinglike cake is one of my favorites. Yucca root, or tapioca, is available in Latin markets and many well-stocked supermarkets.

> 2 pounds yucca (tapioca) root, peeled and grated
> 2 cups sugar
> 1 teaspoon salt
> 2 (14-ounce) cans light coconut milk

Preheat oven to 350F (175C). Lightly grease an 11×7-inch baking dish and set aside.

In a large bowl, mix together the yucca, sugar, and salt until well combined. Add the coconut milk, stirring well to combine. Transfer to the prepared baking dish.

Cover loosely with foil and bake on the center rack 1½ hours. Uncover and bake another 30 minutes, or until browned and bubbly. Let cool completely on a wire rack (mixture will set as it cools). Cut into squares and serve at room temperature. Alternatively, cover and refrigerate up to 3 days and serve chilled.

PER SERVING: Calories 303 • Protein 4g • Total Fat 8g • Sat. Fat 7g • Cholesterol 0mg • Carbohydrate 57g • Dietary Fiber 0g • Sodium 210mg

Thai Tapioca Pudding with Mango

MAKES 6 SERVINGS

This incredibly simple yet delicious tropical pudding can be made with fresh papaya or pineapple instead of the mango, or a combination of all three fruits, if desired. You can omit the remaining uncooked coconut milk from the recipe, if desired, for a lighter dessert.

> 2½ cups light coconut milk
> 1 cup mango nectar
> ½ cup water
> ½ cup sugar
> ¼ cup quick-cooking tapioca
> 1 teaspoon pure vanilla extract
> 1 cup chopped fresh mango

In a medium saucepan, stir together 1 cup of the coconut milk, the mango nectar, water, sugar, and tapioca. Let stand 5 minutes. Bring to a full boil over medium heat, stirring constantly. Remove from heat and stir in the vanilla; let cool 20 minutes (mixture will thicken as it cools). Add the chopped mango and stir gently yet thoroughly to combine. Serve warm or at room temperature, with the remaining coconut milk passed separately. Or cover and refrigerate completely cooled pudding a minimum of 3 hours or overnight and serve chilled.

PER SERVING: Calories 240 • Protein 3g • Total Fat 10g • Sat. Fat 9g • Cholesterol 0mg • Carbohydrate 38g • Dietary Fiber 1g • Sodium 41mg

Belize-Style Sweet Potato Pudding

MAKES 12 SERVINGS

PER SERVING: Calories 310 • Protein 3g • Total Fat 9g • Sat. Fat 7g • Cholesterol 0mg • Carbohydrate 57g • Dietary Fiber 2g • Sodium 24mg

This rich Belizean pudding, or *pone*, is delicious warm or chilled.

- 1⅓ cups regular coconut milk
- 1⅓ cups light coconut milk
- 2¼ cups sugar
- 1½ pounds sweet potatoes, peeled and finely grated
- ¼ cup raisins, preferably golden
- 1 tablespoon canola oil
- ½ tablespoon pure vanilla extract
- ½ teaspoon ground ginger
- ¼ teaspoon ground cinnamon
- Pinch salt

Preheat oven to 350F (175C). Lightly oil an 8-inch-square baking dish, place on a baking sheet with a rim, and set aside.

In a large bowl, combine both coconut milks and sugar; stir until the sugar dissolves. Add the remaining ingredients and stir well to combine. Pour into the prepared baking dish and carefully transfer on the baking sheet to the center of the oven. Bake 1 hour. Reduce temperature to 250F (120C) and bake 1 more hour, or until a golden crust forms and a knife inserted halfway from the center comes out almost clean. Let cool about 30 minutes before serving. Serve warm or at room temperature (the pudding will firm as it cools). Or cover and refrigerate completely cooled pudding up to 3 days and serve chilled.

Beverages

In tropical climates the world over, fresh fruit juices from pineapple, mango, guava, and orange are natural thirst-quenchers. Throughout Cambodia, orange juice is sipped by straw straight out of the fruit. In the Florida Keys and Thailand, bitter limes are mixed with sugar and water and transformed into refreshing limeade—salt is added in the Southeast Asian version as a counterpoint to the sweetness. Many fruit juices are traditionally blended into shakes with coconut milk, fruit, sugar, and ice; in Vietnam, avocado often is included. The trendy smoothie blends are paradise in a glass—they're almost fat-free, and serve triple-duty as breakfast, snack, and dessert. Best of all, these shakes and smoothies are as easy as one (assemble ingredients), two (puree in a blender), three (pour). Not to be forgotten are the sophisticated mixed drinks, where a veranda to watch the sunset and sip your colada is required. Cheers!

Vietnamese Avocado Shakes

MAKES 1 GENEROUS OR 2 SMALL SERVINGS

This thick and rich drink is more an exotic dessert for two, and can be eaten with a spoon.

   1 medium ripe avocado, peeled, pitted, and
      quartered
   ¼ cup light coconut milk
   2 to 3 tablespoons sugar, or to taste
   1 cup ice cubes

Combine all the ingredients in a blender. Cover and blend until smooth. Serve at once.

PER SERVING: Calories 471 • Protein 6g • Total Fat 35g • Sat. Fat 8g • Cholesterol 0mg • Carbohydrate 43g • Dietary Fiber 5g • Sodium 46mg

Banana-Chocolate-Coconut Milkshakes

MAKES 3 SERVINGS

For an even thicker shake, use full-fat coconut milk.

   1 (14-ounce) can light coconut milk
   2 tablespoons unsweetened cocoa powder
   ¼ cup sugar
   1 teaspoon vanilla extract
   1 medium ripe banana, sliced
   8 large ice cubes

Combine the coconut milk and cocoa powder in a blender; blend until thoroughly combined. Add the sugar, vanilla, and banana; blend until smooth. Add ice cubes one at a time, blending until thick. Serve at once.

PER SERVING: Calories 278 • Protein 5g • Total Fat 15g • Sat. Fat 13g • Cholesterol 0mg • Carbohydrate 35g • Dietary Fiber 1g • Sodium 54mg

Coconut-Mango Shakes

MAKES 2 SERVINGS

You can partially thaw a cup of frozen mango cubes to make this delicious shake any time of the year.

   1 cup chilled orange juice
   1 cup cubed mango, partially frozen
   1 cup chilled light coconut milk
   ½ to 1 teaspoon sugar

Combine all the ingredients in a blender. Cover and blend until smooth. Serve at once.

PER SERVING: Calories 179 • Protein 3g • Total Fat 6g • Sat. Fat 5g • Cholesterol 0mg • Carbohydrate 31g • Dietary Fiber 2g • Sodium 26mg

Guava Smoothie

MAKES 1 GENEROUS OR 2 SMALL SERVINGS

Guavas, considered by many to be super fruits, are very rich in vitamin C, and contain significant amounts of vitamins A and B, and calcium to boot. The skin of a ripe guava is usually yellow and yields to gentle pressure from the thumb. To finish ripening a green guava, enclose it in a paper bag with a banana and leave at room temperature until the guava starts to soften.

- 1 ripe guava, peeled, halved, seedy center removed
- 1 ripe banana, peeled and quartered
- 1 cup fresh orange juice
- ½ tablespoon sugar
- 1 teaspoon fresh lemon juice
- 4 large ice cubes

Combine all the ingredients in a blender. Cover and blend until smooth. Serve at once.

PER SERVING: Calories 288 • Protein 4g • Total Fat 2g • Sat. Fat 0g • Cholesterol 0mg • Carbohydrate 70g • Dietary Fiber 8g • Sodium 6mg

Guava Spritzers

MAKES 4 SERVINGS

Frozen guava concentrate is available in Latin and Caribbean markets as well as many well-stocked supermarkets.

- ½ (12-ounce) can frozen guava or pineapple juice concentrate, thawed
- 3 cups lemon-lime soda, chilled
- Ice, to serve

In a one-quart pitcher, gently stir together the juice and soda until well combined. Serve at once, over ice.

PER SERVING: Calories 150 • Protein 1g • Total Fat 0g • Sat. Fat 0g • Cholesterol 0mg • Carbohydrate 38g • Dietary Fiber 0g • Sodium 22mg

Florida Keys Limeade

YIELDS ABOUT 1½ QUARTS

This simple yet delicious drink is the ultimate thirst-quencher.

- 5 cups water
- ¾ cup superfine sugar
- ½ cup fresh Key lime juice, or equal parts fresh Persian (regular) lime juice and lemon juice

In an 8-cup container, stir all ingredients until thoroughly blended. Cover and refrigerate a minimum of 3 hours or up to 5 days. Serve chilled.

PER 1 CUP: Calories 102 • Protein 0g • Total Fat 0g • Sat. Fat 0g • Cholesterol 0mg • Carbohydrate 27g • Dietary Fiber 0g • Sodium 0mg

COOK'S TIP: *You will need about 9 to 12 Key limes to yield ½ cup juice.*

Pineapple–Key Lime Spritzers

MAKES 8 SERVINGS

If you can't use fresh pineapple juice, reconstituted pineapple juice from frozen concentrate is preferred to the canned variety.

½ cup superfine sugar

3 cups pineapple juice, preferably fresh

½ cup fresh Key lime juice, or equal parts fresh
    Persian lime juice and lemon juice

1 liter seltzer or sparkling water, chilled

Ice, to serve

In a half-gallon pitcher, mix together the sugar, pineapple juice, and lime juice. Refrigerate until chilled, a minimum of 1 hour. Just before serving, gently stir in seltzer. Serve at once, over ice.

PER SERVING: Calories 105 • Protein 0g • Total Fat 0g • Sat. Fat 0g • Cholesterol 0mg • Carbohydrate 27g • Dietary Fiber 0g • Sodium 2mg

Thai Limeade

MAKES 6 SERVINGS

The oil from the lime skins provides the unique flavor of this popular Thai refreshment. Just make certain not to steep the rinds too long, as the drink will be unpleasantly bitter.

6 fresh Persian limes, halved, juiced (about ¾ cup),
    and rinds reserved

½ cup sugar

2½ cups boiling water

½ teaspoon salt

2 cups ice, plus additional, to serve

Place the lime juice in a 6-cup pouring container and set aside.

In a medium saucepan, combine the lime rinds and sugar; add the boiling water and let steep 5 minutes (very limy) to 10 minutes (slightly bitter), but no longer. Add the salt, stirring well to combine. Strain warm liquid into juice. Add ice cubes and stir well. Cover and refrigerate a minimum of 3 hours, or up to 5 days. To serve, pour into individual glasses filled halfway with ice. Serve at once.

PER SERVING: Calories 73 • Protein 0g • Total Fat 0g • Sat. Fat 0g • Cholesterol 0mg • Carbohydrate 19g • Dietary Fiber 0g • Sodium 178mg

Mango Smoothies

MAKES 2 SERVINGS

Loaded with vitamin C and fiber, this tangy tropical smoothie is as healthful as it is delicious.

1 ripe banana, sliced

1 cup unsweetened orange-pineapple juice, chilled

1 large mango (about 14 ounces), peeled, pitted,
    and cubed

½ cup cubed fresh pineapple

4 large ice cubes

In a blender, combine the banana and juice; cover and blend until smooth. Add the remaining ingredients; cover and blend on highest speed until smooth and slushy. Serve at once.

PER SERVING: Calories 202 • Protein 2g • Total Fat 1g • Sat. Fat 0g • Cholesterol 0mg • Carbohydrate 51g • Dietary Fiber 4g • Sodium 4mg

Mango and Melon Coladas

MAKES 2 GENEROUS OR 3 SMALL SERVINGS

This colada is delicious enough for dessert. For a terrific smoothie, simply leave out the rum.

2 cups cubed fresh cantaloupe

1½ cups cubed fresh mango

3 tablespoons cream of coconut, such as
    Coco López

2 tablespoons fresh lime juice

2 tablespoons superfine sugar

4 ounces light rum

2 cups crushed ice

Combine all ingredients in a blender. Cover and blend until smooth. Serve at once.

PER SERVING: Calories 400 • Protein 3g • Total Fat 9g • Sat. Fat 7g • Cholesterol 0mg • Carbohydrate 51g • Dietary Fiber 4g • Sodium 20mg

Mango Mimosas

MAKES 5 SERVINGS

Treat your brunch guests to a sophisticated taste of the tropics with these exotic mimosas.

1 cup pureed fresh mango pulp (from about
    1 medium mango)

1 bottle chilled champagne or other dry sparkling
    wine

Strain pureed mango pulp through a fine-mesh sieve into a small bowl. Just before serving, gently pour champagne into a large bowl. Gently mix in mango puree until just combined, taking care not to overmix, as the champagne will loss its bubbliness. Ladle into cups and serve immediately.

PER SERVING: Calories 154 • Protein 0g • Total Fat 0g • Sat. Fat 0g • Cholesterol 0mg • Carbohydrate 12g • Dietary Fiber 1g • Sodium 1mg

Mango-Peach Freeze

MAKES ABOUT 3 (1-CUP) SERVINGS

The marriage of mango and peach is a heavenly one.

2 mangoes (about 12 ounces each), peeled, pitted,
    and chopped

1 (12-ounce) can peach nectar, chilled

⅔ cup crushed ice

Combine all the ingredients in a blender. Cover and blend until smooth. Serve immediately.

PER SERVING: Calories 157 • Protein 1g • Total Fat 0g • Sat. Fat 0g • Cholesterol 0mg • Carbohydrate 41g • Dietary Fiber 3g • Sodium 11mg

16 ounces (2 cups) unsweetened pomegranate juice

16 ounces (2 cups) ginger ale

Juice of 1 to 2 limes

Ice, to serve

In a 5-cup pouring container, gently stir together pomegranate juice, ginger ale, and lime juice until well combined. Serve at once, over ice.

PER SERVING: Calories 113 • Protein 1g • Total Fat 0g • Sat. Fat 0g • Cholesterol 0mg • Carbohydrate 29g • Dietary Fiber 0g • Sodium 23mg

VARIATION: *To make Mangosteen-Ginger Spritzers, substitute unsweetened mangosteen juice, also high in beneficial antioxidants, for the pomegranate juice. Mangosteen juice is available for order online and can be purchased at Asian and specialty food markets.*

Frozen Mango Margaritas

MAKES 2 SERVINGS

For optimal flavor, make sure the mango is fully ripe.

1½ cups chopped mango

3 ounces tequila

1 ounce Cointreau or other orange liqueur

¼ cup fresh lime juice

3 tablespoons superfine sugar

2 cups ice cubes

Combine all the ingredients in a blender; cover and blend until smooth. Serve at once.

PER SERVING: Calories 304 • Protein 1g • Total Fat 0g • Sat. Fat 0g • Cholesterol 0mg • Carbohydrate 47g • Dietary Fiber 2g • Sodium 3mg

Strawberry-Kiwifruit Smoothies

MAKES 2 GENEROUS OR 3 SMALL SERVINGS

You can use packaged frozen strawberries in this recipe, but make sure they are individually frozen, and not in juice.

1 cup unsweetened pineapple juice

2 ripe bananas, quartered

3 small kiwifruit, peeled and quartered

1 cup medium strawberries, frozen solid

Place all the ingredients in a blender. Blend at a low setting for 1 minute. Increase speed to a high and blend until smooth. Serve at once.

Pomegranate-Ginger Spritzers

MAKES 4 SERVINGS

This is a delicious nonalcoholic way to get those beneficial antioxidants from the pomegranate. For a party, double or triple the recipe and serve in a punch bowl, garnished with thin slices of lime, if desired.

Tropical Smoothies

MAKES 2 SERVINGS

Kiwifruit, mango, papaya, and pineapple-orange juice
load this drink with vitamin C, while the banana adds
potassium and fiber—yum!

1 large or 2 small bananas, quartered

2 kiwifruit, peeled and quartered

½ cup chopped mango

½ cup chopped papaya

1 cup pineapple-orange juice, chilled

4 large ice cubes

Combine all the ingredients in a blender. Cover
and blend until smooth. Serve at once.

Metric Conversion Charts

Comparison to Metric Measure

When You Know	Symbol	Multiply By	To Find	Symbol
teaspoons	tsp	5.0	milliliters	ml
tablespoons	tbsp	15.0	milliliters	ml
fluid ounces	fl. oz.	30.0	milliliters	ml
cups	c	0.24	liters	l
pints	pt.	0.47	liters	l
quarts	qt.	0.95	liters	l
ounces	oz.	28.0	grams	g
pounds	lb.	0.45	kilograms	kg
Fahrenheit	F	$5/9$ (after subtracting 32)	Celsius	C

Fahrenheit to Celsius

F	C
200–205	95
220–225	105
245–250	120
275	135
300–305	150
325–330	165
345–350	175
370–375	190
400–405	205
425–430	220
445–450	230
470–475	245
500	260

Liquid Measure to Liters

¼ cup	=	0.06 liters
½ cup	=	0.12 liters
¾ cup	=	0.18 liters
1 cup	=	0.24 liters
1¼ cups	=	0.30 liters
1½ cups	=	0.36 liters
2 cups	=	0.48 liters
2½ cups	=	0.60 liters
3 cups	=	0.72 liters
3½ cups	=	0.84 liters
4 cups	=	0.96 liters
4½ cups	=	1.08 liters
5 cups	=	1.20 liters
5½ cups	=	1.32 liters

Liquid Measure to Milliliters

¼ teaspoon	=	1.25 milliliters
½ teaspoon	=	2.50 milliliters
¾ teaspoon	=	3.75 milliliters
1 teaspoon	=	5.00 milliliters
1¼ teaspoons	=	6.25 milliliters
1½ teaspoons	=	7.50 milliliters
1¾ teaspoons	=	8.75 milliliters
2 teaspoons	=	10.0 milliliters
1 tablespoon	=	15.0 milliliters
2 tablespoons	=	30.0 milliliters

Index

About the Author

Donna Klein specializes in writing vegan cookbooks with a primary emphasis on authentic ingredients and minimal use of meat, dairy, and egg substitutes. She is also the author of *The Mediterranean Vegan Kitchen*, *The PDQ (Pretty Darn Quick) Vegetarian Cookbook*, *Vegan Italiano*, and *The Gluten-Free Vegetarian Kitchen*. Her food articles and recipes have appeared in the *Washington Post*, *The Yoga Journal*, *Body and Soul Magazine*, *Vegetarian Gourmet*, *Veggie Life*, *The Herb Companion*, *VegNews*, and *Victorian Decorating and Life Style*.

Ms. Klein studied at Le Cordon Bleu in Paris, and is a popular vegetarian cooking and food writing instructor in Montgomery County, Maryland, where she lives very happily with her daughters, Emma and Sarah, and adopted dog, Trevor.